T0319917

Internal Controls
Policies and Procedures

Internal Controls
Policies and Procedures

Rose Hightower

WILEY

John Wiley & Sons, Inc.

This book is printed on acid-free paper. ∞

Copyright © 2009 by John Wiley & Sons, Inc. All rights reserved.
Published by John Wiley & Sons, Inc., Hoboken, New Jersey.
Published simultaneously in Canada.

No part of this publication may be reproduced, stored in a retrieval system, or transmitted in any form or by any means, electronic, mechanical, photocopying, recording, scanning, or otherwise, except as permitted under Section 107 or 108 of the 1976 United States Copyright Act, without either the prior written permission of the Publisher, or authorization through payment of the appropriate per-copy fee to the Copyright Clearance Center, Inc., 222 Rosewood Drive, Danvers, MA 01923, 978-750-8400, fax 978-646-8600, or on the web at www.copyright.com. Requests to the Publisher for permission should be addressed to the Permissions Department, John Wiley & Sons, Inc., 111 River Street, Hoboken, NJ 07030, 201-748-6011, fax 201-748-6008, or online at http://www.wiley.com/go/permissions.

Limit of Liability/Disclaimer of Warranty: While the publisher and author have used their best efforts in preparing this book, they make no representations or warranties with respect to the accuracy or completeness of the contents of this book and specifically disclaim any implied warranties of merchantability or fitness for a particular purpose. No warranty may be created or extended by sales representatives or written sales materials. The advice and strategies contained herein may not be suitable for your situation. You should consult with a professional where appropriate. Neither the publisher nor author shall be liable for any loss of profit or any other commercial damages, including but not limited to special, incidental, consequential, or other damages.

For general information on our other products and services, or technical support, please contact our Customer Care Department within the United States at 800-762-2974, outside the United States at 317-572-3993 or fax 317-572-4002.

Wiley also publishes its books in a variety of electronic formats. Some content that appears in print may not be available in electronic books.

For more information about Wiley products, visit our Web site at http://www.wiley.com.

Library of Congress Cataloging-in-Publication Data:

Hightower, Rose.
    Internal controls policies and procedures / Rose Hightower.
        p.   cm.
    Includes bibliographical references and index.
    ISBN 978-0-470-28717-0 (paper/website)
        1. Auditing, Internal.   2. Corporate governance.   3. Managerial accounting.   I. Title.
    HF5668.25.H54   2009
    657'.458—dc22

                                                                    2008022105

10   9   8   7   6   5   4   3   2

About the Author

Rose Hightower

Rose is an accountant, professor, author and owner of IDEAL Consulting Solutions International, LLC. She earned an Accounting degree while in Canada and a Master's degree from Syracuse University. Rose has lived and worked in Toronto and New York.

As an energetic, proactive program manager with extensive Fortune 500 experience in identifying and resolving challenges in finance, process management and organizational development. Her career reflects results-oriented leadership with strong creative problem solving and analytical skills. Rose has over 30 years of business experience working with small, medium and corporate clients to improve their efforts and direction in leadership development.

As an accountant, Rose has participated, managed and had oversight responsibilities within various accounting and finance departments including twenty years at IBM, identifying and resolving challenges in finance, process management and organizational assessment.

IDEAL Consulting Solutions International, LLC a business specializing in redesigning accounting and finance processes, providing tools and skills necessary to improve business operations. The IDEAL™ philosophy is to provide valued added assessments and transfer skill. Current projects include the design and implementation of documentation programs improving them to address significant accounting deficiencies.

With a life long interest in learning, Rose has taught the mechanics of accounting and finance to college and university students within Canada and the States. Teaching has kept her interest and excitement about the topic fresh and current and combining her real world experience with textbook concepts has provided a additional value to her students.

Rose is the author of Accounting and Finance Policies and Procedures also published by John Wiley and Sons and which serves a prequel and companion to this manual. Within these manuals, she packages current research and proven experience in a ready to use solutions.

You may contact the author by visiting www.idealpolicy.com.

About the Web Site

As a purchaser of this manual, *Accounting and Finance Policies and Procedures,* you have access to the supporting web site: www.wiley.com/go/icpolices

The web site contains everything within the book. This download is an accumulation of Microsoft Word, Excel, and PowerPoint documents.

The password to enter this site is: controls

Contents

How to use this Manual

Whether you are a large public for-profit corporation or a small independent, there is benefit and value in adopting an internal control program.

This manual is structured as the final product and includes everything you need to document your internal controls program. These documents must be customized and adapted to fit into your company's culture and environment. Throughout the manual there are exercises that, when complete, will assist by providing input to the internal control program and determining your company's internal control posture. Using the URL, www.wiley.com/go/icpolicies download the book and customize it. Follow the document layout and adjust the scope and process flow using your Company's language and procedure. Everything contained within the book is contained within the URL download.

In addition to considering this manual a reference or a "how to," use it as a workbook. As you read through the chapters, perform the exercises to deepen your awareness, identify and prioritize your strategies, and enable employees to be part of the solution. As you review this manual, complete the exercises as you go and you will have a customized internal control program and plan.

In addition to providing some background as to why internal controls are important, this manual includes internal control program-specific policies, procedures, and testing guides—basically everything you need to launch an internal control program. This manual is a companion book to the *Accounting and Finance Policy and Procedure* manual also offered by John Wiley & Sons and available at www.wiley.com/WileyCDA/WileyTitle/productCd-0470259620.html.

This download is an accumulation of Microsoft word, Excel, and PowerPoint documents and Visio charts named and numbered in accordance with the Table of Contents. The downloadable files are distributed on an "as is" basis without warranties.

This download is available for your personal use within your company and must not be further distributed or used for resale. Permission to download the manual is achieved by procuring the book. This book and the downloadable version contain general information and are not intended to address specific circumstances or requirements. The author does not give any warranties, representations, or undertakings, expressed or implied, about the content's quality or fitness for a particular purpose.

For additional program information or support, contact me as the Policyguru via policyguru@idealpolicy.com or visit www.idealpolicy.com.

Preface

To: Chief Financial Officer, Chief Compliance Officer, and Internal Control Program Manager

Do you worry about . . .

- Achieving objectives?

- Being resilient enough to adapt to change in time?

- Managing risks intelligently?

- Recognizing opportunities?

Do you know where your risks are and how to prioritize them? Does your staff have the resources and support they need to recognize and mitigate these risks? Could your company benefit from improved accounting and finance processes?

Having a strong internal control department enables managements to deal with rapidly changing economic and competitive environments, shifting customer demands and priorities and identifying when and where to restructure for future growth.

This manual is brought to internal control, accounting, and finance leaders and professionals who are tasked with implementing a program that will:

- Identify opportunities for effectiveness and efficiencies and reduce risk

- Engage the workforce

- Comply with external governance and reporting requirements such as Securities and Exchange Commission reporting and Sarbanes-Oxley compliance

The Internal Controls department is tasked with a role and responsibility that is more than just governance, risk, and oversight. This manual deals with those topics and presents tools and techniques which can address CEO/CFO worries.

Internal control is more than a role and responsibility; it is a philosophy, culture, and way of thinking. This manual integrates the governance objectives with internal control basics and provides tools and techniques which when applied provide valuable information to the executive leadership and other stakeholders.

As I began researching and preparing this manual, I realized that most large public companies were using and describing the Committee of Sponsoring Organizations of the Treadway Commission (COSO) framework in the same way. That is both good and bad news. The good news is that there is considerable evidence and proof that the COSO framework is the generally accepted standard and that there is a consistent look and feel to customized manuals. Internal control program managers become subject matter experts on implementing the framework.

The difficult news for an author is on how to make this subject matter fresh and new. So, although the lists may seem familiar, I hope I bring a fresh, new commonsense approach to applying the framework. Since my strength is in accounting and finance processes and process management, my philosophy is to embed COSO into the very processes we live and work with every day.

Whether you are a large public company or a small independent, the philosophy and approach will add value to your bottom line. The approach is based on laws and regulations and follows a commonsense approach to applying continuous process improvement techniques.

This manual is made up of three parts and includes a discussion of the governance journey, the internal control program, and the internal control testing guides. The manual contains exercises, self-assessments, and various other tools and techniques that can and should be adapted to your control environment.

Many of the concepts presented have been part of the repertoire of the best process-driven companies with the tools and techniques used in other proven models and approaches. This manual brings these concepts together in a fresh way ready for customization and implementation and aimed to achieve bottom-line results. There will be references to Sarbanes-Oxley and COSO; you may recognize the style of self-assessment tools, process management, and project management techniques. These all come together as a road map to implement or refresh your internal control program.

The documents should be used as a starting point for constructing, revitalizing, or documenting your company's internal control program. The program and the testing guides must be personalized and customized to meet your company's needs. Replace my company's (IDÆAL, LLP; used only at the beginning of some documents) name with your company's name. Follow the document layout and adjust the scope and process flow using your company's language and procedure.

Welcome to an exciting process. As you work through the process, the outcomes will present you with insights and opportunities about your company that you may not be currently aware of. Use this manual as a starting point to assess the maturity of the internal controls program. As you address each of the processes, if the documentation process comes "easily" (i.e., is currently available, is followed by most if not all of your company's subsidiaries and locations; is measured and used as a basis for continuous process improvement) then the process is very mature and there should be no surprises.

Whether you use this manual as a reference, workbook, or guide, congratulations on taking this step and acquiring this valuable resource.

Rose
Rose Hightower
Policyguru@idealpolicy.com
www.idealpolicy.com

GOVERNANCE JOURNEY

BIG G TO LITTLE g GOVERNANCE JOURNEY

Investments in public offerings such as stocks drive the economy. Recent history and current events indicate that stock markets can be unstable for a variety of reasons. In order to protect investors and shareholders, external or public governing organizations have created laws that require companies to provide investors and shareholders with current, accurate, and relevant data and information. Governance is about creating an environment and process for those laws, rules and regulations.

Within this section, there are references to COSO and SOX; if you need a refresher, at the end of this chapter is a summary of these important initiatives.

What is governance? According to the International Federation of Accountants (IFAC), *governance* refers to a set of responsibilities and practices exercised by management with the goal of providing strategic direction and tactical guidance to ensure that company goals and objectives are achieved, risks are identified and managed appropriately, and resources are assigned responsibly. The key message is that governance is a process that, when practiced, reinforces integrity and accountability and demonstrates leadership.

Notice that the definition is not limited to publicly owned companies and is not limited to laws and regulations. There are lessons to be learned from the public companies that have had to deal with the roller coaster impact to their market and asset values. Other "not so public" companies can benefit and reap the bottom line benefits of adopting the tools used on the governance journey. So, if you are a small or private company, there are cautions and benefits that you need to pay attention to.

What is governance about? Governance is about creating and maintaining an ethical work environment, it is about establishing and following the rules; it is about transparency and disclosure. Governance is about creating and following a process to establish, communicate, implement, and measure the principles, rules and regulations required to conduct business.

Where does governance come from? From an accounting and finance point of view, external or big G Governance originates from laws and regulatory organizations such as the Securities and Exchange Commission (SEC), the Financial Accounting Standards Board (FASB) and the Public Company Accounting Oversight Board (PCAOB).

Externally, these governing organizations propose principles, rules and methodologies that are aimed at increasing integrity in the quantitative and qualitative information presented to potential investors and shareholders. To comply with external governance, leaders must find a way to communicate and integrate these externally driven rules and regulations into internal business practices and processes.

Big G Governance originates from sources external to the company while little g governance originates from inside. Some of the forces behind big G Governance include:

- Market stability, which is driven by investors and those in a position of oversight requiring accurate, complete and transparent information

- Political and economic stability which is driven by local governments imposing economic principles and rules on specific industries

- Financial stability which is often identified as the measure between stock prices and asset values

Internal Use Only

As part of big G Governance, those who are asked to implement the rules are asked to provide input to those regulatory bodies and agencies; for example, public companies satisfy quarterly financial reporting requirements. Those companies and other interested parties provide comments as to current and future direction. The SEC and PCAOB review and evaluate the submissions and comments to ultimately determine the adequacy of current regulation and how these regulations can and must be improved. The SEC and the PCAOB are ultimately responsible for the oversight of compliance with the big G Governance accounting and finance laws and rules.

Compliance with external big G Governance is demonstrated by satisfying reporting requirements and for company leaders to attest to the accuracy and completeness of what is reported. Because the leaders cannot oversee *every* aspect of *every* transaction, leaders translate and integrate the external laws and rules into internal processes, policies and procedures resulting in a little g governance regulatory environment.

The objective of little g governance is simply to integrate big G Governance rules into company processes and comply with reporting and disclosure laws and regulations.

Corporate or little g governance is defined as a process, initiated by the company's board of directors, managers, and other personnel to apply a strategy across the company that will achieve:

- compliance with applicable laws and regulations

- Transparency and reliability of all public reporting and information dispersed for accurate and timely decision making

- Proper (i.e., effective and efficient) functioning of the company's processes, including positive impact on the community; fair and honest dealings with customers, vendors, and employees; compensation; and evaluation of management

Internal or business governance is marked by the review, analysis, and documentation of internal practices and processes required to get work done. Internal business processes define how work is organized and performed; defining the touch points for review, approval and escalation. The business process owners are charged with designing processes that are compliant and yet operate efficiently and effectively.

For our purposes, the term *little g governance* is broadly used to indicate the internal adoption of the external rules and regulations with corporate governance being the bridge between external requirements and expectations and internal processes and resource constraints.

Why governance, why now? It's the law.

Big G and little g governance creation has to be dynamic, that is, it must be able to respond to changing environments with processes incorporating inputs from various constituents, including businesses, investors, creditors, government, and international sources with the purpose of defining and refining governance principles and rules.

For most companies, the focus is on little g governance and the tasks needed to satisfy compliance and oversight regulations. As for any business, there must be identifiable value in the action. The program to establish and oversee little g governance must be about increasing profit contribution to the company through improved process management and decision making.

Little g governance is about creating an internal environment and culture that satisfies internal decision making and external financial reporting. Therefore, while big G Governance is about the law, little g governance is about translating and integrating those laws into the fabric of the business. Little g governance:

- Provides accurate, complete and timely data and information required for informed decision making by customers and other stakeholders

- Provides the workforce with the tools and resources required to act and holding individuals accountable required for a high-performance workforce.

- Leverages the company's core competencies and work systems to manage and improve its key processes. It is about knowing what business you are in and creating an environment to succeed.

Little g governance is about ensuring that operational processes are defined, measured, and reviewed while continuing to achieve the company's goals and objectives and satisfying big G Governance reporting requirements. As part of oversight, operational processes need to be documented and risk assessed to ensure compliance with internal decision making and external reporting.

The journey from Big G to little g governance, to risk and oversight and back to Big G is demonstrated in the following flowchart. Notice that the role and responsibility of little g governance is to implement big G into the operational side of the business and the evaluation and monitoring side with risk/oversight activities. As business areas within the company execute processes, data and information, reports both formal and informal are escalated to the leadership team. The executive leadership and the board of directors are ultimately responsible for the effective and efficient operation of these processes and report the company's outcomes to the big G governance agencies.

Flowcharting the Governance Journey

External regulatory bodies issue directives and guidance. Companies receive and assess these requirements and develop plans to integrate them into their operations or evaluate the risk of not fully implementing them.

Often, it takes time and resources to respond to the directive, and in the meantime, there is risk. The company needs to assess the requirements and determine where within their operations and to what extent they need to make changes to their processes. This assessment requires understanding and evaluating the company's specific processes and risks. When the company decides where and how to implement process changes, a transition plan and project are initiated and integrated within the operational side of the business. During the transition period and thereafter there may be remaining risk to the company that requires monitoring and periodic reassessment.

Once implemented and deployed, processes are updated and the impact of the change in regulation is measured via the processing of transactions. The effectiveness and efficiency of the operational processes is overseen by programs that measure risk and compliance.

The company uses risk assessment techniques to assess the risk of not conforming or not fully conforming. If the decision is to not accept the risk, then operational processes are updated. If the decision is to accept a level of risk, then the risk needs to be managed with oversight built into the risk management process.

With the results of operational processes confirmed, and the impact and effect of risks identified, reports are issued to executive leadership and the board of directors. Once approved, they release external reports to satisfy external regulatory reporting requirements.

Additions, deletions and changes to the external rules and regulations occur as the external regulatory bodies receive company reports and feedback and as those agencies evaluate other economic environmental indicators. The governance journey is complete.

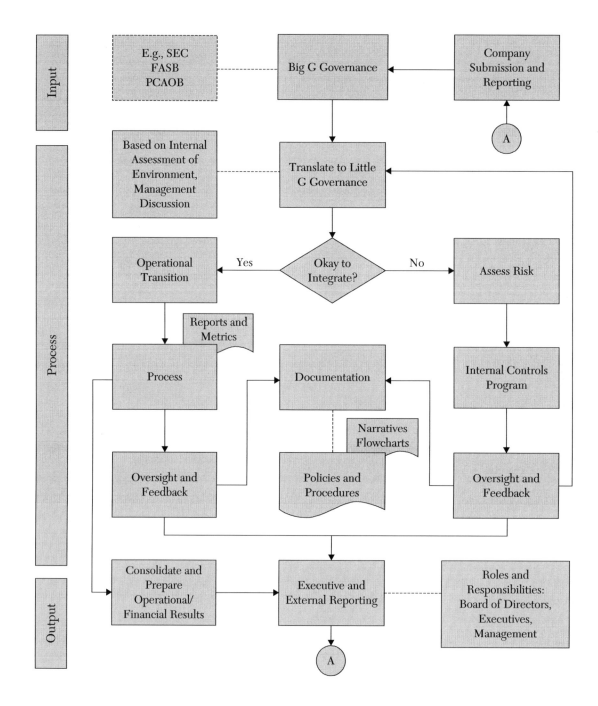

APPENDIX

SOME BACKGROUND INFORMATION ON COSO, SOX AND PCAOB

Every internal control manual today, refers to the Committee of Sponsoring Organizations of the Treadway Commission (COSO) Framework and the Sarbanes-Oxley Act (SOX). For those not familiar with these initiatives, following is a brief overview and positioning of these important milestones as they relate to the internal control governance journey.

COSO Framework

The Committee of Sponsoring Organizations of the Treadway Commission (COSO) in 1992 issued *Internal Control–Integrated Framework* to help businesses and other entities assess and enhance their internal control systems. This framework has been recognized by executives, board members, regulators, standard setters, professional organizations, and others as an appropriate comprehensive Framework for Internal Controls. For further information on COSO go to www.coso.org.

This book neither replaces nor modifies the framework, but rather provides guidance on how to integrate it within your internal control environment. Volumes have been written to discuss and describe the COSO concepts; rather than emphasizing COSO, this manual uses COSO as a tool and guide to implement your customized program. The internal control process begins with management's setting financial reporting objectives relevant to the company's particular business activities and circumstances.

Once set, management identifies and assesses a variety of risks to those objectives, determines which risks could result in a material misstatement in financial reporting and determines how the risks should be managed through a range of control activities. Management implements approaches to capture process and communicate information needed for financial reporting and other components of the internal control system. All this is done in context to the company's control environment, which is shaped and refined as necessary to provide the appropriate tone from the top. These components are monitored to help ensure that controls continue to operate properly over time.

The COSO components include:

- *Control Environment* which is an indicator of the level of control consciousness of the company. It is the basis for all the other components providing direction, discipline, and structure.

- *Risk Assessment* represents the identification and analysis of relevant risks to achieving objectives. This component forms the basis for how risks should be identified, managed, and reported.

- *Control Activities* are embedded in the operational and financial processes and ensure that necessary actions are taken.

- *Information and Communication* identifies, captures, and communicates upstream and downstream data and information.

- *Monitor* refers to the process that assesses and evaluates process effectiveness, efficiency and compliance in addressing the internal control objectives. Included within the monitor component of COSO is the responsibility to report on the company's internal control posture.

Monitoring Challenges in Attaining Cost-Effective Internal Controls

This particularly is the case where managers view control as an administrative burden to be added onto existing business systems, rather than recognizing the business need and benefit for effective internal control that is integrated with core processes. Among the challenges are:

• Obtaining sufficient resources to achieve adequate segregation of duties

• Management's ability to dominate activities with significant opportunities for management override control

• Recruiting individuals with requisite financial reporting and other expertise to serve effectively on the board of directors and audit committees

• Recruiting and retaining personnel with sufficient experience and skill in accounting and financial reporting

• Taking management attention from running the business in order to provide sufficient focus on accounting and financial reporting

• Maintaining appropriate control over computer information systems with limited technical resources

The COSO framework recognizes that an entity must first have in place an appropriate set of financial reporting objectives. At a high level, the objective of financial reporting is to prepare reliable financial statements, which involves attaining reasonable assurance that the financial statements are free from material misstatement. Flowing from this high-level objective, management establishes supporting objectives related to the company's business activities and circumstances and their proper reflection in the company's financial statement accounts and related disclosures. Efficiencies are gained by focusing on only those objectives directly applicable to the business and related to its activities and circumstances that are material to the financial statements.

Sarbanes-Oxley

The Public Accounting Reform and Investor Protection Act of 2002 is commonly referred to as the Sarbanes-Oxley Act, named after its sponsors, U.S. Senator Paul Sarbanes and U.S. Representative Michael Oxley. The Sarbanes-Oxley Act (SOX) requires that all public companies do something that they probably should have been doing all along: assign the chief executive officer (CEO) and the chief financial officer (CFO) authority over the company's internal controls and the opportunity to demonstrate competent and transparent governance.

The major sections of SOX that affect this topic include:

• Section 301, which relates to accounting and auditing complaints

• Section 302, which addresses disclosure procedures and controls, including the quarterly CEO/CFO certification

• Section 404, which addresses internal controls over financial reporting certification and attestation

• Section 409, which requires the rapid disclosure of material events

SOX requirements are based on fundamental principles of good business. Every business whether required to comply with SOX or not, benefits from implementing and paying attention to internal controls. The benefits of a strong internal control structure and program are that it delivers business value far beyond the mandatory compliance with SOX regulations. There are two sections within SOX that require mention here: sections 302 and 404.

Section 302 focuses on management's responsibility. CEOs and CFOs must personally certify that they are responsible for disclosure controls and procedures. Each quarterly filing must contain an evaluation of the design and effectiveness of these controls.

Section 404 mandates an annual evaluation of the company's internal controls program. The rule requires management to base its evaluation on a recognized framework such as COSO. Executive management is directed to support its evaluation with sufficient evidence, including documentation. Section 404 additionally places responsibilities on the external auditors, who must audit management's assessment and issue a related audit opinion.

Together, SOX and COSO have provided the mandate and defined the approach that internal control departments are to use. Companies that focus merely on legal compliance with the act will miss the potential benefits of using the act's provisions as a catalyst for company-wide change. Companies can leverage the SOX provisions to improve employee efficiency and productivity, streamline operations, and make better financial decisions through timelier, more transparent financial information. The act represents an opportunity to elevate corporate integrity, restore investor confidence, and move the economy forward.

There is additional information on the Sarbanes-Oxley Act and how it is integrated within the internal control program in the chapter "Quarterly Subcertification Program." For additional information on the Sarbanes-Oxley Act, go to www.sec.gov/about/laws/soa2002.pdf.

PCAOB

The Public Company Accounting Oversight Board (PCAOB) receives its mandate from section 102 of the Sarbanes-Oxley Act of 2002, which requires accounting firms to be registered with the board if they prepare or issue audit reports on U.S. public companies.

The PCAOB is a private-sector nonprofit organization created by SOX to oversee the auditors of public companies to order to protect the interests of investors and further the public interest in the preparation of informative, fair and independent audit reports.

The PCAOB audits the auditors and provides reports to the public. The PCAOB is mandated to provide, communicate and test compliance with generally accepted auditing standards. Additional information for the PCAOB can be found at http://www.pcaobus.org/.

RISK ASSESSMENT

We live in unstable and volatile times, where a company's ability to conduct business or its very life can be denied by forces seemingly outside its control. There seems to be a never-ending list of factors that require a company to always be diligent. These factors include but are not limited to impacts from events that involve:

- Corruption, fraud
- Economic cycles
- Globalization
- Increasing regulation
- Litigation
- Piracy of intellectual property

- Natural disasters
- Supply chain constraints, restraints
- Geopolitical unrest
- Competitive or industry consolidation
- Consumer demand
- Cyber crime

Assessing or not assessing these risks brings its own price tag in the form of missed opportunities, information and program overload, growing risk aversion and a high cost for failure. The result is a renewed scope and focus for risk, including the company's preparedness for recognizing and managing risk when it presents itself.

Well-run and successful companies know how to use risk to their advantage. Within their organization they have those who monitor and even seek risky opportunities with the purpose of driving innovation and seeking commercial advantage. These same companies also know that resources are drained and wasted when there are inappropriate levels of risk. Understanding the difference is vital.

Innovation and thrill-seeking opportunities may become the domain of sales, marketing, and research and development. There is disproportionate financial risk when innovation and thrill-seeking are not aligned with the company's long-term goals and objectives or when appropriate levels of due financial, technical and operational diligence are not performed *before* investment in these pursuits occurs.

Operational risk occurs when there are unacceptable levels of waste identified by effectiveness and efficiency measures. Financial risk presents itself when budget or plan objectives are not met and when there are gaps within internal control procedure that indicate an opportunity for fraud or misuse may occur.

Our focus in this manual is on the type of risk that compromises your internal controls posture. This includes operational and financial risk.

What is risk? Risk is about being prepared for the unexpected; whether fortuitous or perilous. Risk is about anticipating what is not planned and being confident and able to apply critical thinking faster than the competition. Risk management involves a process of planning, organizing, leading, controlling, and communicating in order to minimize the effects of risk on an organization's capital and earnings.

Using a total company or total enterprise view, management expands the depth and breadth of processes to include not just risks associated with accidental losses but also with financial, strategic and operational situations.

What is risk about? Risk is about understanding its nature and adopting a respectful watchful approach. Companies that understand risk and its place in running a business use it to mitigate unnecessary threats and may even be able to win and make money by taking intelligent risks. Risk management adds value to the bottom line when it provides opportunities for cost savings through identifying and correcting operational inefficiencies, when it promotes "out of the box" thinking, when it opens opportunities to leapfrog the competition. Risk is about being confident and prepared for action.

Not all risk needs to be avoided. For instance, refer back to the Governance flowchart. When big G Governance rules and regulations are received, an assessment needs to be conducted to determine what, if any process is affected. Once the affected processes are identified analysis is required to determine the best approach to comply with the regulation including a cost-versus-benefit analysis. The decision may be to:

- Accept the regulation and integrate it within the current process

- Accept the regulation and integrate it within a redesigned process developing a transition process plan

- Accept the regulation and determine a top level management approach to meet the regulatory reporting requirements and not integrate it within the process

- Partially accept the regulation and integrate it within the current or redesigned process. The part of the regulation not adopted is also considered risk and must be managed. Those areas not adopted must be fully documented including rationale as to why it cannot be adopted at this time. Where possible, mitigating controls must be adopted and monitored collecting evidence to demonstrate a "good faith" effort when regulators call on the company. Even with documentation and mitigating controls, regulators may still consider anything less than full adoption a nonconformation to the law. Consider the cost of potential penalties and risk to the company's reputation if nonconformance is the decision.

Why risk management, why now? It's the environment we live and work in.

Opportunities for risk permeate every aspect of the organization including those points where the external environment imposes specific constraints and/or demands specific information. The following table lists and describes the various types of risks we, as accounting and finance professionals often encounter.

Type of Risk	Description
Business continuity	Assurance that systems and business activities are redundant and recoverable in the event of natural disaster or operational failure.
Business environment and governance	Is an indicator of the company's culture; sets the tone of the organization, business unit, or function; influences the control consciousness of its people; and is the foundation of risk management and internal control, providing discipline and structure.
Change management	Company leaders and employees are unable or unwilling to implement process / product / service improvements quickly enough to keep pace with the changing marketplace.
Compliance	A measure of conformity with applicable laws and regulations, as well as internal policies and procedures.
Customer satisfaction/reputation	The risk that the company's goods and/or services do not consistently meet or exceed customer expectations because of lack of focus on customer needs.
Data security	The protection and safeguarding of sensitive and critical information and the physical assets that support information technology.
Employee health and safety	Health and safety risks are significant due to lack of controls which exposes the company to potentially significant workers' compensation liabilities.
Financial reporting	The risk that financial reports issued to regulatory bodies, existing and prospective investors and lenders include material misstatements or omissions of material facts.

Type of Risk	Description
Human resources	The ability of personnel to effectively manage operating activities, including staff acquisition, staff retention, communication skills, empowerment, accountability, delegation, authority, integrity, judgment, and training.
Legal	Risk that laws and litigation possibilities are not adequately factored into the management decision-making process.
Operational and processing	Ongoing business operations including internal (e.g., culture, people, and process) and external (e.g., competitive, political, and social environment) factors.
Planning	The company's business strategies are not responsible to environmental change, are not driven by appropriate inputs or an effective planning process and are not communicated consistently throughout the organization.
Pricing/contractual commitments	Fluctuations in prices of commodity based materials or products result in a shortfall from budgeted or projected earnings.
Regulatory/industry environment	Regulators impose changes to the industry regulatory environment that result in increased competitive pressures or changes to operational processes.
Reporting	Relates to internal and external reporting and are affected by the preparer's knowledge of generally accepted accounting principles (GAAP), as well as additional regulatory and internal accounting principles.
Risk management	Addresses the company's exposure to loss if market and credit conditions change or if sales, credit, and financing limits are not properly established, updated, or monitored.
Technology	Infrastructure failure (e.g., information systems and telecommunications and/or processing limitations), including failure to properly assess impact of rapidly changing technologies.

Risk and fraud are not the same and fraud deserves a few words. There are generally three requirements for fraud to occur: motivation, opportunity and personality. The degree of motivation is usually dependent on situational pressures and may present itself in the form of a need for money or personal satisfaction or to alleviate a fear of failure. Opportunity refers to having access to a situation where fraud can be perpetrated, such as weaknesses in internal controls, or by necessity or proximity within the operating environment, management styles and corporate culture. Personalities include a personal or behavioral characteristic that demonstrates a willingness to commit fraud. Personal integrity and moral standards need to be "flexible" enough to justify the fraud, perhaps out of a need to feed their children or pay for a family illness.

It is more difficult to mitigate fraud than to mitigate risk. It is difficult to have an effect on an individual's motivation for fraud, since few employees share that level. Personality can sometimes be changed through training and awareness programs. Opportunity is the easiest and most effective requirement to address by developing and implementing effective systems of internal controls. While the occasion for fraud cannot be eliminated, with intelligent supporting programs, the opportunity for it can be diminished by creating an environment of diligence and taking appropriate action at appropriate levels.

Exercise in Evaluating Process Risk

A company's respect for risk shows itself in the company's eagerness for or desire to avoid risk. A company's risk threshold is determined based on the amount of risk exposure or potential adverse impact from an event that the company is willing to accept. As the company reaches its threshold for risk, risk management treatments and business controls are implemented to bring the exposure level back within acceptable levels.

Following is a simple exercise which can be conducted by you or with a select team. Generally the types of things which worry you most attract risk. Without overthinking it, answer the questions with your first impressions, then rate and plot them on the risk matrix.

- Which processes or areas do you think currently have the most risk exposure? Consider using a top-down approach to identify those areas where the highest impact would occur if an internal control weakness was found. Review your financial statements, profit-and-loss statement, and balance sheet. List those accounts that have the largest balances (e.g., revenue, inventory, taxes). It would be helpful to identify what you think the risk might be in these areas.

- Given that you have not conducted any research or investigation, to which of these areas are you prepared to allocate resources? The point being that if these areas worry you and you can name the risk demon and are prepared to spend time and money to find out more; then this is something significant that requires your attention. Consider quantitative as well as qualitative financial and operational impacts for the probability and likelihood that the event will occur.

- What level of risk requires a formal response strategy to mitigate the potentially material impact? In other words, do you want to eliminate all risk, or are you willing to live with certain levels of risk?

Map the risks on the grid according to an impact and probability matrix and group the risks as to those you are willing to:

- *Accept*—retain within the business structure and provide resources to monitor and track

- *Mitigate and control*—establish thresholds and controls to ensure that if pursued the risk will be monitored and tracked and if not pursued a transition plan is established to eliminate it from the business structure

- *Share*—consider alternatives on how the risk may be shared with customers, vendors, suppliers or others

- *Avoid*—eliminate from the business structure and prevent the risk at its source

Risk Matrix

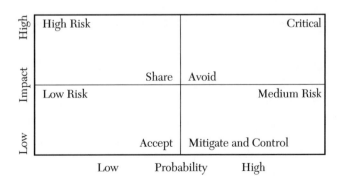

Once your responses are plotted on the above grid, identify what you can or are willing to do to mitigate the risk or test the controls. I've included a few typical examples in the table below to get you started.

To broaden your reach, ask process owners or business area managers to take a few minutes and complete the following providing input for the process areas that "keep them up at night." For about a 20-minute time investment, you could receive input for about 80 percent of the key risks areas.

List Processes	Select an appropriate level of risk you are willing to accept			
	Accept	**Avoid**	**Reduce**	**Share**
A/R—credit administration: Opportunity is to reduce or eliminate customer credit assessments	Accept credit sales from any customer listed as part of the Fortune 500	Customers who are assessed as insolvent	Reduce risk by performing credit assessment for deals over $50K	For "at risk" customers, share the credit risk by asking one-third of the sales price up front
A/P—invoice processing	Accept three-way match between purchase order, invoice, and receiving report	Do not accept invoices without appropriate management-level approval	Reduce the risk by accepting a two-way match between the invoice and receiving report on selected preidentified purchases	

Analyze and prioritize the list to provide a starting point for your risk management process.

Note to reader:

The word *process* is used throughout this text and refers to a definable, repeatable, predictable, measurable, integratable series of tasks. For a process to be complete, it must have **all** these dimensions:

- *Definable* in that there is a specific scope encompassing the series of tasks; there is a beginning and an end. There are defined inputs, defined work activities and defined outputs. There are no tasks which remain undefined to the process. Example: G equals E plus F.

- *Repeatable* in that there are consistent, recurring tasks which make up the process. To ensure consistent outcomes, each time the tasks are undertaken they are performed in the same way. There is little or no room for variation to the sequence of the tasks. Example: task E always precedes task F.

- *Predictable* in that once the tasks begin, consistent, comparable outcomes result. It can be computed so that when the inputs are known the outputs are expected and if the outputs are known the inputs are calculable. Example: E plus F equals G.

- *Measurable* in that performance measures are embedded into the process as an indicator of the predictability of the process. Example: If 1E leads to 1F then 1E is a preelection of 1F.

- *Integratable* in that processes are dependent on, connected and interact with other processes. Example: C plus D equals E.

If the objective of an effective control is to ensure that a definable, repeatable, predictable, measurable outcome occurs each time a process is followed, then why not produce documentation in support of the process?

Note that you could have a definable process and still not have control, if you haven't designed the appropriate control elements into the process. Therefore, it is a myth that a defined process equals control *or* that documentation equals control.

OVERSIGHT

Where there are rules and where there is risk, there is opportunity and oversight. For example, there are rules about driving on highways, let's say 60 miles (100 kilometers) per hour. There are opportunities with high-precision cars, and risks with inadequate drivers to break those rules. It should be no surprise, then, that there is oversight. However, oversight is more than just policing or catching violators; there has to be consequence. Therefore, risk, oversight, and consequence are closely related.

Where does oversight come from? Oversight is included within the big G Governance rules and regulations, including but not limited to the Securities and Exchange Commission (SEC), Sarbanes-Oxley Act, and the Public Company Accounting Oversight Board (PCAOB). In addition to providing oversight of others, each of the big G Governance organizations has oversight responsibility for its own rules and regulations. For example, the PCAOB oversees the auditors who provide audits and opinions about a company's financial position.

What is oversight? *Oversight* is defined as watchful care, careful scrutiny, and intervention. An effective oversight approach has the capacity to influence business leaders, operations, and organizational cultures. Successful oversight programs are proven to reveal waste, fraud, and abuse; protect individual rights; ensure compliance with the law; and evaluate a business's performance.

Oversight is designed to look at everything that is done in an objective and independent manner. Oversight programs review, monitor, and supervise the execution and implementation of policies and procedures, to assure that laws are faithfully executed. As with the PCAOB, oversight programs review the processes and programs responsible for reviewing, monitoring, and remediation. Therefore, as the PCAOB audits the auditors, internal oversight reviews the effectiveness and efficiency of internal audit and controls. In order to provide independence and objectivity, a primary principle of oversight is to separate those within the oversight function from executive and operational management.

What is oversight about? Oversight is about establishing a program for addressing questions of potential risk and providing a check and balance to ensure compliance with principles, rules, policies, and procedures. As with governance and risk, oversight is a process, part of a program used to improve the integrity, credibility, and accountability of the information presented for decision making. As a program, governance and oversight must apply program and process disciplines to monitoring themselves.

Oversight is about assigning the policing role to auditors and those who audit the auditors. One aspect of the auditing role is to provide watchful care and scrutiny that the company is complying with external rules and regulations. The consequences for noncompliance may be significant and include:

- Fines imposed on the company, the executive, and/or the board of directors

- Loss of stock market value

- Public humiliation and loss to company image and reputation, including a loss of customers, employees, and vendors

- Disbarment of business licenses, which means that the company is no longer able to conduct business

One of the functions of internal control is to provide a preventive or early warning signal when weaknesses are present. The internal control program identifies the governance issues requiring monitoring and the internal processes that have the greatest opportunity for risk. As the PCAOB does with external auditors, the internal control function must monitor those processes that oversee compliance within the company, including the effectiveness of the internal audit process.

Internal Use Only

However, the program is not limited to just providing company oversight; to be effective there must be oversight of the program itself. That is, internal controls must monitor and measure how effective its program is in providing and monitoring governance. As part of the COSO guidance, the internal control program must also be evaluated.

Why oversight, why now? To hold leaders accountable. The challenge of accountability is to demonstrate that governance policies and procedures are implemented throughout the company. The power of using oversight as a process is to encourage leaders to venture out of the office, review operations, change policies, reallocate resources, and test audit controls.

The role of internal controls as a best practice is to provide data and information that will assist the company in implementing effective and efficient processes and hold responsible leaders accountable.

Use the following table as a starting point to identify where oversight is needed. The exercise is to recognize and rate the importance and performance of the oversight principles.

Next to each statement, rate how important the principle is within your company and rate how well you think you are doing in satisfying that principle. Use a high, medium, and low rating, and as with the other exercises in this unit, go with your first impression. As a company leader, you should have insight and judgment as to what is important and how well it is operating.

Importance refers to how important these principles and practices are to you in running your business, and performance refers to the degree these practices are embedded into your corporate culture and environment. Be honest—the results will help you improve.

Oversight Principles	Practices for Oversight	Importance	Performance
Strategy, mission, planning	The governing body (i.e., board of directors and senior executives) shall: • Provide strategic direction and monitor management to achieve company goals and objectives. • Ensure that the entity complies with all relevant laws and regulations. • Communicate between the company and stakeholders. • Identify and monitor key areas of risk and the tolerance appetite for risk; key performance indicators.		
Oversight bodies	The governing body shall name subordinate committees and/or departments to aid in discharging its oversight responsibilities. These committees and/or departments shall have: • Resources and independence needed to execute their duties. Committee members shall have the necessary skills, knowledge, and competencies to ensure effectiveness. • A clear mandate to identify their membership, responsibilities, and accountability. • A defined process to access, monitor, and test appropriate and relevant processes and information. • A schedule of regular meetings with defined agendas and minutes to keep track of actions taken or to be taken. • Defined procedures for the early reporting of significant events.		

Oversight Principles	Practices for Oversight	Importance	Performance
Transparency and disclosure	Management shall demonstrate principles of integrity, accuracy, completeness, and timely disclosure to the governing subcommittees and/or departments. Governing subcommittees and department members shall: • Satisfy themselves that they have received objective, accurate, complete, and timely information before rendering an opinion or making a decision. • Be subject to evaluation by the governing body in regard to their performance and effectiveness.		
Ethical environment	The governing body shall: • Develop, communicate, and test the company code of conduct. • Provide a confidential (i.e., whistleblowing) process covering fraud, corruption, and other risks.		
Audit, risk, and compliance	Executive management shall be responsible: • For the design, implementation, monitoring, and integration of big G Governance into little g governance policies, procedures, practices, and activities. • To establish an effective internal audit and internal control function to provide independent feedback as to management's ability to mange the company.		

For those items rated:

- High in importance and high in performance—congratulations, you have achieved best-practice status.

- High in importance and low in performance—consider developing an action plan to close the gap.

- Low in importance and high in performance—consider whether you are spending too much time and resources.

- Low in importance and low in performance—consider missed opportunity and/or exposures by not meeting or addressing this important principle.

Proper execution of an oversight program produces results and improves the profitability. In my opinion, when companies are not seeing bottom-line results from their oversight program, the role and responsibility for oversight is misplaced. The oversight program has probably been compromised by lack of a clear mandate, resources, or scope. When the oversight program provides baby-sitting and policing without providing the result of increased accountability, then it has become not only ineffective but powerless.

When process owners look to the compliance department, internal audit, or internal controls to determine where and when controls must be "designed into" a process and for defining the types of control activities to test schemas or validate data, then the oversight program has lost its independence and objectivity. My advice is to get back to basics, apply project/process management techniques, define roles and responsibilities, and design local control activities and oversight testing activities into each process based on an acceptable level of risk.

You know you have too much or misplaced oversight when:

- It gets in the way of innovation and creativity.

- It does not add value.

- It exerts political influence.

- No attention is paid to the results.

- The objective becomes more "gotcha" and destructive versus monitoring for improvement and constructive.

- Meetings to plan the planning of oversight activities take precedence over and exceed the time and resources it takes to conduct actual oversight activities.

Applying a successful oversight program within the organization involves:

- Independence and objectivity

- A regular, systematic approach regardless of the scope or functional business area

- Comprehensive review and analysis addressing all processes

- Incorporating the use of input from other check-and-balance activities such as key performance indicators

- Performance by professional individuals knowledgeable in the areas of conducting audits and internal controls as well as the functional areas being audited or tested

- The functional organization

- Drawing the line between careful inspection and micromanagement

- Documentation with action items identified and follow-through

- Results reported up the hierarchy chain of command and executive leaders

According to SOX regulations, the board of directors and executive leadership are responsible for overseeing the effectiveness of the company's internal control and disclosure control. Oversight is so important that, if the independent auditors determine that the board is not fulfilling its oversight responsibilities, this failure would be a "material weakness."

Not only is the board responsible for oversight of internal control, the board is actually a component of internal control. The board's oversight of the financial reporting function, the internal audit function, the risk management function, and the relationship with the independent auditors is an element of internal control. As described earlier, the board and executive leadership are responsible for providing direction and translating big G Governance to little g governance implementation, and they are responsible for completing the journey by overseeing that the implementation has complied with the big G Governance regulations.

DOCUMENTATION

Critical to operationally implementing little g governance and linking it to risk and oversight is communication and documentation.

Where does documentation come from? Documentation is all around us—some formal such as charters, policies, procedures, and instructions; and some informal such as checklists, forms, and e-mails. Along the governance journey, *all* documentation is subject to scrutiny and review. Consider recent investigations where seemingly innocent e-mails and memos caused a company's downfall.

Refer to your company's records and information management and/or information handling policies and procedures. In addition to other important topics such as legal hold and destruction, these policies and procedures define what documentation is and is not, how it must be classified, where it must reside, and how long it must be retained. How well employees comply with these rules will have an enormous impact on satisfying governance. These policies and procedures must identify the classification, use, and retention of such documentation.

At an organizational level, a best practice is to be a high-level process flow linking the company's processes and locations. This could be achieved simply with an organization chart or using process flow, the objective to link sub-processes to higher-level processes and to ensure that the "handoffs" between processes are addressed as control points. As a hint, you will generally find control issues at the process "handoff" points.

What is documentation? *Documentation* refers to the act of authentication, providing substantive evidence and proof. *Documents* refer to the formal and informal written audit trail, describing and proving that the fundamental process qualities, elements, and criteria exist, therefore serving as a form of communication, instruction, and due diligence.

By establishing a company-wide policy-and-procedure program and using that program as a basis for measuring compliance, leaders set the tone that internal controls are important and must be considered part of everyone's business. Internal controls must be built into each process, and there must be planned reviews and testing to ensure that those controls are executed as intended.

In order to demonstrate that a controlled environment exists, the process must demonstrate that it is definable, repeatable, predictable, measurable, and integratable; to prove that the process is all of those things, it must be documented, monitored, and controlled.

Management must be careful to distinguish between the documentation of internal control and the internal control itself. Creating a document that describes the controls is *not* the control. The control must be part of the *process* used by the *people* to carry out those documented policies and procedures. It is a myth to think that documentation equals internal controls or that no documents mean no internal controls exist. The process may have controls built in, and documentation itself may be lacking. The documentation process must also be evaluated.

Having said that; documentation is the backbone of the internal control framework. There are different acceptable ways to document control procedures, including observation, narratives, and flowcharts. Software application documentation tools may be used to facilitate this process, and many reputable software companies can be found on the Internet.

Since the passage of The Sarbanes-Oxley Act (SOX), many companies have developed computer software products that aid in complying with the internal control provisions of the act. These software tools typically center on helping companies automate the documentation of internal control procedures while monitoring schedules for review, testing, and remediation.

The first purpose of an automated tool typically is to serve as a repository for all process instruction and documentation. In those instances where the documentation of the control or the control itself either does not exist or is otherwise deficient, the software may allow the company to efficiently document existing policies or design and document new ones.

Since the control objectives include completeness and accuracy, it is ideal to have this type of complete documentation trail. However, most companies operate between the ideal and an ad hoc documentation basis that is, completing documentation only when it is called for and not worrying about aligning it with other processes. For smaller companies, this approach may be useful in that the owner oversees all the processes. Smaller companies may use memoranda and instructions as a substitute for formal policies and procedures. For larger companies, an ad hoc approach to documentation signals an opportunity for improvement.

Determining an appropriate level of documentation is dependent on who will be using the documentation. I recommend taking time to prepare useful documentation, as it can and should be used when training new employees, when base-lining or reengineering the process, and when deciding which parts of the process could be eliminated, transferred, or outsourced.

In addition to the higher-level policies and procedures, useful documentation for testing internal controls comes in the form of:

- *Narratives*—identifying the step-by-step list of activities or tasks performed to produce the desired output. These are sometimes referred to as desk procedures. These descriptions would typically identify contacts and sources of the input, testing and proving that the source input is correct, complete, and accurate. The narratives would include reference to systems and spreadsheets, types of analysis performed, criteria for decision making, and names of those who are required to review and/or approve steps within the process. Finally, it would identify where (i.e., which system or database), when, and to whom the output is sent.

- *Flowcharts*—whether as simple process flows or as role-oriented "swim lane" flowcharts, flowcharts are a practical visual aid to demonstrate how the process is organized. Process flowcharts emphasize the flow of the process including data, information, and decision points, while swim lane charts emphasize a person's role and responsibility.

- *Internal control questionnaires*—which aren't really a description of the process but rather a checklist to identify the likely areas or lack of control activities. These are generally adapted from internal audit work papers, identifying typical monitoring and testing points within the process.

In performing internal control reviews and testing, an example of a typical documentation environment might reveal a weakness. The general ledger manager describes a fair reflection of the actual policy and procedures. A discussion with the monthly accrual accounting employee reveals additional details of the procedural inputs, confirming some of the procedures pointed out by the general ledger manager; however, new details or key changes to the process are disclosed. Finally, when examining the final output, it is discovered that key authorization controls were not included in the procedures, discussed by the general ledger manager or employees performing the task. In this case, there may or may not be a control weakness; however, there is a documentation weakness.

In assessing the adequacy of the documentation, management determines whether *control objectives* have been considered. The testing guides presented in this manual have been structured to identify and consider each of these control objectives:

- Data and information integrity, which includes completeness, accuracy, and timeliness

- Authorized and executed in accordance with formal delegation of authority

- Safeguarding the company's assets and those assets entrusted to the company

- Segregation of duties in order to promote operational effectiveness and efficiency and not compromise the integrity of the company through opportunities for error, misstatement, or fraud

- Automate where and when possible as in the form of information technology controls

In testing the control objective, you have to evaluate the control and the documentation separately with the result classified as:

- *Sufficient controls and documentation.* That is, the documentation allows management and the external auditor to authenticate the process and:

  - Determine whether the policy, procedure, and processes are adequately designed.

  - Perform reviews and tests to validate the deployment and operating effectiveness of the controls.

- *Controls exist and documentation is considered informal, communicated verbally, or otherwise not documented.* Suitable documentation must be developed to facilitate an evaluation of the effectiveness of the design of the control.

- *Controls do not exist or do not follow the written documentation.* The process owner must design, implement, and document new control procedures and/or implement a controlled process.

What is documentation about? Documentation is about definition and communication providing direction and substance when used for reporting purposes. Using a top-down approach, documentation is about establishing and communicating the principles, rules, and behaviors to the greater employee population. Documentation is used to provide authority and accountability to employees to act within defined parameters. Using a bottom-up approach, documentation is about informing management about how work actually gets done, that is, identifying the steps required to process transactions.

Regardless of the method used to document new or existing controls, the goal remains the same—to accurately describe the company's control procedures and internal control posture, as they currently exist. The preparer of this documentation should have an in-depth understanding of:

- The entity's current operations and existing control procedures

- Internal control concepts, as described in the COSO framework

- The financial reporting process

- The assertions and disclosure requirement represented in the financial statements

Once the documentation becomes established as an accurate reflection of internal control, and standardized updating procedures are in place, actual changes to the processes must be reflected in the documentation. At least annually, process owners must review and attest that the documentation is current and accurate.

Why documentation, why now? According to the Securities and Exchange Commission (SEC), Office of the Chief Accountant, accounting documentation, policy, and/or procedures make up 99 percent of ineffective internal controls over financial reporting issues. That bears repeating: **99 percent of the issues related to internal controls over financial reporting are due to a lack of or noncompliance with documentation.**

In my opinion, this means there is a disconnection or risk between the top-down management intent and the bottom-up management review of what is actually being performed. Having an effective and efficient documentation program mitigates the risk. It sounds like a simple fix—providing instructions that are in compliance with the rules and then measuring compliance to those instructions.

Developing an adequate understanding of the processing environment is critical to performing internal reviews and testing. Documenting an understanding of the process, related controls, and key roles and responsibilities can be achieved through process narratives and flowcharts. Once these documentations are confirmed as accurate, they provide a baseline for performing risk analysis, internal control testing, and implementing process improvements as necessary.

Notice that documentation is required regardless of the outcome of monitoring and testing. Documentation becomes a due diligence function required to execute the internal control plan, rather than just part of an audit trail for the findings.

The degree to which the external auditors may rely on tests performed by the company to evaluate the effectiveness of internal control is a matter that is addressed in the Public Company Accounting Oversight Board (PCAOB) Auditing Standard No. 2, "An Audit of Internal Control over Financial Reporting Conducted in Conjunction with an Audit of Financial Statements." Basically, if your internal control program has integrity and depth, the external auditors may rely on the results of the company's internal control program to reduce the amount of on-site testing and audits required, bottom line, saving the company external auditor fees.

Then why is it so difficult to correct and implement? The documentation process is tedious work, requiring coordination and decisions between different functional departments and management. Typically, creating documentation is an iterative process that involves individuals at various levels of responsibility discussing processing steps, related responsibilities, and process metrics or outputs. For more information on establishing a successful accounting and finance policy-and-procedure program, refer to the *Accounting and Finance Policy and Procedure* text produced by John Wiley and Sons and located at http://www.wiley.com/WileyCDA/WileyTitle/productCd-0470259620.html.

Questions arise as to the extent of documentation needed to deem internal controls effective. The answer, of course, is: it depends. Documentation of business processes, procedures, and other elements of internal control systems is developed and maintained by companies for a number of reasons. One reason is to promote consistency in adhering to desired practices, while other reasons indicate that documentation assists communication, creates expectations of performance, assists in education and training, and, of course, provides evidence supporting transactional process. Documentation is reviewed and tested for its consistency, completeness, and accuracy.

The level and nature of documentation varies widely by company. Larger companies usually have more operations to document or greater complexity in financial reporting processes, and therefore find it necessary to have more extensive formal documentation. Smaller companies often find less need for formal documentation such as in-depth policy manuals, system flowcharts of processes, organization charts, or job descriptions. They might document human resources, procurement, or customer credit policies with memoranda and supplement the memoranda with guidance provided by management in meetings.

Determining the level and complexity of the documentation is a matter of judgment and needs to be decided based on the value and use that a documentation program would contribute to the company's success.

Remember to document and test the internal control process itself. Since the internal control program is a critical business process, it, too, shall be documented, monitored, and tested as to its effectiveness and efficiency.

What type of internal control indicators do you collect to support your internal control posture?

READINESS CHECKLIST FOR DOCUMENTATION

To evaluate the effectiveness of documentation, consider the following self-assessment or internal control readiness checklist. Answer **Yes** or **No** to the following questions. A **No** response indicates an opportunity for improvement.

Question	Yes	No
Process Descriptions:		
A) Does the process narrative summary have the preparer's name?		
B) Does the process narrative summary have the approver's name (where applicable)?		
C) Are the relevant policies and procedures noted on the summary?		
D) Are the policies and procedures retained in the company-approved documentation repository?		
Process Maps:		
A) Do the maps indicate inputs and outputs for each activity?		
B) Are there any estimates or assumptions in the process? Is the methodology explained/documented in the narrative?		
C) Have risks and controls been documented where the risk and control occurs?		
D) Does every risk identified on a process step have a control and vice versa?		
Information Technology:		
A) Is the specific database referenced where process information exists?		
B) Does the narrative indicate which database?		
Risk Checklist:		
A) Are there any risks/controls that apply to the whole process?		
B) Is the risk defined adequately enough to explain what could go wrong?		
C) Does every risk link to at least one control?		
D) Does every risk statement contain the cause and effect?		

INTERNAL CONTROL
PROGRAM

INTERNAL CONTROLS PROGRAM

Internal controls are more than rules; they embody a company's principles, trust, values, and culture. Internal control activities are more than walking a process to see if it matches to the documentation. Internal control is much more than standardizing processes; it includes demonstrating that decisions are made based on applying principles and documenting the assumptions, criteria, and evidence used to make decisions.

Internal controls is the part of the governance journey that has responsibility to assess, test, monitor, evaluate, and report on the status of implementing big G Governance.

What are internal controls? *Control* refers to a set of activities used to guide, manage, and regulate toward a directive. Internal control refers to a skill developed and applied within a company, which uses judgment to assess and determine compliance. Those who exercise internal control must have the power and authority to actuate and remediate findings.

Internal controls refers to a program of activities established to catch and monitor a potential exposure that could result in a significant error, omission, misstatement, or fraud. An internal controls program (Program) is the core where big G and little g governance, risk, oversight, documentation, and assessment come together.

The internal control program provides reasonable assurance and oversight for processes that:

- Establish parameters to delegate power or authority to guide and regulate economic activities such as those demanded by external regulations and identified within internal policies and procedures.

- Test and report on compliance with those established parameters.

- Evaluate operational effectiveness and efficiency.

- Assess the reliability of financial reporting.

- Report on compliance with applicable laws and regulations.

- Supports the remediation effort by examining the limits of authority as defined in the first step.

The program consists of a specific set of policies, procedures, and activities designed to address opportunity, risk, and uncertainty.

What is internal controls about? Internal controls is about assessing risk, providing oversight, and reporting on the company's control posture. Often confused with internal audit, in many companies' internal controls has become subordinate to internal audit. Internal controls and internal audit are the same in that their purpose is to add value and improve an organization's operations. They both use auditing techniques and analytical tools to assess and evaluate the business environment.

Internal controls differs from internal audit in that it is not just about assessing and evaluating a company's compliance posture in an oversight capacity, but the internal control function needs to be a proactive participant in defining, documenting, communicating, educating, testing, and supporting the company's operational and financial goals and objectives. Many companies use internal controls as a penalty-free audit where department and process managers may render opinions and decisions about business practices and the implementation of big G Governance.

Internal auditors are generally interested in validating data and reports at the end of a cycle with the purpose of rendering judgment and an opinion. Internal controls are generally interested in validating the operational and financial process used during a cycle with the purpose of exposing weaknesses and identifying areas for improvement.

To summarize and use language that we accountant types might better understand, internal auditors evaluate and assess a process "as at" a point in time, while internal controls professionals evaluate and assess transactions over a "period of time."

Where does the model and requirement for internal controls come from? Internal controls are part of the governance cycle that originates from external laws and regulations and is translated into internal strategies policies and procedures that, when deployed, are used to produce data, information, and reports to those same external organizations where the laws originate.

Internal controls starts with a strong control environment, is "owned" by management, and is the responsibility of every employee. Internal controls must be designed into and embedded within business processes and not "bolted onto" as oppressive "thou shall not" rules.

The Committee of Sponsoring Organizations of the Treadway Commission (COSO) in 1992 issued *Internal Control–Integrated Framework* to help businesses and other entities assess and enhance their internal control systems. Executives, board members, regulators, standard setters, professional organizations, and others have recognized this framework as an appropriate comprehensive model for internal controls.

As a result of addressing and responding to SOX requirements, most internal control departments have experienced resource constraints and unrealistic time demands. As a result, the historic internal control mandate is very different than the present internal control mandate. Historically, internal controls reviewed operational and financial processes and provided resources to research, investigate, and address business practice–type issues (known today as compliance). Today, mainly because of the regulatory workload, internal control testing has generally excluded operations and is focused on validating that appropriate levels of review and authorization are present. Consequently, the internal controls function is generally not a value-add function nor are they invited to the table as a valued member of the team. In too many companies, internal control managers are battle weary from fighting the "kill the messenger" wars.

Following are the signs that your internal controls program is not working the way it was intended to work:

- Do employees say "I didn't know that"? If so, this is a signal that there is inadequate knowledge of the company's policies, procedures, or governing regulations.

- When you ask an employee who performs a specific task and they answer with "We trust 'A,' who does all of those things," this could be a sign of inadequate segregation of duties.

- If there are shared passwords, unlocked offices, or cash not secured, then there is inappropriate access to and safeguarding of assets.

- When you hear, "You mean I'm supposed to do something besides initial it?" there is incomplete form without substance.

- When the documentation reads "Just get it done, I don't care how," that is a sure sign of control override and a strong indicator of other "tone from the top" issues.

- When the excuse is "People are people and mistakes happen. You can't foresee or eliminate risk," then there are inherent limitations and there is a mismatch between the jobs employees are asked to perform and the data and skills made available to them.

This manual goes back to the historical roots of internal controls and incorporates process management, financial management, and audit techniques to execute the Program.

Why internal controls, why now? To ensure compliance with the law, and to hold the leaders accountable for processes and decisions that make up the environment where we work.

Broken processes often can be remedied through the use of an effective internal control program, and it is not an accident that these indicators of broken processes mirror the COSO framework.

1. Lack of adequate management oversight and accountability and failure to develop a strong control culture (links back to COSO's control environment)

2. Inadequate assessment of the risk of certain activities, whether on or off balance sheet (links back to COSO's risk assessment)

3. The absence or failure of key control activities, such as segregation of duties, approvals, verifications, reconciliations, and reviews of operating performance (links back to COSO's control activities)

4. Inadequate communication of information between levels of management, especially in the upward communication of problems (links back to COSO's communicate and remediate)

5. Inadequate or ineffective use of monitoring activities including internal control and audit programs (links back to COSO's monitor, evaluate, and report)

Benefits realized from a well-implemented internal control program include:

- Increased operational effectiveness, reliable financial reporting

- Increased profitability

- Improved documentation of controls and control process evaluation

- Improved definition of controls across the organization, including the crucial relationship between controls and risk

Companies with effective controls experience improvements in operational effectiveness, efficiency, communication, reliability, flexibility, and resiliency. Companies with effective controls have an ability to execute as planned, allocate resources predictably, and provide consistent and reliable data and information available for decision making and reporting.

The resurgence of an emphasis on internal controls has spurred a return to implementing and testing according to its historic mandate. Market leaders know how to leverage the knowledge gained from the internal control program to create measurable value across the entire organization.

A following chapter presents the program charter with objectives to provide:

- Operational effectiveness—to identify and correct defects within processing of transactions, producing products, and/or delivering services

- Operational efficiency—to identify and correct delays in processing transactions, producing products, and/or delivering services

- Oversight of the internal controls over financial reporting (ICOFR)—which includes the data and information submitted externally to satisfy government and reporting regulations

- Oversight and internal controls for all other applicable laws and regulations—as defined by the countries and areas where the company conducts business

Program versus Process

Why an internal control program and not just an internal control process? A program is more than a process. The program guarantees that there is a process whereby the program's objectives must be researched, decided and implemented. A program manager is constantly looking to validate the program's objectives and approaches to ensure the best possible fit for the company. A process manager is looking to execute with consistency, refining the execution but not necessarily looking to expand or change the process mandate or scope.

Notice that the first objective within the internal control charter is to establish an internal control program.

Example:

A transactional or operational process is a group of cohesive tasks and activities that, when implemented, produce a product or service. A process begins with defined inputs and ends with defined outputs. The execution of how input gets converted to output is the process. Each execution of the process requires discrete input and output, and although the process may interact across departments or functions for input and/or output, the process itself is contained within one department or functional group.

Accounts receivable (A/R) collections process has the objective of following predefined tasks to facilitate the collection of valid outstanding A/R from customers. The process includes:

- *Input:* Data and information regarding invoices sent by the billings department

- *Process:* Defined procedures instructing A/R collectors as to the timing and process they are to use when approaching customers

- *Procedural steps:* (1) Running a customer aging report, (2) identifying and selecting those customers whose billings are now due to the company, (3) communicating with those customers to gain remittance or resolution of the invoice, (4) escalating procedures for customers who remain in default, (5) record correspondence and communication efforts and outcomes with customer, (6) prepare outputs

- *Output:* Report on the status of overdue accounts. Note that the application of cash collected is another process and is not a defined output of the collections department.

A program differs in that it is a series of processes that are linked and require only periodic changes or updates to the base input such as when rules and regulations change. The execution part of the program generally crosses functional lines and includes a cycle that may impact the entire company.

An accounts receivable (A/R) program has the objective of optimizing its A/R policies and procedures to maximize sales and reduce company risk. The program includes:

- *Input:* (1) Company goals and objectives (e.g., sales and A/R measures such as days' sales outstanding); (2) sales terms and conditions. Note: Sales plan is optional input in that if there will be a shift to only market to Fortune 500 customers rather than mass marketing, this could affect the A/R program strategies; (3) sales returns; (4) external input from Dun and Bradstreet, credit agencies, and customers; (5) cash deposit reports from treasury

- *Program scope:* Credit administration, collections, cash applications

- *Program procedures:* (1) Evaluate and assist with establishing company goals and objectives regarding sales terms and conditions; (2) staff and assign resources to perform the necessary A/R procedures, ensure staff is trained, skilled, and has access to appropriate systems; (3) establish staff hierarchy with delegations of authority; (4) execute credit administration, collection, cash applications; (5) reconcile customer accounts; (6) prepare, review, and analyze customer status reports for sales and management; (7) prepare input for journal entries, accounting reporting; (8) prepare, review, and analyze A/R effectiveness and efficiency reports for management; (9) evaluate A/R program

- *Output:* (1) Customer status reports used as input to sales; (2) journal entries and accounting reports used as input to general accounting and external reporting; (3) continuous improvement for A/R program

A program and a process are the same in that both are definable, repeatable, predictable, and measurable; both are integrated within the fabric of the company and both require documentation.

Financial, Operational, and Performance Risk, Controls, and Testing

Financial and operational controls exist in assessing risk and are defined as follows:

- *Operational risks* are transactional or events based and affect the "way" work is designed, executed, monitored, or measured. Operational risks refer to the type of internal opportunities and weaknesses that affect processes and impact achieving the company's operational goals and objectives. Operational risks occur when processes are not executed in an effective and efficient manner and assets are not safeguarded or are exposed to abuse by fraud, theft, or other environmental conditions. All inappropriate operational risk has a financial impact.

- *Financial risks* are the result of operational risks and represent the financial outcomes of an ineffective, inefficient process. Financial risks may also occur when the accounting treatment is not updated to reflect changes to financial reporting requirements and are considered noncompliance risks.

- *Performance risks* come about when the company and process owners are driven to achieve specific key performance indicators, regardless of the cost to operational or financial integrity. Performance risks are often designed to bypass operational and financial controls and require deliberate action and collusion.

Internal Control over Financial Reporting

Big G Governance prescribes the rules and standards for management's assessment and reporting on the status of internal controls over financial reporting (ICOFR).

- The Sarbanes-Oxley Act (SOX) directed the Securities and Exchange Commission (SEC) to adopt detailed rules to implement the requirements of the act relating to internal control. Specifically, sections 302 and 404 of the act identify the internal control assessments to which management must attest.

- External auditor standards are defined by the Public Company Accounting Oversight Board (PCAOB). These standards describe the approach, required tests, and other guidance that the entity's external auditors are expected to follow when reporting on management's assertion about the effectiveness of internal control. The PCAOB audits the auditors to ensure that these standards are followed.

- According to SOX and the SEC, management's report on internal control effectiveness is required to disclose the criteria against which management assesses effectiveness. The generally accepted criteria is to follow the Committee of Sponsoring Organizations of the Treadway Commission's (COSO's) *Internal Control–Integrated Framework.*

The COSO integrated framework includes financial and operational controls recognizing that operational controls have an indirect effect on the amounts and disclosures reported in the financial statement. The COSO framework identifies internal controls as relevant to achieving company objectives for operational, financial, and compliance goals.

The internal control testing guides included in this manual address both financial and operational control objectives, recognizing that processes are dependent not only on each other but on the operational aspects, that is, the cause-and-effect relationship between operational data and financial reporting requirements. Therefore, it is recommended that the approach to internal controls take into consideration the historical roots of the internal controls discipline and include operational and financial oversight.

The internal control objective is to establish a program that is made up of processes that, when implemented, produce not only internal control outcomes but an assessment of the overall program itself.

COSO provides the generally accepted internal control framework, and it is made up of five interrelated components:

1. Control environment
2. Risk assessment
3. Control activities
4. Information and communication
5. Monitor, evaluate, and report

Following is a definition of the framework components, including a self-assessment to help you measure how well your company has adopted this framework.

APPENDIX

SELF-ASSESSMENT FOR THE INTERNAL CONTROL FRAMEWORK ACCORDING TO COSO

COSO defines the elements and scope of internal control as a framework to be used by those who oversee big G and little g governance. Following each of the COSO elements are some self-assessment questions.

As with the previous self-assessment exercises, complete this by youself or with a select group. The reasoning is that, as the executive, you know your business best and what worries you. When considering your response to those questions, apply the scoring matrix that follows to give you a baseline self-assessment score.

How well do you think you are doing with incorporating the COSO framework within your company and your internal controls departmental activities? Using the definitions and questions listed after each of the COSO sections, rate your company as to the degree that these elements have been incorporated into the operational approach, deployment, and results. Use the following scoring scale to give yourself a grade. You must satisfy earlier grades before proceeding to the next level.

Notice that the scale progresses from ad hoc to serving as the benchmarked company and that as you move up the scale, there are more requirements for a deeper, more integrated deployment. Results that demonstrate that the approach and the deployment have caused the improvements are required to achieve ratings in the higher categories.

Don't be discouraged if you score low; follow the scoring road map to improve.

The scoring scale is defined as:

- **Up to 20 percent—ad hoc,** which means:

  - No clear approach; issues are corrected as they arise.

- **Up to 40 percent—awareness,** which means:

  - Approach includes strategic, tactical, and operational activities.

  - Resources are assigned to internal control activities.

  - Deployed in some areas of the business.

- **Up to 60 percent—deployed,** which means:

  - Approach is deployed in most areas of the business.

  - Internal control measurements are gathered and communicated to management for action.

- **Up to 80 percent—results,** which means:

  - There is a direct cause and effect on improved internal control measures due to the deployment of the approach.

- **Over 80 percent—benchmark,** which means:

  - Results are sustained and the company's internal control program is shared with other companies and industries.

Score Sheet

Up to Percent (%)	Control Environment	Risk Assessment	Control Activities	Information and Communication	Monitor
Up to 20%—Ad Hoc					
Up to 40%—Awareness					
Up to 60%—Deployed					
Up to 80%—Results					
Over 80%—Benchmark					

1) The **control environment** establishes the overall tone, or culture, of the organization, which exercises a pervasive influence on all control functions. The principles of a controlled environment need to be documented, communicated, and integrated within each of the processes. A company's overall tone and control objectives might include becoming a process-driven company. In a process-driven company, each process and employee is part of process value chain that is continually monitored and managed for continuous improvement with objectives for reaching best-in-class, best-of-breed, or world-class status.

   - Has the executive leadership identified an overall control strategy and assigned appropriate resources to execute the strategy?

   - In support of this overall control strategy, list the types and frequency of communication that demonstrates the tone from the top.

   - Would the general employee population be able to articulate the company's control strategy and environment? If you are unsure, ask.

   - How is the control strategy managed, monitored, and improved to ensure that it is meeting executive leadership goals and objectives? Does this strategy trickle down to those who execute the process?

2) **Risk assessment** is a process that identifies the risks to achieving the internal control objectives. This process forms the basis for designing control activities to mitigate those risks. For example, the risk assessment considers measurements, tools, and job aids that assist employees in evaluating the efficiency (i.e., number of defects) and effectiveness (i.e., cycle time) of each process. Once the baseline process and measures have been established, risks need to be identified and quantified.

   - Has the company defined and identified the operational areas or processes where unacceptable levels of risk may be present? Is there a functional business area identified to assess, monitor, and track these processes?

   - What is the approach used to define, identify, quantify, and report on the status of risk thresholds?

   - Is there a tool that allows any employee to report on transactional events or processes that may have inappropriate levels of risk?

   - Are risk-related issues investigated, tracked, and resolved in a timely manner? Are "band-aid" control fixes replaced with changes to the process where controls are designed in?

   - How is the risk strategy managed, monitored, and improved to ensure that it is meeting executive leadership goals and objectives?

3) **Control activities** are policies and procedures designed to identify and mitigate risks to achieve company success and internal control objectives. Their goal is to optimize performance, proactively prevent control failures (such as errors in financial statements or employee fraud), and reactively detect failures that occur.

- What is the approach used to define, identify, measure, and report on the status of control activities?

- How are control activities identified and incorporated into the company's documentation? Who reviews and approves these control activities as being adequate to meet the company's goals and objectives?

- Is there a process to measure, collect, and report on the effectiveness of these control activities? What type of action has occurred to respond to inappropriate levels of control?

- How is the process of monitoring and reporting on control activities measured, reported, and improved?

4) **Information and communication** refers to systems that disseminate financial and operational information. Such systems must effectively deliver information both internally and externally, and receive information from both internal and external sources.

For example, management must design and develop processes that are appropriate to the way the company is organized and operated. Management must authorize employees to act or execute the processes. Employees must be skilled and trained and have access to the information required to perform their jobs. To control the organization, management must receive timely, accurate, and complete reports. To comply with regulatory requirements, an organization must be able to produce accurate reports on a timely basis. Effective information and communication requires systems to be both well designed and well controlled. Design ensures that the right kind of information is sent and received both internally and externally, with controls to ensure that the information is complete, accurate, and timely.

- Are there information and communication policies and procedures (e.g., records and information management and information handling), in place to protect company informational assets?

- List the types of controls built into information and communication policies and procedures. Who reviews and approves these control activities as being adequate to meet the company's goals and objectives?

- Is there a process to measure, collect, and report on the effectiveness of these internal controls? What type of action has occurred to respond to inappropriate levels of control?

- How is the process of monitoring and reporting on control activities measured, reported, and improved?

5) **Monitoring, evaluating, and reporting** integrates the four elements of internal control, described above, and is an essential characteristic of an effective system of internal control. Regular and continuous monitoring of the control environment, risk assessment, control activities, and information and communication provides continuous feedback to the effectiveness and efficiency of these control elements.

Monitoring occurs at all levels of the organization, from the board of directors to individual employees.

- Are monitoring, evaluating, and reporting considered value-add activities? Are the monitoring, evaluating, and reporting functions separated from those functional areas that provide operational support?

- Are there defined tools used for analysis and decision making? Are these tools evaluated for their effectiveness?

- Is the internal control program itself monitored, evaluated, and reported to validate that the appropriate level of risk, control, and control activity is implemented throughout the company? How has the internal control program been improved over the years?

- Have the executive and board of directors received training at least annually on governance, compliance, and internal control procedures?

Note to Reader:

Internal controls have been an important component of successful companies for decades prior to the issuance of the Sarbanes-Oxley Act. Internal controls became an embedded discipline within process controls and process management. Long before Sarbanes-Oxley and long before masters of business administration (MBAs) influenced the business world, a solid internal control environment could be used as a tool and technique to meet and accelerate the achievement of business goals, objectives, and profitability targets.

If you have worked through the simple, yet powerful exercises presented in this and previous chapters, you have a good baseline or profile of your company's internal control posture. Use this as valuable input in customizing your internal control program.

The following chapters are designed to assist your company in the adoption and measurement of a solid internal control program. At strategic points, job aids and tools are introduced to assist with the establishment and measurement of internal controls.

Following are some quick fixes you can do right now to improve:

- Implement segregation of duties where duties are divided or segregated among different people to reduce risk of error or inappropriate actions. No one person has control over all aspects of any transaction.

- Make sure a person delegated approval authority authorizes transactions that are consistent with policies and procedures.

- Ensure that records are routinely reviewed and reconciled by someone other than the preparer or person processing the transaction to determine that transactions have been properly processed.

- Make certain that equipment, inventories, cash, and other property are secured physically, counted periodically, and compared with item descriptions shown on control records.

- Provide employees with appropriate training and guidance to ensure that they have the knowledge necessary to carry out their job duties, are provided with an appropriate level of direction and supervision, and are aware of the proper channels for reporting suspected improprieties.

- Make sure policies and operating procedures are formalized and communicated to employees. Documenting policies and procedures and making them accessible to employees helps provide day-to-day guidance to staff and will promote continuity of activities in the event of prolonged employee absences or turnover.

INTERNAL CONTROL PROCESS

In order to create value for the company, an internal control program shall be designed to address the company's short- and long-term needs. Whether those needs refer to improving process effectiveness and efficiency, market value, customer, investor, and employee confidence or just satisfying external reporting requirements, an internal control program is a valued tool.

Following is the flow of the overall program, process flow, and narrative. Since we have decided to use the Committee of Sponsoring Organizations of the Treadway Commission (COSO) framework as our model, it is embedded within the process and the phases are referenced as:

1. Control environment
2. Risk assessment
3. Control activities
4. Information and communication
5. Monitor, evaluate, and report

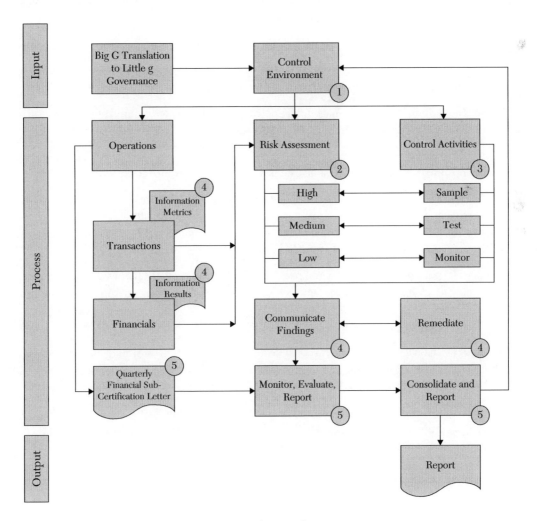

Narrative for the Process

> **Note to reader:**
>
> In describing the steps, the word *should* (i.e., with should meaning "ought to but not necessarily will be") is used. This is not intended to be a conditional statement but rather to demonstrate that there is a choice to use some or all of the guidance presented. If the guidance is not followed, then an equal alternative must be substituted. I recognize that presenting detail techniques to a broad audience may be too severe for smaller companies and not robust enough for other companies; the use of judgment, common sense, and cost/benefit analysis must be used in the discussions with the internal control executive sponsors and cross-functional supporters.

1. Control Environment

If you refer to the earlier process flow from governance, you'll notice that the input to this process is produced when big G Governance is translated to little g governance. The translation step means that big G rules and requirements have been adopted by the company and embedded into processes. The role and responsibility for implementing a control environment and setting the right tone is with the board of directors, the chief executive officer (CEO), and the chief financial officer (CFO).

The control environment shall include statements to define and/or reinforce the tone from the top expressing:

- *Value to the company.* The control environment must state that the ultimate success of all projects is rooted within the company's values and the company values its culture of integrity, honesty, and high ethical standards.

- *Tone at the top.* In addition to senior management's setting the tone, resources must be made available, including people with the appropriate skills, time, information technology, and interruption to operations and money.

- *Authority to act.* Business area and process owners must have the authority to establish and exercise operational control, allocate resources, and make critical decisions as to when and where controls are needed.

The board of directors (BOD) must understand the company's opportunities and constraints and advise company executives as to organizational structure, levels of acceptable risk and control strategies. The audit committee of the BOD is responsible for interfacing with the internal and external auditors and internal controls for the purpose of overseeing the monitoring, evaluating, and reporting responsibilities of management.

Senior leadership is responsible for implementing the strategies approved by the BOD. The senior leadership emphasis for this step is to ensure there are suitable and consistent activities to support the control environment such as communication, providing adequate resources and time to implement, and holding process owners accountable and responsible for process outcomes.

Jointly, the BOD and senior leadership are responsible to promote high ethical and integrity standards and to establish a culture within the organization that emphasizes and demonstrates the importance of internal controls. These standards are reflected in the internal controls strategy and objectives.

If you don't have a BOD, then use your company advisors in a similar manner. It is important to receive an objective review and analysis from independent parties. Regardless of whether you are a public or private company, it is important to take time and consider what levels of risk and controls are strategically important and which control objectives require attention.

Big G Governance guidance to management indicates that the approach management uses must be principles based, direct effort to the highest-risk areas where material misstatements may occur, and be tailored to facts and circumstances. It is important to design an internal control program that is right for your organization.

Because of the emphasis Big G Governance places on principles and scope, I've discussed these as separated sections. As part of your internal controls program, it will save a lot of time and debate to define the principles and control objectives that are expected to be universally followed; having these agreed up front assists in refining the scope to be reviewed and the types of control activities that will validate the objective. Choose and customize the principles that are appropriate to your company. You should find these principles stated in one form or another within the company's code of ethical conduct or other compliance policies.

Hint: Use the principles to develop clear "tone from the top" communication messages in support of the program.

Internal Control Principles and Control Objectives

Principles are universally accepted standards that signal satisfactory behavior. Internal control principles serve as fundamental assumptions that communicate specific characteristics when assessing and evaluating the company's internal control status. Principles occur to support policies and procedures and represent the due diligence that must be embedded into operational and financial process design and implementation.

Each of the internal control testing guides identifies control objectives and activities designed to test the existence and systemic use of the principles within processes. In designing your internal control program, you must identify and document the principles that are important and how these are defined within your organization. Following is a list describing internal control principles and objectives integrated within this program:

Compliance with laws and regulations refers to big G Governance and requires that accounting and finance professionals are aware of current and future laws and regulations. Although they do not have to be subject matter experts, they must be able to demonstrate that they subscribe to and use resources that provide a level of information appropriate for their role and responsibility.

Compliance with company policies and procedures refers to little g governance and requires that accounting and finance professionals keep current and participate in cross-functional activities that affect the strategic, tactical, and operational nature of the company's current and future policies, procedures, processes, and programs. All transactions ultimately affect the financial statements, either quantitatively or qualitatively; accounting and finance professionals must be thoroughly familiar with the processes involved. As a control, this requires documentation to support an adequate methodology and a sound approach to address cross-functional needs.

Compliance with contract terms and conditions requires that the company honor its authorized and approved commitments. The company has an obligation to customers, partners, vendors, employees, and investors to ensure that contract terms and conditions are clear, understandable, consistently applied, and enforceable. As financial professionals, we attest that assets and liabilities reported on the balance sheet are bona fide rights and obligations of the company as at that point in time.

Authorization is defined by the delegation of authority and allows employees to make commitments or representations on behalf of the company. Management defines and communicates the criteria for recognizing economic events and authorizing transactions. Reference the chapter on authorization and approval. Note that there is a difference between authorization and approval, with some companies choosing to highlight the difference within responsibilities: *authorizers* are assigned the power to influence and make decisions and commitments, while *approvers* follow a process to substantiate, corroborate, and authenticate. Also known as the *propriety of transactions principle,* this ensures that there is a culture and environment where transactions and activities are appropriately reviewed and authorized prior to execution.

Internal controls over financial reporting includes control objectives to address that:

- **Payments are paid, recorded, and reflect** authorized transactions that are the result of purchased or committed obligations made on behalf of the company. Payments are made according to a specific timetable and in agreement with contractual arrangements. Cash or other assets are disbursed and recorded according to generally accepted accounting principles (GAAP).

- **Payments are received, recorded, and reflect** authorized transactions that are the result of sales or committed entitlements due to the company. Receipts are collected in accordance with a specific timetable and in agreement with contractual arrangements. Cash or other assets are received and recorded in accordance with GAAP.

- **Transactions are recorded** in a timely manner and represent activity belonging to the entity involved and are classified in accordance with company defined rules and procedures (i.e., chart of accounts). Transactions are generally recorded in the period they are received and accepted by the company. Exceptions must be in accordance with the company's policies and procedures.

- **Disclosure** as a control is required for purposes of transparency. Whether internally or externally focused, disclosure requires that there is sufficient and appropriate documentation to support the treatment of transactions, indicating that there is a clear audit trail as to what and how data was analyzed, decisions made, and actions taken.

Disclosure is also a requirement for regulatory purposes. Similar to disclosure as a control, disclosure for regulatory purposes requires that the company's policy and/or procedure and related background information is shared. In addition, disclosure for regulatory purposes may require:

- Roll-forward activity analysis showing the closing balance from one period plus/minus totals by activity type to arrive at the closing balance for the current period.

- Segmented presentation of data and/or information showing the closing balance showing the subtotals by logical classifications.

- **Operational and financial reviews** are performed by authorized reviewers. The reviewer is responsible to examine the area in question and:

  - Validate that the supporting documentation matches the content and context of the transaction and that any assumptions made are in accordance with company policies and procedures and GAAP.

  - Validate that the calculations are accurate by reviewing the source of the data and testing the formulas.

  - Analyze the results and findings to ensure they are complete and "make sense" given the purpose, content, and context of the transaction.

  - Evaluate the transaction as being required, in agreement with company policy and procedure and authorized. Once evaluated, reviews may be forwarded to others who have a "need to know."

Effectiveness and efficiency of operations reviews refers to safeguarding the company's core competencies as being critical for sustainability and the continued operations of the company.

- **Reconciliations** are performed between the source documentation and the general ledger and/or between contracts and the processed transaction in order to:

  - Validate that only legitimate and authorized activity is processed.

  - Validate that amounts are accurately calculated.

  - Match the inflow of cash or other assets equals the amount of addition of company benefits *or*

  - Match the outflow of cash or other assets equals the amount of reduction of company obligations.

  - Ensure that reviews have been performed.

Integrity is made up of accuracy, completeness, and timeliness. Integrity occurs when transactions and other events and circumstances transpire during a specific period and are recognized in that period. The items in the financial statements are properly described and classified as well as fairly presented in conformity with generally accepted accounting and company policies and procedures. There are no unrecorded assets, liabilities, or transactions and no omitted disclosures.

- **Accuracy** refers to the correctness, exactness and truthfulness of the data and information presented. Accuracy refers to the physical existence of tangible assets, liabilities, and equity and the existence of the company's rights and obligations as to intangible assets, liability, and equity. Accuracy of valuation refers to the validation and approval of assumptions made to quantify transactions at appropriate amounts.

- **Completeness** refers to the wholeness or comprehensiveness of the data and information presented. All transactions and events that should have occurred and have actually occurred refers to the concept of occurrence which is included with completeness.

- **Timeliness** refers to the adherence to a processing or operational schedule and the dating of the process and control points along that timeline. Timeliness also refers to the correct reporting of transactions in the period they should have been reported in.

Segregation of duties refers to the identification and assignment of key roles and responsibilities where roles must be separated in order to mitigate the risks such as misrepresentation, fraud, and collusion. Adequate segregation of duties reduces the likelihood that errors, intentional or unintentional, will remain undetected by providing for separate processing by different individuals at various stages of a transaction. The basic design is that no one employee or group of employees shall be in a position to both perpetrate and conceal errors or irregularities in the normal course of executing their responsibilities.

Roles and responsibilities must be clearly defined to ensure that no one person has complete control over more than one key processing function, such as authorizing, approving, certifying, disbursing, receiving, or reconciling.

Resource constraints may limit the number of employees, sometimes resulting in concerns regarding segregation of duties. In those cases, management must take action by adding control features to compensate for the resource inadequacy. These actions may include managers reviewing system reports of detailed transactions; establishing peer reviews for selected transactions; providing oversight during counts of physical inventory; reviewing supporting documentation for journal entries prior to approval and independently reconciling account balances.

Safeguarding assets refers to the custodial and security arrangements for the company's tangible and intangible property and assets. Control of assets includes asset classification, assignment, movement, and use.

The company's assets include its customers, qualified vendors, and partners; employees; products and services; cash; marketable securities; inventories, property, plant and equipment; patents; trademarks; and goodwill as well as the processes and results of those operations such as data and information.

Management must clearly identify the personnel who have primary custodial responsibility for each category of assets, critical forms and records, processing areas, and processing procedures. To the extent possible and practicable, responsibility for the physical custody of an asset must be vested with employees who have no responsibility for and are denied access to accounting for the asset.

Determining the Scope Using a Top-Down approach

According to Big G Governance guidance, companies may use a top-down, risk-based approach to determine an appropriate scope for identifying the relevant operational and financial reporting risks. To determine the range for the internal control activities (e.g., ongoing monitoring of key indicators to engaging a full audit) financial management must identify the financial reporting elements including accounts and disclosures that have a significant dollar or volume amount and which if misstated would have a material or significant effect.

To apply the top-down risk based approach, begin with the financial reporting accounts and drill down to the sub-account or process level to identify those accounts that have a high: (1) volume of transactions, (2) dollar throughput, and/or (3) process risk.

Then evaluate those financial reporting elements as to risk by identifying: (1) "what could go wrong," (2) the underlying financial reporting or fraud risk, and (3) where potential errors, omission, and misstatements may occur. For this stage of the evaluation, consider which of the control objectives has the potential for being violated or deficient.

There should be a list of accounts and a description of the type of risk. Rank the accounts and risks based on the magnitude of the accounts and likelihood of misstatements.

Plot these results on a risk matrix according to their probability and impact rating. Develop appropriate level of control activities which identify the effectiveness of the control environment.

The control environment influences and provides input and direction for implementing operational processes, risk assessments, and the control activities.

Within the control environment, early warning signs that internal controls may break down occur when management sets unrealistic targets, when rewards depend on performance, and when there are upper and lower cutoffs to bonus plans. Internal controls need to be especially vigilant when it comes to poor segregation of duties where there is a high degree of decentralization, when weak or poor internal audit results have been documented, and where there are penalties for improper behavior, whether these behaviors are insignificant or unpublicized.

Once you have defined the scope, begin to put together the schedule, selecting the best time within the financial and reporting cycle to review and test controls within the selected accounts and/or processes. Some items to consider when scheduling the control review and/or testing include:

- Timing of review and/or testing as to be in "real time" (e.g., observing the process) or after the fact

- Level of detail required for the review and/or testing

- Since testing occurs after the fact, select a time within the reporting cycle that would have enough transactional volume to choose a meaningful sample size.

Note that the schedule at this point is tentative, given that activities and resources have not yet been assigned.

Operations

Business area managers and process owners are responsible for establishing and promoting controlled processes that provide reasonable assurance that:

- Data and information published either internally or externally has integrity; that is, it is accurate, reliable, complete and timely.

- The company's resources (i.e., its people, systems, data and information, assets, and client goodwill) are adequately protected.

- The resources are acquired economically and employed effectively.

- Operational transactions are monitored for continuous process improvement.

Quarterly, as part of the quarterly subcertification process, business area managers and process owners must attest that they are in compliance with company policies, procedures, and external laws and regulations. Refer to the later chapter on the quarterly subcertification to implement this part of the program.

2. Risk Assessment

A risk assessment program shall be implemented that includes activities to:

- Classify processes as having high, medium, or low risk.

- Determine the company's risk threshold.

- Monitor, evaluate, and report on the processes as to their exposure to risk.

Business area and process owners are responsible to identify and evaluate internal and external factors that could adversely affect the achievement of the company's goals and objectives and to reflect those findings in their business plans and reports to senior management.

Use a top-down approach to identify key processes and account balances that must be considered in-scope for a risk assessment. Refer to the section on risk to help identify areas with higher risk or use the section above to determine the in-scope areas for internal control testing. Select those processes and areas that pose a critical or high-risk level and where the company needs to share, mitigate, or control risks as the first process areas to test. Processes that rank in the quadrant where there is medium or low risk may be tested using less rigorous testing techniques.

Selected business area representatives, advisors, and senior management may offer additional accounts and/or processes as input to be tested based on current and future strategies. The scope for internal control testing is then reviewed and approved by the CEO, the CFO, and in-house legal counsel and presented to the BOD and the members of the audit committee. This select group must take responsibility to:

- Review and approve the internal control plan.

- Ensure that the right accounts and processes are monitored and evaluated.

- Oversee execution of the plan and ensure that it has proper resources and ongoing executive support.

Within the risk assessment early warning signs that internal controls may break down occur when there is no risk assessment program; when risks, however low, seem to be clustered around the same process or functional area; or when risks seem to occur at the same point within the process or financial cycle. Internal control representatives need to be especially vigilant when it comes to functions working in silos and not sharing information; low risks in one area may snowball as they progress down the line to where they become significant.

3. Control Activities

When designing control activities, consideration needs to be given to whether the control needs to be detective or preventive, what level of control activity is required, and how it will be tested.

Detective and Preventive Controls

Controls are identified as either detective or preventive, with preventive controls preferred. Preventive and/or detective differences may change based on the type of event and where/how the control is initiated.

- *Detection*—refers to checks and balances that occur after the transactional event has occurred and is designed to identify an error, omission, misstatement, or fraud. Detective controls are important where there are weak or broken processes or where preventive controls are not designed into the process. General controls considered detective in nature include comparing budget to actual results, comparing period-over-period results, monitoring performance indicators, and following up on unexpected results or unusual items.

- *Prevention*—refers to control procedures designed within and becoming part of the process. Preventive controls are designed to prevent errors, omissions, misstatements, or fraud from occurring before processing the activity. General controls considered preventive in nature include written policies and procedures, limits to authority, attaching supporting documentation, questioning unusual items, and no blank signed forms.

Consider this list a "prompt" to identify the types of detective and preventive controls that should be addressed in all processes. Remember that whether a control is considered preventive or detective depends on the type of transactional event, the event frequency, and whether it is performed as part of or separate from the process.

Example:

- When accounts payable (A/P) invoices are reviewed and authorized for payments by ensuring a three-way match prior to releasing the invoice for payment, it is considered a preventive control. When the quantity and price extension on the vendor invoices are checked after the payment has been made, it is a detective control.

- When a credit analysis is performed prior to a credit limit or customer set up in accounts receivable (A/R), it is a preventive control. If all new customers are automatically granted A/R credit with credit assessments performed only if there are collection issues or when credit requests exceed a predefined dollar threshold, then the credit assessment is a detective control.

- When payroll runs are authorized as long as they are consistent period over period, it is considered a preventive control. If variances to the payroll run are only reviewed and resolved monthly, then it is a detective control.

Type of Control	Preventive / Detective
Compliance with laws, GAAP, and company policies and procedures	Detective
Compliance with company policies and procedures	Detective
Compliance with contract terms and conditions	Detective
Authorized and approved transactions	Preventive

(Continued)

Type of Control	Preventive / Detective
Internal controls over financial reporting	
• Payments paid and recorded	Preventive
• Payments received, deposited and recorded	Preventive
• Transaction recorded	Preventive
• Disclosed	Detective
• Reviewed	Preventive
• Reconciliation	Detective
• Integrity	Preventive
• Accuracy	Preventive
• Completeness	Preventive
• Timeliness	Preventive
• Segregation of duties	Preventive
• Safeguard assets	Preventive

Control Activities

Select control activities that are commensurate with the level of risk as identified in the risk assessment. Document the control activity procedure, the evidence collected, and the results of your findings.

Control activities refer to those specific actions designed to produce evidence in support of the control objective and may include some or all of the following techniques:

- Self-assessments performed by process owners using predefined self assessment or audit readiness checklists
- Walk-through and observation performed by peer groups and/or internal control representatives
- Monitoring performed by management and/or submitted to internal controls for review
- Reconciliations between source data and reporting records including period-to-period roll-forward and period-over-period analysis
- Testing performed by management and internal control representatives using statistical or random sampling techniques
- Quarterly subcertification submitted by executive leadership, process owners, and selected business area executives attesting to compliance with company policies, procedures, and internal control requirements
- Remediation of action items resulting from internal control and internal audit reviews

Testing and controlling is a management function and is an integral part of the overall process management. As such, it is the responsibility of managers at all levels to:

- Identify and evaluate the exposures to loss relating to their particular sphere of operations.

- Specify and establish policies, plans, and operating standards, procedures, systems, and other disciplines to be used to minimize, mitigate, and/or limit the risks associated with the exposures identified.

- Establish practical controlling processes that require and encourage administrators, officers, and employees to carry out their duties and responsibilities in a manner that achieves the control objectives.

- Maintain the effectiveness of the controlling processes established and foster continuous improvement to these processes.

Monitoring and Testing

The monitoring and testing of operational transactions validates that identified controls are performing as they were designed. Depending on the complexity of the process (i.e., the number of steps), the activity is to test transactions through computerized and/or manual processes. The tests must address the issues of integrity (i.e., completeness, accuracy, and timeliness).

A cradle-to-grave test direction selects a sample of certain source documents (e.g., vendor invoice, sales transaction, subsidiary ledger balance) and trace them through the operational processes until it reaches the financial statement balances.

A grave-to-cradle test selects a sample of other transactions from the financial statement balance (i.e., the general ledger or reconciliation) back to the source input. The test of transactions in this direction addresses the issue of whether all data contained in a financial account balance is supported by source documentation.

The sample of transactions tested must be documented and selected using generally accepted auditing sampling techniques. Sampling techniques can employ either a judgmental or statistical approach. An example of a judgmental approach is a systematic selection of days of the fiscal year or every 100th transaction in a numerical sequence. A statistical approach would take random samples from among all transactions.

According to auditing standards, the tests of transactions must be designed to test management assertions. Evidence may be classified into one of five categories:

- *Existence or occurrence.* This assertion deals with whether assets, liabilities, and equity included in the balance sheet actually exist on the balance sheet date. Additionally, the assertion of occurrence is concerned whether recorded transactions included in the financial statements actually occurred during the period. This assertion is concerned with the inclusion of amounts that should have been included (e.g., inventory that exists and is available for sale at the balance sheet date).

- *Completeness.* This assertion states that the financial statements include all transactions and accounts that should be presented. This test is concerned with the possibility of omitting items from the financial statements that should have been included (e.g., a sales cutoff test to determine that sales are recorded in the proper accounting period).

- *Valuation or allocation.* This assertion is related to whether the asset, liability, equity, revenue, and expense accounts have been included in the financial statements at appropriate values (e.g., fixed assets stated at the net book value).

- *Rights and obligations.* This assertion is related to whether the assets are the rights of the company and the liabilities are the obligations of the company at the balance sheet date.

- *Presentation and disclosure.* This assertion is related to whether components of the financial statements are properly classified, grouped, or reported separately and disclosed in the financial statements (e.g., liabilities properly recorded as a current or long-term liability).

Even though a control may be embedded within a process, it still needs to be tested. There are times when an embedded control could be bypassed or exception reports ignored because it is "assumed" that the control is working.

A few examples:

Schedules and checklists often serve as controls when schedules and checklists are embedded as part of the process; they operate concurrently at all levels. However, schedules and checklists must still be reviewed and tested to ensure that management activities are identified, with comments and exceptions noted including shortcuts or process "workarounds" (i.e., bypassing the designed process).

Data and information is provided from a single central source is a good automated control; however, the source data must still be verified to ensure that it is complete and accurate and that it is used according to its designated purpose and that errors, omissions, and misstatements of the data are corrected at the source.

To begin planning for the monitoring and testing plan, start with the accounts and processes identified in the risk assessment. Next to each of those accounts and processes list the control objectives that need to be verified with monitoring and testing. Next to each of those control objectives identify the control activities that will be used to provide evidence that the control objective is working (or not). Having an aligned link between account/process, control objective, and control activity is an indicator of a strong internal control program.

Note to reader:

As part of the testing guides, I have included working papers that can be used as a sample for preparing this worksheet. The downloadable version of the book presents this worksheet in Excel format.

This is the technique recommended for use when rolling out the internal control testing guides. As you test and document the internal controls, consider the type of evidence that will be reviewed and the type of assertion that can be made against that evidence. Remember to document the evidence, whether it produces a finding or not.

Within control activities, early warning signs that internal controls may break down occur when control activities are not linked to control objectives, when there is not enough time and resources to execute the control activity plan, or when the unfavorable results are scattered across all control objectives and processes. Internal controls need to be especially vigilant when process managers are continually not prepared or available to participate in the control activities.

4. Information and Communication

Information and communication is about enabling employees by providing pertinent information at all levels of the company and distributing it in a form and time frame that supports the achievement of company goals and objectives.

Senior management is responsible for information and communication activities that support the understanding and execution of internal control objectives. Employees are also responsible for information and communication activities, ensuring that senior management fully understands the process consequences of implementing or not implementing certain control objectives. Information sharing and communication refers to the flow occurring from the top down and bottom up. For employees to be enabled, senior management must clearly identify the environment as open and allow employees ready access to contribute suggestions for improvement. Employees will best know when "checking the checker" controls are ready to be replaced with control-smart learning, planning, and process modeling.

Information and communication objectives are to:

- Ensure adequate and comprehensive internal financial, operational, and compliance data.

- Ensure adequate and comprehensive external market information about events and conditions that are relevant to decision makers.

- Establish effective channels of communications to ensure that employees are aware of policies and procedures affecting their duties and responsibilities.

- Ensure that other relevant information reaches appropriate decision makers.

- Ensure that there are appropriate and secure information systems in place.

Company business area managers and process owners are required to have an effective system of internal controls that responds to changes in the company's environment and conditions; they must take appropriate action to remediate internal control findings and improve process effectiveness and efficiency. In addition, they must have a process proportionate with the complexity and level of risk associated with the company's on and off-balance-sheet activities.

Information and communication must flow from the top down, bottom up, and across the organization providing meaningful, relevant data to allow for prompt decision making and action. The internal control program manager shall issue progress reports at least quarterly or as deemed necessary to all internal parties as well as to the external auditors and outside legal counsel.

Within information and communication, early warning signs that internal controls may break down occur when information and communication flows only in one direction, information is estimated rather supported by data points, or more time is spent on "wordsmithing" rather than remediation. The internal controls program manager needs to be especially vigilant when it comes to a difference between what is being communicated versus the findings and evidence collected.

5. Monitor, Evaluate, and Report

This last phase of the framework and the program's process is to consolidate and report on the findings and remediation efforts *and* to evaluate the effectiveness of the internal control program itself. This information is used to determine the company's overall control position that is required within big G Governance submission.

Classify Findings

Control findings are the result of the analysis and evidence collected from the control activity. As findings are discovered, they need to be classified into one of the following categories, with the most severe deficiency category listed first:

1. **Significant deficiency** conditions in the design or operation of the process and the internal control structure could/would adversely affect the company's ability to record, process, summarize, and report financial data consistent with the assertions of management in the financial statements.

2. **Material weakness** conditions are less severe but serious enough that the design or operation of one or more of the specific process elements could/would have a material impact to the accuracy of the financial statements and if it occurred may not be detected within a timely period.

3. **Reportable conditions** refer to process weaknesses or opportunities for continuous improvement. When discovered, these should be noted so that the process owner may evaluate and/or correct the process before the issue becomes a weakness. These may be "early warning signs" and addressed as neither the process owner nor the internal control representative want to see an identified reportable condition from one testing period show up as a material weakness in another period.

4. **An effective control** condition exists when there were no unexpected results and the internal control is operating within defined parameters and there is no immediate exposure to the company.

Once consolidated, summarize the findings using the following type of scorecard. The information contained on this scorecard identifies the number of control activities performed within the findings classified from 1, Significant Deficiency, to 4, an Effective Control, as described above.

Account/Process	Rating of Control Activity Results			
	1	2	3	4
Accounts Payable				
Accounts Receivable				
Inventory				
Payroll				
Revenue				

When internal control deficiencies are identified, plans to remedy these deficiencies must be documented and implemented as soon as possible.

When a significant deficiency or material weakness is identified, the internal control department must retest the process to ensure that the improvement has occurred. The corrected internal control procedure must be in place and in operation for a period of time prior to the financial reporting date. Management must be able to evaluate the corrected control and conclude that the control is operating effectively. It is recommended that testing continue for at least three consecutive quarters and positive results shown before the deficiency is deemed to be satisfactorily closed.

This type of summary lets you compare accounts and processes at a high level to identify whether the control activities are equal to the level of risk as defined in the scope. It also lets you prioritize and focus on selected processes to remediate the most significant findings first. Information from this scorecard can help you better plan the control objectives and activities that will target high-risk, in-scope accounts and processes.

If the results have a disproportionate number of 3 and 4-rated items, review the objectives and activities to ensure that you have aligned the appropriate level activity to "catch" the appropriate level of risk. Although this is a not a "gotcha" exercise, remember, you selected this list of accounts and processes as being high risk and high impact. If the findings and results are accurate, then it signals that there is something wrong in the risk assessment process.

Be careful not to play a numbers game—more is not necessarily better. Remember that control activities require planning, assigning of resources, and perhaps disruption to the operational flow.

Evaluating the Internal Control Program

Measures must be established to determine the effectiveness of the internal control program itself. For senior management to have confidence in attesting to the company's internal control status, they must have confidence that the program itself is working as it should.

According to COSO, each of the five control elements must be assessed before an opinion can be rendered about the design and effectiveness of the overall internal control program. The assessment rating is satisfactory or unsatisfactory and must be documented with rationale and supporting evidence where and as applicable.

COSO Control Element	Criteria for an Unsatisfactory Rating
Control Environment	• The presence of any one of the control objectives is missing, violated, or inadequate. • There are verified systemic instances of breakdown of control activities.
Risk Assessment	• Risk assessment objectives are incompatible or inconsistent with the control environment objectives. • A risk assessment program is missing, not followed, or inadequate. • Management has not mitigated critical operating risks. • Internal control tests detect risks not previously contemplated by management.
Control Activities	• Key control activities are not functioning as intended. • Management's control activity monitoring is missing, violated, or inadequate.
Information and Communication	• Pervasive lack of knowledge by employees about their control responsibilities. • Customer or supplier complaints and disputes are not resolved or remedial action is not undertaken in a timely manner.
Monitoring	• Key metrics are not identified, collected, and communicated. • Management has not established a means of determining the quality of the internal control program over time.
Overall	• The rating of all components must be considered to determine whether controls provide reasonable assurance that management objectives will be achieved.

Significant deficiencies and material weaknesses must be disclosed if they have not been cleared as of the financial reporting date.

One of the ways the company completes the governance journey is through the quarterly subcertification program. A later chapter discusses this program in depth; however, here is a brief overview. This program and tool has benefits other than aiding in providing support for executive attestation to big G Governance regulatory submissions.

As part of the company's policies and procedures, the internal control department oversees the quarterly subcertification letter also known as the letter of representation. The letter asks selected individuals to certify or attest that the information provided from their business areas of responsibility is complete, accurate, and conforms to the company's code of conduct, policies, procedures, and internal controls; and that the financial results are recorded in accordance with U.S. GAAP.

The letter process and attestation is a job aid, used by internal controls to evaluate and support the company's internal control posture. Comments submitted by the selected process owners and business area executives must be addressed as part of the internal control program.

Submissions and Attestations

According to Sarbanes-Oxley and Securities and Exchange Commission (SEC) governance, the CEO and CFO must submit a report from management and attest to the Company's internal control position with submission of the quarterly 10Q and annual 10K reports.

The report of management contains the following:

- A statement of management's responsibility for establishing and maintaining adequate internal controls over financial reporting.

- A statement identifying the framework (i.e., COSO) used by management to conduct the required evaluation of the effectiveness of the company's internal controls over financial reporting.

- Management's assessment of the effectiveness of the company's internal controls over financial reporting as of the end of the company's most recent fiscal year. Management is not permitted to conclude that the company's internal controls over financial reporting are effective if there are one or more significant deficiency or material weakness in the company's internal controls over financial reporting.

- A statement that the external auditor has issued an attestation report on management's assessment of internal controls over financial reporting.

Within the monitor, evaluate, and report phase, early warning signs that internal controls may break down occur when monitoring activities are sporadic, skipping reporting periods, and when evaluation techniques are inconsistently applied in order to show less damaging results. Internal controls need to be especially vigilant when it comes to censoring results.

With the attestation and submission of the financial reports to big G Governance regulatory agencies, one cycle of the governance journey is complete.

The following documents are presented in support of the program:

- Internal control program policy and procedure
- Internal control program charter
- Internal control plan

Policy and Procedures		
Procedure No. B02a	Section: Corporate	Page 1 of 3
	Internal Control Policy and Procedure	
Department Ownership	Issue/Effective Date:	Replaces previously issued

Prepared by: Date	Approved by: Date	Authorized by: Date

Scope

The document applies to all IDÆAL LLP's legal entities, subsidiaries, and business units.

Policy

It is IDÆAL LLP's (Company) policy to establish and maintain an internal control program (program) to serve as oversight for and test the company's operational and financial effectiveness and efficiency in accordance with designated risk thresholds. This program shall be led and managed by the internal control program manager and have reporting responsibilities to senior leadership, including the chief executive officer, chief financial officer, and the audit committee of the board of directors.

An internal control department shall be established to design, implement and oversee a program that will comply with external laws and regulations as well as promote internal operational effectiveness and efficiencies. The internal control model the company chooses to follow is the Committee of Sponsoring Organizations of the Treadway Commission (COSO) framework.

The internal control department shall establish an annual plan and schedule to identify the current fiscal year's area of focus.

Company processes shall be assigned and owned by process owners who have the responsibility to create integrated (i.e., cross-functional) process maps, policies, and procedures as required. Process owners are responsible for defining and collecting process and financial metrics to ensure the process is executed in an effective and efficient manner. Process owners shall provide key performance indicators, participate in self-assessments and be prepared for internal control testing.

At any time, if anyone (e.g., internal controls representative, process manager, or employee) considers a breach in operational or financial process management has or is likely to occur; it is their responsibility to immediately contact executive leadership and internal controls to investigate.

Procedure

The internal control program as used within the business environment has come to be defined as a program to oversee processes and is required to:

1. Assess risk and evaluate processes as having high, medium or low risk as identified through the company's risk assessment process.

	Policy and Procedures	
Procedure No. B02a	Section: Corporate	Page 2 of 3
	Internal Control Policy and Procedure	
Department Ownership	Issue/Effective Date:	Replaces previously issued

2. Develop control objectives and control activities that are aimed at providing evidence of the effectiveness of the control objective (i.e., that the control objective is working or not).

3. Analyze and consolidate findings from the control activities

4. Evaluate, report, and rate the company's internal control status. The internal controls program manager shall communicate and report those findings and status to the leadership team and the board of directors at least quarterly.

5. Monitor remediation and improvement efforts for those controls that are deemed to need improvement.

In addition to monitoring the effectiveness of the internal control program itself, the internal control department shall follow the COSO model to define and deploy the following phases:

- Control environment

- Risk assessment

- Control activities

- Information and communication

- Monitor, evaluate, and report

At the beginning of each fiscal year, the internal controls program manager shall present a plan that includes testing and oversight for the company's processes and activities. Although a schedule is prepared, internal controls may alter the timing of the scheduled tests so as to conduct random unplanned testing.

Internal controls in cooperation with the process owners perform risk assessments in accordance with the risk assessment model and shall rank processes as to the likelihood and probability of an adverse operational or financial impact to the company.

Risk thresholds are broadly defined as:

- *Low risk:* The process shall be considered to have low risk as long as the measures are within acceptable control limits and there is minimal risk for adverse exposure. Low-risk processes shall be monitored at least monthly with exceptional variances investigated and remediate. When control limits are exceeded for three consecutive periods, the risk is reclassified as medium.

- *Medium risk:* The process shall be considered to have medium risk as long as the measures are within acceptable control limits and there is moderate operational and financial exposure due to adverse activity or when low-risk processes have exceeded their control limit measures. Medium-risk processes are reviewed and tested at least semiannually on a rotating basis. Medium-risk processes may be considered high risk when the control measures become unpredictable and unacceptable.

- *High risk:* The process shall be considered to have a high risk if it is a newly implemented or reengineered process or if it is deemed that the impact of an operational or financial misstatement could have a material impact on operational results and/or financial reporting. High-risk processes require the assignment of a quality review team and must be reviewed and tested at least quarterly.

Control activities and testing guides may include operational reports and measures, financial reports and measures, system-generated control reports, and manual sample testing. Testing guides shall be made available to the process owners prior to the actual testing. Testing guides may be augmented or supplemented based on findings from testing activities.

The internal controls manager shall monitor the program's execution and results and monthly report on the status of schedule attainment, testing activities and findings to the chief compliance officer and the chief financial officer (CFO).

Quarterly, a report shall be submitted to the chief executive officer (CEO) and board of directors for review.

At least annually, the internal controls manager and the chief compliance officer shall provide an in-depth review of the risk assessment and internal control process to the CEO, CFO, and the board of directors.

Control/Areas of Responsibility

This Program shall have oversight by the chief compliance officer and CFO and shall be managed by the internal control program manager.

The internal control program itself shall be monitored and evaluated as to its effectiveness and efficiency.

Internal control testing activities and findings shall be monitored and with reports generated at least quarterly and distributed to the CEO, CFO, and other leadership including the audit committee of the board of directors.

Contact

Chief Compliance Officer

Chief Financial Officer

<table>
<tr><td colspan="3" align="center">**Policy and Procedures**</td></tr>
<tr><td>Procedure No. B02b</td><td align="center">Section: Corporate
Internal Controls Program Charter</td><td align="right">Page 1 of 2</td></tr>
<tr><td>Department Ownership</td><td align="center">Issue Date / Effective Date:</td><td align="right">Replaces previously issued</td></tr>
</table>

Reviewed by: document review Date	Approved by: Date	Approved by: document approved Date

Purpose

Internal controls is a function within corporate governance, separate and distinct from internal audit and compliance, and as such must be sponsored and approved by the executive leadership, implemented at the business area level with responsibility and accountability for compliance held at every level.

IDÆAL, LLP's internal control department conducts independent and objective reviews of the company's operations and procedures. Findings and recommendations are reported as appropriate. The internal control department shall use the Committee of Sponsoring Organizations of the Treadway Commission (COSO) Internal Control Integrated Framework as the basis for the program.

Scope

The internal control department shall oversee the integrity of the company's internal control program as well any outward facing statements concerning the company's internal control or risk posture.

To this end, the internal control department shall prepare a schedule which includes education and training, testing and remediation for the company's process owners, managers, executives, and board of directors.

Meetings

Annually, prior to the beginning of the fiscal year, the internal control program manager shall present a plan to assess the company's internal control and risk posture as well as a plan to remediate or improve operational effectiveness and efficiency. Although primarily focused on financial processes, the internal control department must also consider upstream operational processes. This annual plan shall be reviewed and approved by executive leadership and presented to the audit committee of the board of directors and the external auditors.

At least quarterly, the internal control program manager shall provide progress reports to executive leadership and the audit committee of the board of directors. Quarterly, the internal control program manager shall provide statements to the external auditors as to the status of the company's internal controls and risks.

Policy and Procedures		
Procedure No. B02b	Section: Corporate	Page 2 of 2
	Internal Controls Program Charter	
Department Ownership	Issue/Effective Date:	Replaces previously issued

Responsibilities and Authority

The success of an internal controls project depends upon the endorsement and ongoing support of senior management and the board of directors. Senior management must believe that implementing an internal control program is more than a legal obligation; in the long run, doing so will increase the value of the company.

The internal control program manager shall have the authority, to the extent necessary or appropriate, to secure the participation of subject matter experts and advisors.

Selected business area representatives are invited to assist the internal controls department in the preparation and review of internal processes. All process owners, managers, and employees are expected to fully cooperate and participate in the testing and review process.

The company shall provide appropriate funding and resources to the internal control program manager in order to execute his/her responsibilities.

The internal control program manager shall review and reassess the adequacy of this charter at least annually and recommend proposed changes to the executive leadership for approval. The internal controls department shall review its own performance at least annually and include that performance review with its quarterly reports.

INTERNAL CONTROL PLAN

This chapter lists specific tasks and activities required to develop and execute the internal control plan (plan) and program. The plan incorporates the information presented thus far and the approaches that follow this chapter. The internal control program manager oversees the design and deployment of the plan and is responsible for its outcomes.

The internal controls program manager shall establish the program, which includes activities and tasks to address the Committee of Sponsoring Organizations of the Treadway Commission (COSO) framework:

A. Control environment

B. Risk assessment

C. Control activities

D. Information and communication

E. Monitor, evaluate, and report

In support of planning process and as described below, at the end of this chapter are documents and forms that address:

- Internal control policy and procedure

- Internal control charter

- Roles and responsibilities classified as per the COSO framework

- Authorization and approval process, policy and procedure

- Information and technology—end-user computing, process, policy and procedure

- Account reconciliation process, policy and procedure

- Quarterly subcertification process, policy and procedure, exhibit and PowerPoint training

- Results of control activity testing form

A. *Control environment.* The planning process involves defining the desired scope and outcome objectives for the program.

   This starts with the executive's appointing an internal control program manager and communicating executive support by granting the program manager with access, authority, and resources.

   Together, the internal control program manager and the executive sponsor develop:

   - An internal control program charter providing the authority and mandate to the internal control program manager.

   - The internal control policy and procedure informing employees of their role and responsibility related to this program.

   - Evaluate the need for supporting policies and procedures not otherwise addressed within the company policy and procedure manual.

   - Choose an internal control framework (e.g., COSO); identify control principles and objectives.

   Linking the internal control plan to COSO phase *D: Information and Communication*, the program manager assists the executive team with delivering appropriate tone-from-the-top communication that endorses the control objectives and the ethical standards that must be designed and embedded into all company policies, procedures, and processes.

The internal control program manager develops and gains approval for the internal control activity plan and schedule, ensuring that all major processes are covered at least once annually and that there is time allotted for remediation retesting and unscheduled testing engagements. The schedule must allow time for consolidation, assessment, and evaluation in time for quarter-end financial reporting to regulatory agencies.

The internal control program manager prepares an overview of how the internal control process is organized and managed and gains approval from the sponsoring executive, the audit committee of the board of directors, and the independent external auditors.

The internal control program manager provides education and training for employees, process managers, executives, and the board of directors as to their role and responsibility in the internal control program. The training should include documentation to assist with each of the constituent groups understanding their role and responsibility.

B. *Risk assessment.* Assess and define the existing control procedures.

The internal control program is assessed for risk, identifying the impact to the financial statements and/or disclosure regulations if omissions, errors, or mistakes are found within the program itself. The internal control program manager must also consider establishing measures and control activities to ensure that the internal control program is operating as designed.

Using risk assessment techniques identifies the processes and/or accounts that need to be included within the current year's program. Conduct a risk assessment to provide understanding, visibility, and ranking of the:

- Current infrastructure and the degree to which existing procedures meet or fall short of the internal control objectives defined in the first stage.

  - Define the control principles, objectives, and activities that will be used to assess the processes and/or accounts in scope.

- Likely causes of error, omission, and misstatement.

  - Identify significant financial reporting elements including accounts, disclosures, and relevant assertions prone to material misstatement.

  - Significant financial reporting elements are those accounts where there is considerable volume of transactions and/or dollars such as revenue, inventory, and cash. Determine "what could go wrong" for each relevant assertion, considering the underlying processes and subsequent steps where potential errors can occur. Rank the risks according to the magnitude and likelihood of a material misstatement.

- Areas where fraud may occur.

Referring back to the internal control process flowchart, the internal control program manager may use the input acquired through the quarterly subcertification process to identify focus areas for the coming quarter.

As optional input, the internal control program manager may request that process managers conduct an internal control readiness or self-assessment and submit results to internal controls representatives. This is an appraisal concerning the existence and adequacy of controls currently in place to ensure operational and financial process effectiveness and efficiency and compliance control objectives.

- Of course, before this can be done, the internal control program manager must have generic assessments ready to distribute to the process managers.

Using the COSO framework, establish and design control activities to test the control objectives, ensuring that the results of the control activities will indeed provide evidence that the control objective is working or not working as designed. Estimate the time it should take to conduct the proposed activities.

From this initial assessment, the internal control program manager summarizes the input to identify which processes must be considered in-scope for this year's internal control testing and which are "at risk" or contain the opportunity for significant exposure.

Once identified, the list is prioritized and assigned a place on the schedule.

- It is recommended that a top-down, risk-based approach be used to isolate those processes and/or accounts that must be considered in-scope. Refer to the risk section within the governance journey for additional detail.

Plan the schedule so as to minimize disruption to business operations, and to allow time to measure and test a typical set of transactions. Consider how frequently the identified processes and/or accounts need to be evaluated. Allow time in the schedule for retesting of specific areas where remediation efforts needed to be implemented and monitored. Communicate the plan and schedule to senior executives for their review and input. Management discretion may choose to add processes/accounts for testing. Communicate the plan and schedule to process owners.

The best way to plan the schedule is to:

- Have a list of the processes and accounts that will be tested and the types of control activities that will be used. Estimate the time it takes to fulfill the testing obligations allowing extra time to address "surprise" findings and to revisit weak areas.

- List the accounts and processes on a calendar, aligning the timing with the operational cycle in order to maximize the testing scope and sample size.

- Assign internal control resources to conduct the testing allowing time for the internal control representative to follow up on unanticipated findings, weak areas, or areas recently remediated. Additional time is also required for the internal control representative to analyze the evidence and document the findings.

Communicate the program and what is expected to process managers or, if possible, include within the training. It may not be possible if this is the first year that the internal control program is being rolled out; otherwise, there should be enough history and detail for the internal control program manager to have the control activities and schedule prepared with the training material.

To serve as an independent observer over the internal controls program, someone from internal audit and/or compliance tests and monitors the program for effectiveness and efficiency. In more sophisticated business operations, instead of one internal control program manager there may be a committee made up of cross-functional representatives from internal controls, legal, information technology, human resources, finance, and internal audit to oversee the internal control program, including plans, findings, areas for improvement, remediation and communication.

The internal control plan is shared with the audit committee of the board of directors and the external auditors and provides updates at least quarterly as to the status of the program activities and results.

C. *Control activities.* Identify and document controls specific to operational and financial risks within a centralized document repository.

An internal control document repository shall house the internal control plan, control principles, objectives, activities, process and/or account narratives, process flows, results of the control activities, and evaluation of the results. To the degree practicable consider cross-referencing this repository with the company's policy-and-procedure document repository.

If there is no in-house repository, consider researching and evaluating one of the many software programs specifically designed for this application. Customize this plan, the policies and procedures and the templates presented in this manual to populate the internal control repository.

In smaller companies, a repository might be as simple as a folder on a shared drive or printed documents housed within a central file cabinet or binder.

Control Activity/Testing Engagement

The control activity engagement shall mirror and be less formal than an internal audit engagement. We are looking for the same level of professionalism as with an internal audit; however, the objective is to test and repair rather than test and report. As a best practice, internal control findings are considered a benefit to the process and provide useful feedback for the process manager.

- At the beginning of each fiscal year, the chief financial officer or executive sponsor and the internal control program manager notify the business and process owners of the coming year's plan and schedule, mentioning that the schedule is subject to change. Not every process requires the same level of scrutiny, so some process managers may have to submit key performance indicators, while others will have their operation interrupted for more invasive testing activities.

- In order for the process manager to plan for a disruption to the process or the allocation of personnel to the control activity, provide a reminder notice to those areas, which will be tested. Provide the process manager with the readiness checklist so they can prepare for the control activity engagement. Prior to the start of the control activity engagement, the process manager should notify the staff to be prepared and fully cooperate.

  It may be appropriate to have a discussion prior to beginning the control activities. This provides both the internal control representative and the process manager with the opportunity to discuss the goals and objectives as well as the best approach to be used to verify the status of the control objective. The internal control representative should come prepared to build relationships, set the tone, and enlist the process manager's cooperation.

- The internal control project representative or team perform the control activities as planned and gather evidence. The internal control program team shall be professional and use a variety of techniques to gather data and information. If the risk assessment and planning was adequately addressed, the scope and method for the control activity should have been clearly defined.

  The process manager should be prepared to share data and evidence in support of the objective. As a best practice, the process manager knows which control objective and control activities will be used, so they can present their evidence and documentation trail to the internal control representative.

  The internal control representative shall ask questions and listen, as these are effective testing techniques to determine if there are additional previously unidentified risks or if the evidence presented supports the objective being tested. Learning how to ask direct and open-ended questions and fully listening to the response provides the internal control representative with a valuable aid to more fully discover how well the control objective is actually working.

Evidence must be presented as a reliable, accurate depiction in support of the control objective. The internal control representative must document the control activity and the approach used to collect an appropriate level of evidence.

When performing testing, it is important to select a sample of transactions to review. When determining the size of the sample to collect, consider that the size must be large enough to draw inferences regarding overall compliance and yet manageable to review in the given period. It is common to establish threshold limits prior to selecting the sample.

Example: If you are testing for the accuracy of the physical inventory, you may want to have an inventory report run that identifies the quantity and book value of the inventory. The control objective is accuracy and the control activity is to validate the physical count by reperforming the count. The two areas of inventory you are interested in testing include (1) high volume and low value and (2) high value. Let's assume there are 1,000 different product numbers for the high volume and low value and 20 product numbers for the high value. You may choose to validate the inventory count by randomly selecting 200 of the high volume and low value and counting all 20 product numbers for the high value.

Depending on the type of inventory, the test to validate the high-volume low-value inventory might be to weigh a unit of one for each product number and then weigh the entire product number and divide to see if the weighed physical count reconciles to the actual physical count. If it is correct or close for all 200 samples, then no further testing is required; if it is not correct or close, then actually counting several within this sample is required, and expanding the sample size may be in order.

The test to validate the high-value inventory is to physically recount the entire high-value inventory. Since you are reproducing the control, if there is any discrepancy, evaluate whether additional controls are required, such as retaining the high-value inventory in a separate secured area of the warehouse. The control objective has now been broadened to include safeguarding the asset.

- Once the evidence is collected, it must be evaluated to determine if the evidence is aligned with and supports the control objective. Sometimes the evidence collected shows a deficiency in a different objective.

Example of misalignment: If the control objective is to test for *accuracy* that the bill of lading on shipping orders are matched to sales orders before the goods are shipped and the control activity looks for *authorization* that the sales and shipping orders are approved, then there is a misalignment of the objective and the activity. A different control activity must be planned.

Example of unplanned discovery: We are testing for accuracy that all sales orders are fully processed but the test evidence shows that although accurate, not all sales orders are recorded in the period they are supposed to be recorded in. The evidence leads the internal control representative to identify and list *timeliness* as a new control objective, control activity, and evidence on the testing form. Remedial action is required.

- Once the evidence is gathered, the internal control representative analyzes the evidence to prove or disprove if the evidence supports that the control objective is working.

The analysis step may be supported with using such tools as variance analysis, process control charts, performance run charts, reconciliations, tree diagrams, and fishbone charts—basically any type of analysis that the internal control representative is comfortable in using and is appropriate for the process being reviewed.

- Using the Internal Control—Result of Control Activity Testing form, the internal control representative summarizes the tests and results. The results of each test, whether positive or negative, must be recorded to demonstrate that the internal control representative exercised an appropriate level of due diligence when reviewing the process.

  In addition, those items that indicate a deficiency need to be identified and classified for remedial action.

- The internal control representative reviews the Result of the Control Activity Testing form with the process owner, and together they determine an appropriate plan for remediation.

- The internal control representative submits the form to the internal control program manager, who then consolidates it with the other submitted test forms in order to evaluate and analyze the status of the company's internal controls.

As the internal control program manager reviews the findings, there may be similar findings across functions that signal a systemic issue, which may require further testing and subsequent remediation.

The internal control program team shall recommend integrating the control activities with technology to provide automated controls where possible. The process manager or internal control program team shall identify the significant applications including end-user computing applications such as spreadsheets that support the significant financial reporting elements.

For items that require remediation, process managers are to take corrective action and the internal control program manager must establish plans for subsequent retesting actions.

D. *Information and communication.* Prepare and distribute reports.

  As soon as the internal control testing is complete or at least quarterly if only key measures are reviewed, the internal control program team evaluates the findings, and prepares and distributes progress reports to process managers identifying those control activities performed and the corresponding results. Process managers are expected to reply with remediation and/or corrective action plans and an estimated completion date.

  At least quarterly, the internal controls program manager consolidates results accumulated from control activities. The results are classified according to risk (i.e., impact to the financial statements) and probability of occurring, with all material weaknesses and significant deficiencies highlighted on the report. From this ranking, the internal control program manager determines the company's overall internal control rating and the effectiveness of the internal control program.

E. *Monitor, evaluate, and report* requires that the internal control program manager consolidate the findings and review the internal control status with senior managers and leaders.

  The findings and review are presented include a summary of the internal control plan, progress on implementing the plan, results of the testing activities, and recommended areas for improvement and disclosure. The results are presented to the audit committee of the board of directors and to the independent external auditors.

  It was pointed out earlier that internal controls and audit are different processes with different objectives serving different constituents. However, to the degree that the internal controls program is effective and efficient, the independent external auditors will view the contribution from internal controls as part of the company's control environment and reduce the scope of their audits, thereby reducing the independent external auditor fees to the company. This monitoring section of COSO is aimed at evaluating the effectiveness of the internal control program.

To support the big G Governance CEO and CFO attestation, the quarterly subcertification letter asks select individuals who have or should have intimate knowledge of the company's processes to attest and subcertify along with the CEO and CFO. During the quarter the internal control program manager maintains a list of processes, process owners, and their financial and legal counterparts. A matrix is prepared, which serves as the distribution list for the quarterly subcertification letter and related questionnaire. Prior to the end of the quarter and allowing enough time for the internal control program manager to distribute, receive, evaluate, and resolve issues, the quarterly subcertification letter program is initiated.

The internal control program manager consolidates the data and information from the risk assessment, the control plan and activities, and the internal control program itself and the quarterly subcertification program and prepares a report. The report is reviewed with the CEO the CFO and then distributed to the audit committee of the board of directors and independent external auditor.

ROLES AND RESPONSIBILITIES

Control Environment Representing Management Oversight

The board of directors is responsible for:

- Approving internal control strategies and policies

- Understanding the risks the company is subject to

- Setting the acceptable level of risks

- Ensuring that senior management takes the necessary steps to identify, monitor, and control the risks

- Approving the organizational structure

- Ensuring that senior management is monitoring the effectiveness of the internal control system

The audit committee of the board of directors is responsible for monitoring, overseeing, and evaluating the duties and responsibilities of management, the internal audit activity, and the independent external auditors as those duties and responsibilities relate to the company's processes for controlling its operations. The committee is also responsible for determining that all major issues reported by the internal audit activity, the external auditor, and other outside advisors have been satisfactorily resolved.

Senior management is responsible for:

- Implementing the strategies approved by the board of directors

- Establishing appropriate internal control policies

- Monitoring the effectiveness of the internal control system

Jointly, the board of directors and senior management are responsible for:

- Promoting high ethical and integrity standards

- Establishing a culture within the organization that emphasizes and demonstrates to all levels of personnel the importance of internal controls

Managers are responsible for establishing a network of processes with the objective of controlling the operations in a manner that provides the board of directors reasonable assurance that:

- Data and information published either internally or externally is accurate, reliable, complete, and timely.

- The actions of company officers, managers, and employees are in compliance with the company policies, standards, plans and procedures, and all relevant laws and regulations.

- The company's resources (including its people, systems, data/information bases, and client goodwill) are adequately protected.

- Resources are acquired economically and employed effectively; quality business processes and continuous improvement are emphasized.

- The company's internal controls promote the achievement of plans, programs, goals, and objectives.

Risk Assessment

Senior management is responsible for:

- Identifying and evaluating internal and external factors that could adversely affect the achievement of the company's objectives

- Continually evaluating the risks affecting the achievement of the company's strategies, goals, and objectives

Control Activities

Senior management is responsible for:

- Establishing an appropriate control structure to ensure effective internal controls

- Establishing control activities at every business level

- Periodically ensuring that all operational areas are in compliance with established policies and procedures

- Ensuring that control activities are an integral part of the daily operations

- Ensuring that there is appropriate segregation of duties and that personnel are not assigned conflicting responsibilities

Controlling is a function of management and is an integral part of the overall process of managing operations. As such, it is the responsibility of managers at all levels to:

- Identify and evaluate the exposures to loss relating to their particular sphere of operations.

- Specify and establish policies, plans, and operating standards, procedures, systems, and other disciplines to be used to minimize, mitigate, and/or limit the risks associated with the exposures identified.

- Establish practical controlling processes that require and encourage administrators, officers, and employees to carry out their duties and responsibilities in a manner that achieves the control objectives outlined above.

- Maintain the effectiveness of the controlling processes established and foster continuous improvement to these processes.

- Be prepared to cooperate when internal controls notify them as to review scope and schedule. They must promptly reply to reporting conditions and remediate in a complete and timely manner. They must notify internal controls when unusual or nonroutine transactions or results present.

The process owner needs to:

- Perform a risk assessment.

- Understand the likely causes of error, omission, and misstatement.

- Scope the processes and activities to be performed.

- Establish a schedule to perform those activities.

- Assemble existing policies, procedures, processes, and instructions, including risks and controls.

- Produce evidence of operating effectiveness and efficiencies.

- Identify, monitor, and track opportunities for improvement efforts.

- Monitor, track, and report on efforts to remediate deficiencies.

Information and Communication

Senior management is responsible for:

- Ensuring adequate and comprehensive internal financial, operational, and compliance data

- Ensuring adequate and comprehensive external market information about events and conditions that are relevant to decision making

- Establishing effective channels of communications to ensure that all staff are aware of policies and procedures affecting their duties and responsibilities

- Ensuring that other relevant information is reaching the appropriate personnel

- Ensuring that there are appropriate information systems in place that cover all activities of the company

- Ensuring that information systems are secure and periodically tested

Monitor, Evaluate, and Report

Senior management is responsible for:

- Monitoring the overall effectiveness of the company's internal controls on an ongoing basis

- Monitoring key risks on a daily basis

- Evaluating each key risk separately

Jointly, the board of directors and senior management are responsible for:

- Ensuring an effective and comprehensive internal audit of the internal control system

- Ensuring that the internal audit function reports directly to the board of directors or its audit committee and to senior management

Senior management is responsible for:

- Ensuring that internal control deficiencies are reported in a timely manner to the appropriate management level and addressed promptly

- Ensuring that material internal control deficiencies should be reported to senior management and the board of directors

Evaluation of internal controls belongs to everyone.

Company entity general managers and controllers as well as functional business unit leadership:

- Requiring all business areas and company subsidiaries to have an effective system of internal controls that is consistent with the nature, complexity, and risk of the company's on- and off-balance-sheet activities and that responds to changes in the company's environment and conditions

- Taking appropriate action against companies with inadequate internal control systems to ensure that the internal control system is improved immediately

INTERNAL CONTROL – PLANNING, TESTING AND REMEDIATION WORKSHEET

Available in the URL download is an Excel worksheet with the following columns. For your convenience, the download is pre-populated with process/account, control objectives, and control activities as described in the internal control testing guides from Unit 3 of this manual.

Process/Account

- Using a top-down assessment approach, list the significant processes and/or accounts that require testing.

- After the risk assessment has been performed and the risks identified prioritize and classify the risks, assign an executive sponsor to oversee the investigation and management of the risk. Ideally, the process would be engineered to eliminate and/or mitigate the opportunity for omission, error, mis-statement and risk.

Control Objective/Risk

- Identify the control objective or risk element that must be documented or tested.

- Designate your own control objectives or use the ones identified and defined within testing guides presented in the manual.

Control Activity

- Identify the planned control activity that must be documented or tested.

- Design your own control activities, or use the ones identified and defined within testing guides presented in the manual.

- Remember that the control activity must demonstrate that the internal control representative has defined a substantive activity that will produce sufficient evidence that the control is working. Supporting evidence shall be included or referenced on the Internal Control—Result of Testing form.

Sample Size and Results of Testing

- Describe the approach used to determine the sample size, identify the sample size, and describe the findings that result.

- Reference the Internal Control—Results of Testing checklist and the supporting evidence collected.

- Remember to note where the control objective is working as designed and there are no findings.

- Even if not an immediate control exposure, remember to include areas of concern that may lead to control exposures or where process effectiveness and efficiency opportunities may exist.

Control in Place

- Identify "Yes" or "No" as to whether the control objective is in place and proved by the control activity.

- If "No," then describe the issue and rate the control as: assessment refers to your evaluation as to whether the control is working as it should be. Rate 1 as a significant deficiency, 2 as a material weakness, 3 as a reportable condition, and 4 as an effective control.

Process Owner

- Those items rated as 1, 2, or 3 require a process owner to oversee the remediation efforts. This column is to identify the name of the process owner or person responsible for remediation.

Remediation Actions

- If remediation actions are required, identify the immediate next steps and corrective action plans.

- Remediation actions and next steps should be developed in cooperation with the process manager.

Next Follow-up Date or Due Date

- A follow-up date is required for those issues which cannot be readily corrected. This date should not be more than two weeks from the date of the testing to ensure a timely response from the process manager. The corrective action may require a significant process reengineering plan and periodic meetings to ensure that the re-engineering design corrects the control issues or it may require a documented "work around" which allows employees to monitor and track the opportunity for risk.

- A due date is preferable as the date the issue is corrected and ready for re-testing.

- Allow time for the correction to be implemented and performance indicators to prove that the correction has been deployed; then follow with a retest of the control objective.

AUTHORIZATION AND APPROVAL PROGRAM

Within the company, little g governance defines roles, relationships, and reporting requirements. Organization charts show how work is organized with solid and dotted lines drawn to cross-link functional groups. Direction and accountability become more complicated as cross-functional teams are established for projects.

When there is disagreement or a lack of clarity over who is responsible for what, the development of a process ownership and authorization matrix is recommended. We discuss process ownership maps in other chapters, but here we examine its usefulness in assigning various levels of approval and authorization. Governance and leadership depend on establishing defined roles and responsibilities and encouraging and reinforcing specific behaviors.

Defining the Terms

Often used as synonyms, *approval* and *authorization* are different, requiring different skills and levels of action. The approval role is to accept as satisfactory, to hold a favorable opinion, to prove, and to attest. The approval responsibility refers to a process that encompasses reviewing and testing up to a level that allows the approver to feel comfortable and confident that the data and/or information presented is satisfactory and acceptable. Authorization refers to the person in command with influence and power to make the decision, to grant official authority, or legally commit company funds and/or resources. A subdelegation of authority requires empowering others and is issued from those with authorization to act.

As a control objective, those tasked with the role of approver may or may not have authority; therefore, the roles must be clearly defined and accepted.

> *Example:* The board of directors provides authorization to the chief executive officer (CEO) and chief financial officer (CFO) to operate the company. The CFO subdelegates authorization for capital projects less than $5 million to the chief operating officer (COO); that is, the CFO allows the COO to make decisions about whether to proceed with capital projects; the COO has the ability to enter into formal company commitments for capital projects. In order to not be bogged down with the day-to-day operational aspects of the project, the COO assigns capital project approval to the real estate project manager. Once the COO has authorized the project, the real estate project manager's role is to review and grant acceptance of the project details for execution. In this example, the real estate project manager is not authorized to sign contracts, but is authorized to execute those contracts.

> *Example:* Those who have authorization to sign procurement contracts may subdelegate the approval of those contracts to professional staff within the business finance, and legal units. The approval in this case refers to the reviewing and agreeing that the contract specifics (i.e., terms, conditions, products, services) are accurate and complete.

Delegation of Authority

Authority is derived from the owners of the company. For public companies, authority is identified and granted by the board of directors; for nonpublic companies, authority belongs to the proprietor or partners. From these official positions, a subdelegation of authority may be established based on roles and responsibilities. An example of a company's delegation-of-authority policy and procedure as well as its related matrix follows.

The matrix identifies the types of commitments that the company is likely to require, and it identifies the various positions that are then "authorized" to make those decisions and commitments.

RASCI

Building on this methodology, a company may find the following tool useful as a compliment to the delegation-of-authority matrix. The role assignment is complementary to the one above, providing an additional layer identifying the various functions or operational areas. The role assignment is subordinate to the more formal delegation of authority.

In every organization, in order to get work done, it is important to know who is responsible, who has approval, who provides support, who provides counsel, and who needs to be kept informed. A common methodology is to establish and use the RASCI (responsible, authority, support, counsel, and inform) matrix.

> *Example:* Referring to our procurement example above, only the procurement department is authorized to purchase goods and/or services, while each of the other functional areas are responsible for the purchased products.

> *Example:* The marketing organization may be assigned the authority to bring merger and acquisition requests forward to the CEO, CFO, and the board. However, they must consult with manufacturing, technical support, administration, human resources, and legal. In addition, they must engage research and development and finance in the authorization process and inform sales.

Following are the:

- Subdelegation of authority policy and procedure and the sample delegation-of-authority matrix

- RASCI matrix and instructions

Customize both of these matrices to fit your company's operational and transactional needs.

SUBDELEGATION-OF-AUTHORITY MATRIX

The authorization matrix is made up of the following sections:

A. Annual Budget and Plans

B. Nonbudgeted Capital Projects and Lease Obligations

C. Human Resources

D. Legal

E. Acquisitions, Divestitures, and Joint Ventures/Alliances

F. Procurement

G. Commercial Sales of Licensed Agreements, Product, Professional Services, Intellectual Property Asset-Sharing Agreements

H. Treasury and Intercompany Matters

Definitions as used within the matrix:

- *Acquisition*: Acquiring or purchasing whether by asset purchase, stock purchase, merger, consolidation, or other business combination or otherwise, of any business, line of business, product, product line, assets including intellectual property and other intangible assets, securities, or any other ownership interest in any third party or related entity.

- *Agreements:* Encompass *all* one-time contracts and master agreements.

- *Divestitures:–* Sale or disposition whether by asset purchase, stock purchase, merger, consolidation, or other business combination or otherwise, of any business, line of business, product, product line, assets including intellectual property and other intangible assets, securities, or any other ownership interest in any third party or related entity.

- *Review:* (A) Providing documented feedback within the reviewer's (or corporate committee's) area of functional or technical expertise to the employee (or corporate committee) with decisional authority who, in turn, should consider such feedback prior to approving a transaction; or (B) that where review is conducted by the employee or committee with decisional authority over the transaction, considering of all of the facts and opinions gathered in the due diligence and review process and rendering a documented decision on whether to proceed with the proposed transaction as presented.

- *Delegation of Authority (DOA):* The formal written conveyance from one person to another of the authority to bind the company to a legally enforceable obligation.

Roles and Responsibilities

- *A – Approval/decisional authority:* Employees who have requisite authority emanating from resolutions approved by the board of directors through proper delegations of authority to make a decision to commit or bind the company to a legally enforceable obligation or benefit (transaction). Employees with approval/decisional authority should ensure that all requisition reviews of transactions have been completed and consider them prior to approving transactions.

- *I – Inform authority:* Employees who must be informed about a transaction as early as practicable in the process and, in any event, prior to approval and execution. It is the responsibility of the employee with the approval/decisional authorities to ensure that appropriate stakeholders in the organization are informed about transactions.

- *R – Review authority:* Employees responsible for reviewing proposed transactions and providing documented feedback within the reviewer's areas of functional or technical expertise to the approval/decisional authority employee who, in turn, should consider such feedback prior to approving the transactions.

  - *Authority/signatory authority:* Employees who have requisite authority to sign documents that commit or bind the company to a legally enforceable obligation or benefit. Employees with signatory authority may not necessarily have approval/decisional authority; however, employees with approval authority have signatory authority. Any employee with signatory authority must ensure that all proposed transactions have received all requisite approvals prior to signing any documents that commit or bind the company to transactions.

  - *Payment execution authority:* Employees who have requisition authority emanating from their position in the organization to authorize release of payments for goods, services, and obligations entered into by the company. Any employee authorized to execute payment must ensure that all requested transactions have received the appropriate documented reviews and approvals prior to the payment release. For most ordinary business expenditures, the payment execution authority and approval/decisional authority will be delegated to the same individual.

Areas with Worldwide Authority

In addition to the authorization levels identified within the matrix, the following transactions must comply with their related policies and procedures:

- **Accounting:** An accounting manager other than the originator must approve all journal entries.

- **Contracts:** The worldwide legal department (legal) must approve all contracts and legal obligations made on behalf of the company prior to their execution. Legal may subdelegate contract review of standard contracts to the functional business area. Alterations to company standard contracts and agreements must be approved by legal. All contracts executed on behalf of the company must be executed by at least a vice president and senior officer if not set forth elsewhere in this policy.

- **Human Resources** must provide written approval prior to extending any financial commitments to employees (e.g., hiring, salary or wage increases, incentives, commissions, and bonuses).

- **Information Services (IS)** must approve all purchases of computer-related hardware, software, networks, and peripherals used for internal purposes.

- **Planning:** The financial planning and analysis function approves the company's plan and forecasts.

- **Product and Services Pricing** must be established according to preapproved guidelines and approved by the product/service business unit and the SVP Pricing.

- **Real Estate** commitments to purchase, lease, or rent property on behalf of the company must be approved by the headquarter real estate/facilities function. The treasurer must approve real estate financing arrangements.

- **Sales and/or Services Finance** must approve sales contracts or changes to sales terms and conditions, including delivery, shipment, payment, demo licenses, and future product discounts.

- **Tax:** Income, sales and use or country equivalent, import/export, property, and other tax-related preparations and obligations must be approved or delegated by the corporate tax department.

- **Treasury** must approve *any and all* bank accounts and establishes signing authority for issuing checks and arranging for electronic transfers.

Prepared by:	Approved by:	Authorized by:
Date	Date	Date

Scope/Background

By resolution of the company's board of directors (BOD), the BOD delegates to the chief executive officer (CEO) authority including the authority to subdelegate and redelegate such authority to conduct activities necessary for the operational continuation of the business.

The purpose of this document is to:

- Identify expenditure authorizations in order to provide clear guidance over decision making and accountability company-wide.

- Increase transparency of decision making to enhance operational efficiency.

U.S. and international regulations require documented delegation of authority for public companies:

- Section 103 of the Sarbanes-Oxley Act requires external auditors to evaluate whether a company's internal control and procedures provide reasonable assurance that transactions are being made in accordance with authorizations as subdelegated to management and directors.

- Section 404 of the Sarbanes-Oxley Act, in order to support the effectiveness of the Company's internal control environment, requires that there be written documentation of the subdelegation chain and approval to execute a specific transaction.

- The U.S. Foreign Corrupt Practices Act of 1977 stipulates in its record-keeping and accounting provisions that access to a company's assets include management's authorization (i.e., written delegation and subdelegation authority).

Policy

In accordance with the BOD resolutions regarding this matter; it is IDÆAL, LLP's (company's) policy to establish and delegate authorization to specific functional areas of the business and to specific individuals for the purpose of making commitments, collecting and disbursing cash on behalf of the company.

The BOD delegates to the CEO specific authority and, in turn, the CEO subdelegates authority for certain activities (e.g., review and approval) to certain company officers and employees.

It is the company's policy that authorization be delegated to those areas that are held responsible for the successful implementation of company objectives. The company assigns authorization levels based on the employee's level of responsibility. Commensurate authority is available to meet the needs of proper conduct for the business and therefore reflects the company's strategic principles.

<table>
<tr><td colspan="3" align="center">Policy and Procedures</td></tr>
</table>

Procedure No. B03a	Section: Internal Controls	Page 2 of 4
	Delegation of Authority	
Department Ownership	Issue/Effective Date:	Replaces previously issued

Authorization must be in accordance with the authorization matrix (separate document). In a hierarchical corporate environment, authorization may be delegated following the reporting line of command and must be documented.

Delegation is restricted to full-time company employees.

The CEO, chief operating officer (COO), chief financial officer (CFO), chief administrative officer (CAO), and general counsel establish and delegate authorization limits.

The company's executive management empowers, authorizes, and grants responsibility to specific corporate positions through the company's formal policies and procedures. Each business unit's functional executive and their financial designate should either directly approve every financial commitment made on behalf of the unit *or* document the delegated line of authority. **Functional authorizations must be aligned to the authorization matrix.**

Delegation of Authority

Delegation of authority (DOA) is the formal written conveyance from one person to another of the authority to bind the company to a legally enforceable obligation.

Each geographic and functional business area should document and align the sub delegation limits based on management responsibility. Note that business decisions require review and approval from a business manager, their financial controller or designate.

Delegations of authority may be considered:

- *Short term:* Each manager should establish protocols for delegation when they anticipate being absent due to illness, vacations, leaves, or extended business trips. Delegations should be documented and distributed to the appropriate departments within the business area.

- *Long term:* Any delegation of a long-term nature must be approved by the CFO.

Special Areas with Worldwide Authority

In addition to the authorization levels identified within the matrix, the following transactions must comply with their related policies and procedures:

- **Accounting:** An accounting manager other than the originator must approve all journal entries.

- **Contracts:** The worldwide legal department (legal) must approve all contracts and legal obligations made on behalf of the Company prior to their execution. Legal may subdelegate contract review of standard contracts to the functional business area. Alterations to company standard contracts and agreements must be approved by legal.

- **Information services (IS)** must approve all purchases of computer-related hardware, software, networks, and peripherals used for internal purposes.

<table>
<tr><td>Procedure No. B03a</td><td colspan="2" align="center">**Policy and Procedures**
Section: Internal Controls
Delegation of Authority</td><td align="right">Page 3 of 4</td></tr>
<tr><td>Department Ownership</td><td align="center">Issue/Effective Date:</td><td align="right">Replaces previously issued</td></tr>
</table>

- **Human resources** must provide written approval prior to extending any financial commitments to employees (e.g., hiring, salary or wage increases, incentives, commissions, and bonuses).

- **Planning:** The financial planning and analysis function coordinates the approval of the company's plan and forecasts.

- **Product and services pricing** must be established according to preapproved guidelines and approved by the product/service business unit and the senior vice president pricing.

- **Real estate** commitments to purchase, lease, or rent property on behalf of the company must be approved by the headquarter real estate/facilities function. Facility-related contracts (e.g., landscaping, cleaning, utilities) must be approved by real estate. The treasurer must approve real estate financing arrangements.

- **Sales and/or services finance** must approve sales contracts and changes to sales terms and conditions, including delivery, shipment, payment, demo licenses, and future product discounts.

- **Tax:** Income, sales and use or country equivalent, import/export, property, and other tax-related preparations and obligations must be approved or delegated by the corporate tax department.

- **Treasury** must approve *any and all* bank accounts and establishes signing authority for issuing checks and arranging for electronic transfers.

Planned Spending

Annually, the company approves regional plans that should achieve the business area's goals and objectives. Spending to the authorized plan limits requires approval as per the authorization matrix.

Under no circumstance shall local management authorize spending in excess of budget.

Roles and Responsibilities

The attached matrix identifies specific roles and responsibilities:

A-Approver having authority for final decision and signature.
R-Reviewer having review and analysis responsibility.
I-Requires that information be provided to those in this role.

- **Approval/decisional authority:** Employees who have requisite authority emanating from resolutions approved by the BOD through proper delegations of authority to make a decision to commit or bind the company to a legally enforceable obligation or benefit (transaction). Employees with approval/decisional authority should ensure that all requisition reviews of transactions have been completed and consider them prior to approving transactions.

Policy and Procedures		
Procedure No. B03a	Section: Internal Controls	Page 4 of 4
	Delegation of Authority	
Department Ownership	Issue/Effective Date:	Replaces previously issued

- **Authority/signatory authority:** Employees who have requisite authority to sign documents that commit or bind the company to a legally enforceable obligation or benefit. Employees with signatory authority may not necessarily have approval/decisional authority; however, employees with approval authority have signatory authority. Any employee with signatory authority must ensure that all proposed transactions have received all requisite approvals prior to signing any documents that commit or bind the company to transactions.

- **Inform authority:** Employees who must be informed about a transaction as early as practicable in the process and, in any event, prior to approval and execution. It is the responsibility of the employee with the approval/decisional authorities to ensure appropriate stakeholders in the organization are informed about transactions.

- **Payment execution authority:** Employees who have requisition authority emanating from their position in the organization to authorize release of payments for goods, services, and obligations entered into by the company. Any employee authorized to execute payment must ensure that all requested transactions have received the appropriate documented reviews and approvals prior to the payment release. For most ordinary business expenditures, the payment execution authority and approval/decisional authority will be delegated to the same individual.

- **Review authority:** Employees responsible for reviewing proposed transactions and providing documented feedback within the reviewer's areas of functional or technical expertise to the approval/decisional authority employee who, in turn, should consider such feedback prior to approving the transactions.

Controls/Areas of Responsibility

- Each business area should have a documented list of financial delegation and approval limits that is aligned with the company's authorization matrix.

- All financial commitments undertaken on the company's behalf should be in conformance with the company's code of conduct and other company policies.

- The person granting financial authorization should not be the same person who requests, purchases, or receives the product or service.

- All contracts and documented records require stewardship in accordance with the records information management policy.

- A dedicated business planning and analysis group reviews and tracks results relative to achieving the company's plan and reports variances as part of the monthly performance review package.

- Appropriate level of documentation and authorization signatures should accompany the request for spending and the subsequent set up in the accounting systems.

Contact

Chief financial officer

SUB DELEGATION OF AUTHORITY MATRIX
SUPPORTS THE SUB DELEGATION OF AUTHORITY POLICY AND PROCEDURE

The Authorization Matrix is made up of the following sections	
A	Annual Budget and Plans
B	Non Budgeted Capital Projects and Lease Obligations
C	Human Resources
D	Legal
E	Acquisitions, Divestitures and joint Ventures / Alliances
F	Procurement
	Commercial Sales of Licensed Agreements, Product, Professional Services, Intellectual
G	Property Asset Sharing Agreements
H	Treasury and Intercompany Matters
Definitions	
	Acquisition – acquiring or purchasing whether by asset purchase, stock purchase, merger, consolidation or other business combination or otherwise, of any business, line of business, product, product line, assets including intellectual property and other intangible assets, securities or any other ownership interest in any third party or related entity.
	Agreements – encompass ALL one-time contracts and Master Agreements
	Divestitures – sale or disposition whether by asset purchase, stock purchase, merger, consolidation or other business combination or otherwise, of any business, line of business, product, product line, assets including intellectual property and other intangible assets, securities or any other ownership interest in any third party or related entity.
	Review – a) providing documented feedback within the reviewer's (or corporate committee's) area of functional or technical expertise to the employee (or corporate committee) with decisional authority who, in turn, should consider such feedback prior to approving a transaction; or b) that where review is conducted by the employee or committee with decisional authority over the transaction, considering of all of the facts and opinions gathered in the due diligence and review process and rendering a documented decision on whether to proceed with the proposed transaction as presented.
	Delegation of Authority (DOA) is the formal written conveyance from one person to another of the authority to bind the company to a legally enforceable obligation.
Roles and Responsibilities	
A	**Approval / Decisional authority** – employees who have requisite authority emanating from resolutions approved by the BOD through proper delegations of authority to make a decision to commit or bind the company to a legally enforceable obligation or benefit (transaction). Employees with approval / decisional authority should ensure all requisition reviews of transactions have been completed and consider them prior to approving transactions.
I	**Inform authority** – employees who must be informed about a transaction as early as practicable in the process and, in any event, prior to approval and execution. It is the responsibility of the employee with the approval / decisional authorities to ensure appropriate stakeholders in the organization are informed about transactions.
R	**Review authority** – employees responsible for reviewing proposed transactions and providing documented feedback within the reviewer's areas of functional or technical expertise to the approval / decisional authority employee who, in turn should consider such feedback prior to approving the transactions.

	Authority/Signatory authority – employees who have requisite authority to sign documents which commit or bind the Company to a legally enforceable obligation or benefit. Employees with signatory authority may not necessarily have approval / decisional authority; however, employees with approval authority have signatory authority. Any employee with signatory authority must ensure that all proposed transactions have received all requisite approvals prior to signing any documents that commit or bind the Company to transactions.
	Payment execution authority – employees who have requisition authority emanating from his/her position in the organization to authorize release of payments for goods, services and obligations entered into by the company. Any employee authorized to execute payment must ensure that all requested transactions have received the appropriate documented reviews and approvals prior to the payment release. For most ordinary business expenditures, the payment execution authority and approval / decisional authority will be delegated to the same individual.

Areas with Worldwide Authority

	In addition to the authorization levels identified within the matrix, the following transactions must comply with their related policies and procedures:
	Accounting – An accounting manager other than the originator must approve all journal entries.
	Contracts – The Worldwide Legal Department (Legal) must approve all contracts and legal obligations made on behalf of the Company prior to their execution. Legal may sub-delegate contract review of standard contracts to the functional business area. Alternations to Company standard contracts and agreements must be approved by Legal. All contracts executed on behalf of the Company must be executed by at least a Vice President and Senior Officer if not set forth elsewhere in this policy.
	Global Information Services (GIS) must approve all purchases of Computer related hardware, software, networks and peripherals used for internal purposes.
	Human Resources must provide written approval prior to extending any financial commitments to employees (e.g., hiring, salary or wage increases, incentives, commissions and bonuses).
	Planning – The Financial Planning and Analysis function approves the Company's plan and forecasts.
	Product and Services Pricing must be established according to pre-approved guidelines and approved by the product / service business unit and the SVP Pricing.
	Real Estate commitments to purchase, lease or rent property on behalf of the Company must be approved by the headquarter Real Estate / Facilities function. The Treasurer must approve Real Estate financing arrangements.
	Sales and/or Services Finance must approve sale contracts, changes to sales terms and conditions including: delivery, shipment, payment, demo licenses and future product discounts.
	Tax – Income, sales and use or country equivalent, Import/Export, Property and other tax-related preparations and obligations must be approved or delegated by the Corporate Tax department.
	Treasury must approve <u>any and all</u> bank accounts and establishes signing authority for issuing checks and arranging for electronic transfers.

AUTHORIZATION – DELEGATION, SUBDELEGATION OF AUTHORITY

Authorization – Delegation, Sub Delegation of Authority

	U.S. Dollars	Authorization Levels – refers to a single transaction	BOD	CEO	COO	Human Resources	CFO	General Counsel	Business Unit Manager	Business Unit Finance Manager
A	**Annual Budget and Plans**		R	A	A	A	A	A	R	R
B	**Non budgeted Capital Projects and Lease Obligations**									
	Capital projects not approved as part of the annual budget – Per project aggregate value	Over $10M	A	R	R	R	R	R	R	R
		$5M to $10M		A	R	R	R	R	R	R
		$2.5M to $5M			A	I	R	I	R	R
		$1M to $2.5M					A		R	R
		Up to $1M							A	A
	Capital and Operating Lease Obligations	Over $10M	A	R	R	R	R	R	R	R
		$5M to $10M		A	R	R	R	R	R	R
		$2.5M to $5M			A	I	R	I	R	R
		$1M to $2.5M					A		R	R
		Up to $1M							A	A
C	**Human Resources**									
	Executive – individual employee plans: Recruitment, Hiring, Severance	Any Value	I	A	R	A	R	R		
	Non executive – individual employee plans: Recruitment, Hiring, Severance	Any Value			I	A	A		A	A
	Restructuring and Reorganization initiatives	Over $10M	A	R	R	R	R	R	R	R
		$5M to $10M		A	R	R	R	R	R	R
		$1M to $5M		I	A	R	A	I	R	R
		Up to $1M		I	A	R	A	I	R	R

(Continued)

Internal Use Only

U.S. Dollars	Authorization Levels – refers to a single transaction	BOD	CEO	COO	Human Resources	CFO	General Counsel	Business Unit Manager	Business Unit Finance Manager
Employee benefits, HR policy impact	Over $5M	A	A	R	R	R	R	R	R
	Up to $5M		I	I	A	R	I	R	R
Executive – stock options or equity compensation programs	Any Value	A	R		R	R	R		
Non executive – stock options or equity compensation programs	Any Value	I	A	I	R		R		
D Legal									
Product Liability and Class Action Claims, Corporate Secretary and VP Public Relations needs to be informed of ALL	Over $10M	A	R	R		R	R	R	R
	$5M to $10M		A	R		R	R	R	R
	Up to $5M		I	I		A	A	R	R
Non monetary, Material Settlement			A	R		R	R	R	R
Non monetary, Nonmaterial Settlement			I	I		A	A	R	R
Commercial Litigation and Claims including Patent and Intellectual Property Disputes, Corporate Secretary and VP Public Relations needs to be informed of ALL except less than $5M	Over $10M	A	R	R		R	R	R	R
	$5M to $10M		A	R		R	R	R	R
	Up to $5M		I	I		A	A	R	R
Non monetary, Material Settlement			A	R		R	R	R	R
Non monetary, Nonmaterial Settlement			I	I		A	A	R	R
Labor and Employment Claims, Corporate Secretary and Public Relations needs to be informed	Over $10M	A	R	R		R	R	R	R
	$5M to $10M		A	R		R	R	R	R
	Up to $5M		I	I		A	A	R	R
Non monetary, Material Settlement			A	R		R	R	R	R
Non monetary, Nonmaterial Settlement			I	I		A	A	R	R

U.S. Dollars	Authorization Levels – refers to a single transaction	BOD	CEO	COO	Human Resources	CFO	General Counsel	Business Unit Manager	Business Unit Finance Manager
E Acquisitions, Divestitures, and Joint Ventures/Alliances									
Investment Committee: reviews ALL and is made up of the CEO, COO, Human Resources, CFO, General Counsel, Business Unit Management, Business Unit Finance Management									
Any single Acquisition or Divestiture	Over $10M	A	R	R	R	R	R	R	R
Acquisitions, Divestitures, and Joint Ventures/Alliances with a single or aggregate value	Up to $10M		A	A	A	A	A	R	R
F Procurement									
Purchase or Lease of Goods and Services – VP Procurement must approve ALL	Over $5M	I	A	R	I	R	R	R	R
	Up to $5M			A		A	R	R	R
Procurement (excludes: Mergers, Acquisitions, Licensing Agreements, Royalties, Intellectual Property, Technology)	Up to $500K					R	R	A	A
Professional Services – External Auditors	Annual Contract	A							
G Sales									
Standard Product Pricing – list prices, discounts, Terms and Conditions	Any Value		I	A		A		R	R
Discount within standard range	Any Value							A	A
Discount exceeding standard range	Any Value		I	A		A	A	R	R
Standard Contract language	Any Value							A	A
Nonstandard Contract language	Any Value		I	A		A	A	R	R

(Continued)

U.S. Dollars	Authorization Levels – refers to a single transaction	BOD	CEO	COO	Human Resources	CFO	General Counsel	Business Unit Manager	Business Unit Finance Manager
Commission Plan			I	A	A	A	A	R	R
Payment Terms and Concessions	Any Value		I	A		A		R	R
Licenses/Asset sharing agreements – outbound technology sharing	Any Value		I	A		A	A	R	R
Licenses/Asset sharing agreements – inbound technology sharing	Any Value		I	A		A	A	R	R
H Treasury and Intercompany Matters – ALL must be approved by the Corporate Treasurer									
Cash and Banking – opening, changing, closing accounts – movement of cash – investment of excess cash	Any Value					I			
Investment transactions	Over $10M		I			A	A		
	Up to $10M					I	R		
Financing transactions including debt, issuance or retirement of debt, issuance or retirement of guarantees	Over $10M		I			A	A		
	Up to $10M					I	R		
Transactions incorporating equity components	Any Value	A	A		A	A	A		

RESPONSIBILITY, AUTHORITY, SUPPORT, COUNSEL, AND INFORM (RASCI)

The following procedure can be used to establish the RASCI either at an organizational or process level. As a control objective, RASCI clearly defines the interrelationships and dependencies between functional areas. The various assigned roles may be reviewed and tested to ensure that an appropriate level of due diligence is conducted.

Consider which functional areas or individuals provide the various RASCI roles as described.

Responsible refers to the person or group that actually performs the work and completes the task. The output of being responsible is action and implementation. The person or group who is in charge or has authority is responsible for naming those who are in fact accountable for the design, deployment, and execution of actions. There may be many individuals or groups that will be held responsible for a given process or activity.

Authority refers to the person or group that is held accountable for the work performed. This person has legitimate authority to approve the adequacy of the deliverable. Sometimes referred to as the executive owner or sponsor of a process or project, this person holds the power for go/no go decisions or responds with yes/no decisions. There must be one authority figure and only one authority role assigned per process.

Support refers to the person or group that provides active assistance to complete the task. This person or group may have specific subject matter expertise, provide administrative or logistical coordination, and may be used for some or all of the activities and tasks. For successful outcomes there may be none, one, or many individuals or groups that provide supportive resources. Where there is no supporting role assigned, it means that the full support remains with those identified as responsible.

Counsel refers to the person or group that provides consultative support between any of the persons or groups. Those who provide counsel have information, resources, or capability necessary for decision making or to complete the work. These are generally people with technical expertise regarding rules, regulations, and terms and conditions required in the design, development, and execution of the process or project. For successful outcomes there may be one or many individuals or groups that provide consultation.

Inform refers to those persons or groups that must be notified regarding the progress and/or results. These are individuals or groups with a "need to know" regardless of whether the need relates to courtesy information or is required for complementary processes or projects. Those assigned the inform role must understand the process and how it may or may not integrate with processes under their locus of control. To maintain segregation of duty integrity, the inform role must not be assigned to those who have been assigned responsibility within the authority, support or counseling roles.

As a control objective, development of a RASCI matrix indicates that there are clearly defined roles and that review and testing can be directed to ensure that the cross-functional team has executed their role accordingly. Those responsible must maintain the audit trail, which indicates that review and approval has occurred throughout the process.

An example of a RASCI matrix follows. When constructing the RASCI matrix, use the following steps:

- *Identify processes or activities.* Note that this list is useful for many internal control activities, so taking the time to create and gain approval on this list will assist with many control activities.

- *Identify the roles.* Broadly speaking, roles may follow the organization chart along functional lines.

  - Complete the cells of the matrix by assigning an R, A, S, C, or I. Not every cell needs to be complete; however, there is an advantage to filling every cell if one of the goals of using this matrix is to enhance and enrich cross-functional communication.

- Each process must have only one A, and should only have one R. When more than one R shows up, it is a sign that there is overlap and the potential for confusion. The process needs to be further divided with each party understanding the scope of their responsibility.

- To complete the matrix, assign supporting, counseling, and informing roles to the rest of the roles.

- Resolve areas where there are gaps (i.e., omissions) and duplication where there mustn't be duplications. Once the cells have been completed, remember to gain agreement from the role owners that they have, in fact, accepted their assignment.

Functions / Processes	Research and Development	Manufacturing and Distribution	Marketing	Sales	Technical Support	Finance	Administration	Human Resources	Legal
Research and Development									
Product Management	A/R	S	C	C	S	R	I	I	I
Product Development	A/R	R	C	C	R	R	I	I	I
Intellectual Property	A/R	R	I	I	S	I	I	I	R
Emerging Markets	A/R	C	R	S	C	C	I	I	C
Manufacturing and Distribution									
Production	R	A/R	I	C	S	R	I	I	I
Materials Management	R	A/R	I	I	S	S	I	I	I
Inventory Management	I	A/R	I	R	S	S	I	I	I
Distribution and Logistics	I	A/R	I	C	C	S	R	I	I
Safety and Security	S	A/R	I	I	C	I	R	I	I
Marketing									
Strategic Marketing	C	C	A/R	R	I	S	I	I	I
Geographic Marketing	I	C	A/R	R	I	S	I	I	I
Product Marketing	R	C	A/R	R	C	S	I	I	S
Brand Management	C	I	A/R	R	I	I	I	I	S
Demand Generation	C	S	A/R	R	C	I	I	I	I
Mergers and Acquisitions	R	C	A/R	I	C	R	C	C	C
Sales									
Sales Strategy	R	S	S	A/R	C	R	I	I	I
Sales Plan	S	R	R	A/R	I	R	I	I	I
Sales Operations	S	S	S	A/R	R	S	I	I	S
Technical Support									
Maintenance	S	I	I	S	A/R	S	I	I	I
Technical Support	R	S	I	I	A/R	I	I	I	I
Product Knowledge	R	R	S	I	A/R	I	I	I	I

(Continued)

Functions / Processes	Research and Development	Manufacturing and Distribution	Marketing	Sales	Technical Support	Finance	Administration	Human Resources	Legal
Finance									
Corporate Finance	S	S	S	S	S	A/R	S	S	S
Corporate Accounting	I	I	I	I	I	A/R	I	I	I
Geographic Finance	S	S	S	S	S	A/R	S	S	S
Geographic Accounting	I	I	I	I	I	A/R	I	I	I
Functional Finance	R	R	R	R	R	A/R	R	R	R
Functional Accounting	I	I	I	I	I	A/R	I	I	I
Investor Relations	I	I	I	I	I	A/R	I	I	I
Planning and Budgeting	R	R	R	R	R	A/R	R	R	R
Administration									
Product Pricing	S	I	C	C	I	I	A/R	I	C
Information Technology	C	C	C	C	C	R	A/R	C	C
Procurement	R	R	R	R	R	R	A/R	R	R
Real Estate and Facilities	S	S	I	I	I	R	A/R	S	I
Insurance	I	I	I	I	I	S	A/R	I	C
Human Resources									
Recruitment	C	C	C	C	C	C	C	A/R	C
Retention	C	C	C	C	C	C	C	A/R	C
Training and Development	R	R	R	R	R	R	R	A/R	R
Compensation and Benefits	I	I	I	C	I	C	I	A/R	R
Employee Relations	I	I	I	I	I	I	I	A/R	S
Performance Management	R	R	R	R	R	R	R	A/R	R
Legal									
Law	I	I	I	I	I	I	I	I	A/R
Contracts	I	I	C	C	I	S	C	C	A/R
Compliance and Risk	S	S	S	S	S	S	S	S	A/R

INFORMATION TECHNOLOGY PROGRAM

As technology provides opportunities for growth and development it also carries risks and threats due to interruption of service, theft of data or information and fraud or manipulation of data or information. Information technology (IT) control activities describe procedures that provide assurance that the processes which transport and hold data and information are reliable, safe, and secure. IT controls are essential to protect company-held data and information, demonstrate ethical behavior, and preserve brand reputation and company trust. Within the IT environment, IT controls must present continuous evidence of their effectiveness and that evidence must be monitored, assessed, and evaluated on an ongoing basis.

Different functional areas have different issues and needs regarding IT and IT controls. Marketing and public relations may want to showcase IT improvements as a way to demonstrate competitiveness and innovation. Human resources and compliance areas may have protection against information theft and complying with legislation and regulations. Finance may want to demonstrate improved value for the IT investments by increasing productivity and driving costs down. IT may be driven by managing the complexity resulting from the necessity for diverse technical components working with each while at the same time monitoring the movement of IT assets.

Within information technology there are general and application controls:

- General controls, also referred to as infrastructure controls, apply to all systems, components, processes, and data. General controls include such topics as: information handling and security, administrative access and authentication, the separation of key IT functions to ensure segregation of duties, management of IT asset acquisition and use, backup, recovery and business continuity.

- Application controls are business process specific and include such controls as data edits, separation of duties between transaction initiator from transaction processor or authorizer. Application controls are designed into the software program or system and may be preventive or detective in nature. These controls are generally automated and nondiscretionary; that is they are generally produced whenever the application is opened or used. There are often compensating and redundant controls which provide a clear check and balance to reconcile or validate the data; e.g., foot and cross-foot or the automatic reclassification of amounts remaining in suspense accounts.

As with other functional areas, perform a top-down risk assessment for IT. To assess the current risk status of IT controls, rate (as high, medium, or low) the following items as to their probability that something could go wrong and if that was to go wrong the impact on your company. Once you complete this risk assessment, ask your IT professionals to also provide this quick assessment. Share and compare your ratings and develop a plan to improve.

- Reliance on systems or programs that are inaccurately processing data, processing inaccurate data, or both. Are there some systems or applications that worry you more than others?

- Do you feel you are achieving the most productivity or return for your IT investment?

- Unauthorized access to data that may result in destruction of data or improper changes to data. Identify the types of data (e.g., financial, legal, HR), which if lost or manipulated would have the greatest risk to your company.

- Unauthorized changes to data in master files

- Unauthorized changes to systems or programs

- Failure to make necessary changes to systems or programs

- Inappropriate manual intervention

- Potential loss of data

IT applications must design in and document controls to address these risk areas. IT policies and controls shall be developed to address:

- The level of security and privacy expected throughout the organization

- Classification of information and the rights to access and limitation of use

- Concepts of data and system ownership, authorization required to originate, modify, or delete data

- Recruiting and hiring of staff for sensitive or critical areas

- Disaster recovery and business continuity

- Standards to be used when developing, modifying, configuring, testing, and documenting software implementation

- IT segregation of duties ensures that no one individual has access to or controls all aspects of processing, reviewing and authorizing data. Within the IT environment, there must be separation between systems development and operations.

- The physical safeguarding and protection of IT assets including hardware, software, and networks from accidental or deliberate damage or loss

However, documentation is not enough with technical control activities required to be implemented, monitored and tracked. Standard operational technical controls must be designed into systems and program application set-up parameters, with these controls addressing:

- Access rights assigned to individuals must be allocated and controlled ensuring that the appropriate level of access is granted to only active employees.

- Segregation of duties enforced through system software and configuration controls. The segregation of duties shall be the same as those defined for operational and financial processes.

- Security, intrusion, and vulnerability assessment. IT security shall have preventive and detective controls in place and be continuously monitored for breach, with all noncompliance situations promptly addressed.

- Encryption services applied where confidentiality is a stated requirement.

- Change management process applied to all changes and patches to software, systems, network components, and data.

Technical controls are not just about overseeing the implementation of the applications, they must also address how the applications are used by end users.

Technical control activities identified as end user responsibility include:

- Input controls to ensure data is complete, accurate, timely, and authorized

- Processing controls to ensure data is processed as intended

- Output controls to ensure data is accurate, complete, timely, and authorized

- Data movement is monitored and tracked providing an audit trail

Data, information handling and security control activities address:

- Classifying information and data to ensure data and information is appropriately labeled as internal use only, confidential, or restricted. According to the level of classification, data and information must be protected from unauthorized access, disclosure, or interruption and divulged as and when appropriate

- Authenticating data as employing technical controls to validate data integrity as to its source, access, and use

- Retaining retention controls ensures data is stored and accessible as complete and accurate in accordance with records and information management policies and procedures

- Availability controls ensure that the data and information is available when, where, and in the format it is needed. Availability control issues also includes recovery from loss, disruption, or corruption of data and IT systems.

From the preceding lists, there are layers of technology controls that touch every aspect of your business. Whether through enterprise-wide systems, applications and networks or via local applications, all need to have built-in technology controls.

Ask your IT professionals to also answer the following control questions and compare with the initial assessment above. When performing readiness checklist for information and technology-related controls, consider the following questions and risk assess your responses.

1. For access controls:
   a. Is a restricted list prepared based on job responsibilities?
   b. How and how often is the access list reviewed for accuracy and approved for appropriateness?

2. For exception report controls:
   a. Which systems and applications produce exception reports?
   b. What information is contained in the report?
   c. Who reviews the report and how often?
   d. What follow-up activities are performed for exceptions/errors detected?
   e. How are file transfers reviewed for completeness and accuracy?
   f. How often do file transfers occur?
   g. What system generates the report?

3. For management review/monitoring controls:
   a. How often are reports/results reviewed?
   b. What is the purpose of the review?
   c. Who performs the review?
   d. Are discrepancies and variances logged for corrective action?
   e. Who is responsible for monitoring and tracking follow-up actions until they are resolved?

4. For segregation of duties controls:
   a. Which responsibilities are segregated?
   b. Does this list match to the one used by finance?
   c. Does an organization or department chart exist, and where is it located?

5. For approval or authorization controls:
   a. Are these designed into the system or application or manual?
   b. Do the approval and authorization controls match to the official delegation of authority documentation?

6. For reconciliation controls:
   a. Who prepares and performs the reconciliation?
   b. What is the purpose of the reconciliation?
   c. Who reviews the reconciliation and how is this evidenced?
   d. Is the re-independent sources for supporting reports and systems and how is this documented?
   e. How are differences investigated/resolved?

7. For document processing controls:
   a. Are the IT systems, applications, and procedures documented?
   b. Are documents prenumbered and system generated (e.g., sales orders, invoices)?
   c. How are documents safeguarded (e.g., physical controls over checks, contracts, manual journal entry logs)?

8. For physical asset controls:
   a. Are the systems and applications rated as to their criticality to the business? Is documentation available that describes procedures for monitoring, maintenance, and disaster recovery of these systems and applications?
   b. Is access to assets and related record keeping appropriately restricted, and is it reviewed periodically?
   c. What procedures ensure the accuracy of the related record keeping (activity logs)?

9. For system based controls:
   a. Are there checks and balances designed into the program to ensure that data entry contains valid information (e.g., current date, established dollar range) in order for a record to be accepted?
   b. Is information validated against a master table where applicable (e.g., customer number, product number, vendor number, purchase order number)?
   c. Are master data and tables reviewed and updated regularly to ensure accuracy and completeness?
   d. Are duplicate postings/entries not accepted into the system?
   e. Are accounting period-end cutoff dates enforced by the system?
   f. Are system-based control overrides properly authorized?

END-USER COMPUTING AND SPREADSHEET CONTROL

End-user computing (EUC) describes job situations where professionals utilize computers as supporting tools within the computing environment.

What is EUC? EUC refers to the use and integration of computer-aided tools and approaches that reside on the user's computer rather than on the company's mainframe. EUC is becoming more accepted and is one of the more common and widespread activities carried out in organizations today. More and more, business activities begin and end with computer activities and an end user.

What is EUC about? EUC tools are where the end user has arranged for or provided the programming or customized inquires. The results of this programming are used to determine or analyze transactional activities with the purpose of producing data and information required for journal entries and/or disclosure statements. For accounting and finance professionals, EUC is defined as spreadsheets used in the process to determine financial statement transaction amounts where the amounts are used to produce journal entries and/or support disclosure statements.

Why is EUC important? For accounting and finance professionals, Sarbanes-Oxley regulations require documented controls for internal controls over financial reporting. Developing an EUC policy and procedure and paying attention to EUC controls adds accuracy, completeness, and integrity to the output used for financial analysis and reporting.

Spreadsheets are manual and can easily lead to error, omission or misstatement by such simple changes as inserting or deleting columns or rows and cutting and pasting data. The simple act of opening the spreadsheet could cause an unwanted recalculation of the data. The more heavily a company relies on EUC, the more attention it needs to pay to EUC controls.

Many end users do not have programming disciplines or a sophisticated knowledge of spreadsheet potentials. Most end-user spreadsheet users employ the same standard arithmetic formulas and formatting commands. Programming and formula documentation and designing in controls is often lacking.

In companies where there is a seamless flow of information from the source data entry to financial statement reporting the need for additional EUC controls is not necessary. However in most companies, there is a gap between the software application where the source data is entered and the financial reporting system. Often, a data report is downloaded from the application to a spreadsheet, analyzed, and perhaps reformatted to be uploaded into the general ledger application.

The difference is shown in the following flow.

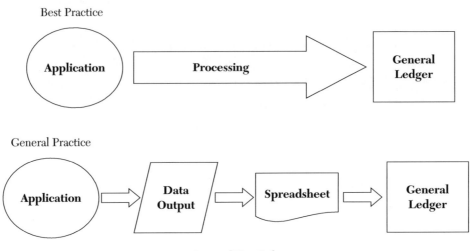

Each handoff point or arrow requires controls to be embedded into the process.

Employees who use EUC are generally performing the roles of preparer, reviewer, file share owner, and security operations.

The internal control for end-user computing requires that these roles be segregated. Typical control responsibilities of each of these groups are listed as:

- The preparer role obviously prepares and formats the spreadsheet by programming the formulas and arranging for the input of source data. Preparers are responsible to document the process with auditable instructions for any user to follow as well as to build in control totals to verify the accuracy and completeness of the data input and output.

- With EUC, the reviewer's role serves as a check to the preparer. The reviewer arranges to test and audit the documentation, spreadsheet formulas, and use of the data input and output. The reviewer confirms that the preparer has used the spreadsheet appropriately and that other than the data input, there were no changes to the formulas or use of the output. Required spreadsheet changes must be documented and approved by data output stakeholders.

- File share owners are responsible for maintaining an inventory of spreadsheets, spreadsheet owners, and a description of their purpose and function. To safeguard the spreadsheet asset, file share owners retain approved spreadsheets on a shared repository. The security operations team oversees access rights to the file share repository and the use of the spreadsheet. The file share owner may have security operations responsibilities as long as they are not the preparer or the reviewer.

A controlled alternative for end-user computing is to deploy the following process. However, depending on the persuasiveness of spreadsheet use, this process could easily become onerous and bureaucratic to monitor. Begin by identifying those spreadsheets that are critical to the company's financial reporting and expand the discipline where it makes sense. The benefits of the program are to provide a consistent and standard format for spreadsheets and introduce and encourage the use of software application design and control disciplines. Include review and approval of data prior to submission to the next process step.

When the preparer needs the spreadsheet, they go to the repository where the spreadsheets are maintained to access it. Before using the spreadsheet, they should perform a review to ensure the spreadsheet format or formulas have not been tampered with. Once they are satisfied, they populate and use the spreadsheet as it was designed. Using the control totals built into the program, the preparer reconciles the input and output data to validate that the data is complete and accurate. The preparer signs the spreadsheet cover sheet to indicate that they have performed the necessary controls. Once the preparer has completed their use of the spreadsheet, the spreadsheet is saved on the official repository.

The reviewer tests the spreadsheet to ensure data and formula accuracy. The reviewer also examines the documentation for auditability. The reviewer signs the spreadsheet cover sheet to indicate that they have reviewed and tested the spreadsheet, data output, and documentation.

The reviewer is often identified as the spreadshet owner.

Cover Sheet example:

End User Computing Spreadsheet Cover Page	
Follow Standard naming Convention for Spreadsheet name	
Name of Spreadsheet	
Date of use	
Definition or Purpose of the spreadsheet	
List specific testing activities or reconciliations performed	
	Report deemed reliable as it is
	Directly run from xxx application. It is traced and agreed with xxx control totals.
	Calculations were re-produced and verified and the schedule was footed
	Data input traced back to source transactions
	Data output traced to next step in the process, e.g., general ledger
Conclusion: Based on the above testing, the data and information calculated and presented appears accurate	
Prepared by	Name_____ Date _____
Reviewed and Approved by	Name_____ Date _____

When changes are required to the spreadsheet, the preparer arranges for the updated spreadsheet to be reviewed by the reviewer and any other interested stakeholders. Their approval is required by for the file share owner to replace the revised spreadsheet on the approved repository. The file share owner monitors and tracks changes to the spreadsheet and updates the spreadsheet inventory as required. At least quarterly, the file share owner reviews and validates the spreadsheets with the spreadsheet owners.

The IT Security operations department maintains a list of authorized users who have access rights to specific spreadsheets and at least quarterly validates that list with the spreadsheet owners.

The documentation and instruction must include a definition of the spreadsheet, reference to reliable source data, instructions to prepare the data output, formulas including use of control totals, data output, how it is analyzed and used, and where it is distributed.

Tips to prevent or detect spreadsheet errors follow, and they should be documented when used.

- Try to **avoid complex formulas**. If its purpose is not obvious, break it into smaller components. This makes errors more apparent and makes the spreadsheet easier to audit.

- **Incorporate validation checks** on data input. For example, use functions like IF (OR A1 < 5000, A1 > 10,000,"out", "in") to check a value is inside a range. This reduces the number of errors on data input.

- Have a **batch total to check the total of data input.** Input a control total, and have the spreadsheet calculate its batch total underneath. This ensures all the data is in the spreadsheet before it is manipulated.

- **Use formulas that foot and cross-foot** when summing data. This provides a cross-check and increases likelihood to catch errors as well as catch insertions of rows or columns if there are errors in formulas.

- Large columns of data **should *not* contain subtotals *and* totals.** This greatly increases likelihood of errors.

- **Try not to hide columns or rows.** If necessary, please indicate the purpose of hidden columns or rows within the spreadsheet definition.

- Develop and use standard **naming conventions.**

The spreadsheet cover page and inventory list should contain such information as:

- Spreadsheet name and owner

- File name and path to access the spreadsheet

- Purpose of the spreadsheet

- Structure and layout including links from other spreadsheets and data input

- Source of the input data

- Assumptions and limitations for the formulas

- Structure and layout of the data output

- Use and distribution of the output

- Preparer's name and date prepared

- Reviewer's name and date reviewed

Policy and Procedure		
Procedure No. B04a	Section: Internal Controls	Page 1 of 2
	End-User Computing – Control of Spreadsheets	
Department Ownership	Issue/Effective Date:	Replaces previously issued

Prepared by:	Approved by:	Authorized by:
Date	Date	Date

Scope

The document applies to all IDÆAL LLP's legal entities, subsidiaries, and business units.

End-user computing applications or use of spreadsheets present a significant risk exposure to the company mainly because:

- Desk reviews by the preparer cannot be relied on to identify shortcomings or risks.

- Preparers do not require special programming analysis or knowledge of internal controls to design or develop a spreadsheet.

- Spreadsheets generally do not have version or access control.

- Spreadsheets may change anytime as they are opened.

Policy

It is IDÆAL LLP's policy that spreadsheets be treated as software applications with controls designed into the formula logic and risk assessed based on source and use of the information provided.

Procedure

Process owners and managers are responsible for identifying the spreadsheets used within their process. Working together, process owners, information technology services, and internal control shall:

- Ascertain how many spreadsheets are in use and which are critical to the business by securing an inventory of spreadsheets and a description of their use. Capture such information as who uses it, for what purpose (i.e., financial or operational), what is the magnitude (i.e., dollar or volume impact of the spreadsheet).

- Assess the current levels of controls protecting those spreadsheets by rating the spreadsheet use according to its complexity and magnitude of the potential risk. Classify the potential risk as high, medium, or low.

  - Complexity is classified as light, intermediate, or advanced.

  - Magnitude of the spreadsheet may be classified as immaterial, material, or critical.

<table>
<tr><td colspan="3" align="center">**Policy and Procedure**</td></tr>
<tr><td>Procedure No. B04a</td><td align="center">Section: Internal Controls</td><td align="right">Page 2 of 2</td></tr>
<tr><td colspan="3" align="center">**End-User Computing – Control of Spreadsheets**</td></tr>
<tr><td>Department Ownership</td><td align="center">Issue/Effective Date:</td><td align="right">Replaces previously issued</td></tr>
</table>

- Confirm that the spreadsheets are operating in accordance with management intentions by testing its integrity and conducting an audit of the spreadsheet input, formulas, and output. Document the results as a baseline by recalculating tracing the input, recalculating and testing the formulas and the labeling and use of the output.

- Improve/implement a system of controls designed to protect the integrity of the spreadsheet. High- and medium-risk spreadsheets need to be protected with manual and system controls such as:

  - Automatic version control

  - Access control with the spreadsheets residing on central server

  - Identification and validation of changes to spreadsheet formulas or formats

  - Spreadsheets shall be backed up to external media

  - Noninput fields shall be password protected.

  - All spreadsheets shall be documented as to owner and use, version, and change control and provide instruction as to the source of the input data, formulas, and processing of data and when, where, and how output should be directed.

Periodically, test and confirm the spreadsheets are operating in an effective manner. Manual controls shall be tested at least quarterly for spreadsheets deemed high risk; at least semiannually for those deemed to be medium risk and at least annually for those deemed low risk. Wherever possible, system controls shall be embedded into the spreadsheet with system and control totals added for review and validation. System controls for spreadsheets shall be reviewed with each run of the spreadsheet.

Control/Areas of Responsibility

Process owners and managers are responsible for the control and use of all spreadsheets used within the process.

The internal controls department shall oversee the use, inventory, and testing of spreadsheets.

As with other software applications, information technology services shall create and maintain the inventory for and access to company-approved spreadsheets (i.e., those identified as high or medium risk).

Contact

Internal control

Information technology services

ACCOUNT RECONCILIATION PROGRAM

If there is one policy and procedure I could implement throughout all accounting and finance organizations, it would be account reconciliation. If every account went through this type of analysis, reviewing and monitoring it would greatly reduce the number of "surprises" and adjustments required and increase the level of financial and reporting integrity.

Internal controls, internal audit, and external audit use account reconciliations as support and evidence of the company's control environment. They rely on account reconciliations on an individual account basis as well as a program basis in order to:

- Assist with "grave-to-cradle" risk assessments

- Identify key control objectives and actions

- Assess adherence to company policies and procedures

- Provide evidence of management review

- Validate the balance sheet account totals

As a control tool within a culture of continuous improvement, account reconciliations means that when errors, omissions, and misclassifications occur, they are corrected at the source and future recurrences are not as likely to occur. When account reconciliations are used as an analysis tool, before the books are closed, this is a preventive control; when they are used after the books are closed, they are detective as well as preventive in that they correct an inappropriate process for the next reporting cycle.

An account reconciliation program begins by having defined accounts. As basic as definitions are, many companies do not have documented definitions for the accounts listed in the chart of accounts. If your company has an accounting manual, then your company is ahead of most. It seems that in this age of constant change, the accounting manual seems out of date as soon as it is populated. However, for communication, education, training, and control purposes, it is still a valued and useful tool. In today's online world, accounting manuals can and should be made available to all, accounting and financial professionals as well as functional units.

The accounting manual identifies the account hierarchy, defines the account, describes the accounting treatment for the types of journal entries that are classified to the account, and provides journal entry examples. Additional information that may be provided would be a reference to accounting literature and a description of how the accounts are organized, that is, chart of accounts and procedures for creating, updating, and rescinding accounts.

However, even if you do not have an accounting manual, a successful account reconciliation program can be achieved. A successful account reconciliation program serves to improve financial integrity by reviewing and monitoring account balances for completeness, accuracy, and timeliness. The program serves:

- As evidence that accounting policies and procedures are understood and followed

- As a link between operational processing and recording transactions

- As documented evidence that the general ledger account balances are valid, appropriate, approved, and adequate

- To discover accounting errors, omissions, and misclassifications in a timely fashion

- As an analytical tool to view the company's activity and results in a different way

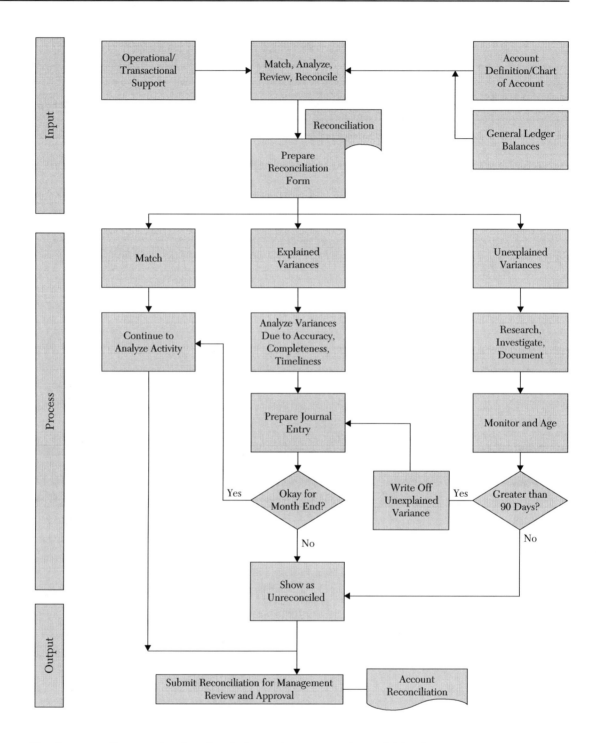

When reconciling items are discovered and analyzed, they point to correcting activities that may or may not require additional controls. Recurring reconciling items signal a systemic issue which must be addressed and may be corrected with:

- Training; hiring appropriate skills; providing better instruction, data, information, or tools; and is generally used to correct errors

- Inserting checklists, system control totals, reviews, and authorization and is generally used to correct omissions.

- Standardizing journal entry and account flow by predefining or preprogramming account classification into instructional guidance and/or systems that may be used to correct misclassifications.

Format and Analysis Techniques

It is important to use standard formats and consistent analysis techniques when analyzing and documenting account activity. However, it is often useful to use a parallel type of analysis to see if a different result occurs. For example, when accounts receivable (A/R) is reconciled to the accumulated outstanding customer balances, it might be useful to analyze and reconcile the A/R general ledger closing balance to the aging report or by geographic location.

Segmenting the information provides a different point of view and maybe a different analytical result. The analysis may not identify control issues but may reveal risks and/or opportunities not previously visited. A change in format and/or analysis when presenting the information in a different way adds value to the review and decision-making process; follow with a parallel analysis for a few periods to bridge the change and see if there is sustained value.

Account reconciliation presentation formats may vary with all format versions containing the general ledger account balance, opening and closing balances, and a list of the activity that occurred during the period. Depending on the volume and type of transactional activity the information may be organized in a variety of ways. A few format alternatives are provided.

This presentation reviews the operational impacts to identify the types of operational events that occur during the period. The benefit with this approach is that it classifies and groups the transactions in logical segments. It could be additions and subtractions as exampled below, by geographic location or by data source. This format may used be referred to as a *roll-forward analysis.*

This type of transactional reconciliation ensures that all the data and information that was supposed to be represented in the closing balance of the account activity has been included. This technique is very useful when there is more than one source of input; whether the source must also have upstream controls built into the manual and/or system processes to ensure that only valid and complete data is input into the account.

Opening Balance from the General Ledger			
Additions as per the transactional support			
Addition adjustments which include errors, omissions and misclassification			
Subtractions as per the transactional support			
Subtraction adjustments, which include errors, omissions, and misclassification			
Closing balance as calculated from above			
Closing Balance from the General Ledger			
If there is a difference between the closing balances, treat this as unexplained activity that requires additional investigation and review,			

This presentation format asks for analysis between the opening and closing general ledger account balance. The difference should be explained by a net of the monthly transactional activity or may be presented in similar segmented detail to the above format. The benefit with this approach is that it ignores business-as-usual transactions and focuses on explaining unreconciled transactions.

This type of transactional reconciliation refers to when the data directed to the account is matched with the data that actually shows up in the account. The account reconciliation analyst confirms that the data that is supposed to be directed to the account is appropriately coded and that the expected transactional volume and amount is recorded in the account.

Opening Balance from the General Ledger			
Closing Balance from the General Ledger			
Difference due to transactional activity that occurred during the period			
Transactional activity grouped by category (e.g., sales activity by region, activity by asset class, activity by portfolio investment, activity by source documentation type or system feed)			
If there is a difference between the transactional activities, treat this as unexplained activity that requires additional investigation and review			

Procedure No. B05a	**Policy and Procedure** Section: Accounting and Finance	Page 1 of 4
	Account Reconciliation	
Department Ownership	Issue/Effective Date:	Replaces previously issued

Prepared by: Date	Approved by: Date	Authorized by: Date

Scope

The document applies to all IDÆAL LLP's legal entities, subsidiaries, and business units.

Policy

It is IDÆAL LLP's (Company) policy to reconcile every balance sheet (B/S) account with a closing balance greater than US$5,000 on a monthly basis in accordance with the accounting and finance close schedule. B/S accounts with a closing balance less than $5,000 must be reconciled at least once a quarter. These analyses and reconciliations are to be prepared and reviewed by the appropriate divisional personnel, with all analysis subject to corporate review and audit.

Account reconciliations shall be forwarded for review and signoff in accordance with the Sarbanes-Oxley (SOX) narratives or the business areas respective financial designate.

Underlying detail, in the form of a subledger or schedule, must support every B/S account balance and such detail must be reconciled to the general ledger on a monthly basis. Any unreconciled difference must be investigated and resolved with adjustments made in a timely manner prior to the end of the quarter. Upon completion of the investigation, any remaining unsupported balance shall be written off.

Procedure

Corporate accounting determines account ownership based on the area that has the most knowledge and control of the account (unless internal control considerations dictate otherwise).

The B/S account balance is determined with the close of the books at each month-end.

- The reconciliation begins with the current year-to-date closing balance as per the general ledger.

- Review the subledger or supporting schedule to summarize the components that correspond to the general ledger's balance. In some cases there may be more than one subledger that needs to be considered.

- Subtract the general ledger and subledger (or other supporting document) closing balances to determine the difference to be reconciled.

- List known adjustments that must be taken during the accounting period. Subtract the total of known adjustments from the difference to be reconciled.

	Policy and Procedure	
Procedure No. B05a	Section: Accounting and Finance	Page 2 of 4
	Account Reconciliation	
Department Ownership	Issue/Effective Date:	Replaces previously issued

- The remaining balance is to be investigated and resolved.

- The reconciliation status is identified as either A, B, or C.

  - Circle **A** if there are no outstanding explanations required.

  - Circle **B** if there are known adjustments and list those that will be taken during the current accounting period.

  - Circle **C** if there is a remaining balance that must be further investigated and list the actions that will be taken during the following accounting period.

- Unreconciled items and amounts must be tracked, aged, and monitored for clearing.

- Each functional business area's controller or financial designate shall review, agree, and sign off on the reconciliation.

- Reconciliations for accounts with closing balances greater than US$1M shall be submitted to corporate accounting for additional review at the end of each quarter.

- The reconciliation shall be prepared using the standard format attached (reference exhibit).

- Account reconciliations shall be completed no later than the 10th business day.

When summarizing the account, use the key components that represent the types of transactions flowing into the account. For example, payroll payable may have the following components: regular salaried full-time employees, regular hourly employees, temporary or partial-period employees, reimbursements, and other. Components that make up an account may mirror the plan input, transaction sources, or areas that will aid in account analysis. It is not acceptable to simply summarize the debit and credit totals. For accounts that are reconciled for the first time, the opening balance must be reconciled.

Differences between the general ledger and subledgers or supporting documentation must be investigated and resolved in a timely, accurate manner. Recurring variances must be investigated and resolved at the root cause, as they may indicate a systemic issue.

- Out-of-balance situations may occur due to:

  1. Natural timing differences

  2. Misclassification (i.e., journal entry to the wrong account)

  3. Miscalculation (i.e., mathematical error in determining the amount of the journal entry that was to be recorded)

  4. Errors where an entry was omitted or recorded multiple times

  5. Other unexplained or a combination of reasons that have not yet been identified

Internal Use Only

<table>
<tr><td></td><td>Policy and Procedure</td><td></td></tr>
<tr><td>Procedure No. B05a</td><td>Section: Accounting and Finance
Account Reconciliation</td><td>Page 3 of 4</td></tr>
<tr><td>Department Ownership</td><td>Issue/Effective Date:</td><td>Replaces previously issued</td></tr>
</table>

- Misclassifications, miscalculations, and errors of omission or duplication must be readily identified and corrected. Corrections shall take place within the following month.

Any individual unreconciled differences greater than US$5,000 occurring at quarter-end or year-end must be disclosed to the chief accounting officer (or a designate). Every effort must be made to understand and resolve such differences in the month the error occurs. If you are not sure if a difference should be considered material, contact corporate financial reporting to discuss and resolve the matter.

Levels to define materiality shall be defined by the chief accounting officer (CAO) and communicated within the quarter-end and year-end instructions. Each month, the CAO shall receive a status of the reconciliation accounts, identifying those that have large unreconciled values (i.e., exceed the materiality thresholds) as well as those that have long term (level C) unexplained variances.

Control/Areas of Responsibility

The functional business area's controller or financial designate is responsible to ensure that balance sheet accounts are:

- Accurately reconciled on a timely basis
- Accurately reflect the recording of all business transactions
- Assets are properly accounted for and expensed
- Liabilities are properly reflected and accrued for

Unreconciled amounts at the end of the quarter must be expensed. The regional controller or financial designate may approve write-offs up to $5,000, while all other write-off amounts must be approved by corporate accounting.

Corporate accounting shall monitor and track the materiality and recurrence of unreconciled balances and review the status quarterly with the CAO.

Contact

Corporate controller

Chief accounting officer

	Policy and Procedure	
Procedure No. B05a	Section: Accounting and Finance	Page 4 of 4
	Account Reconciliation	
Department Ownership	Issue/Effective Date:	Replaces previously issued

Exhibit

Account Reconciliation for the Period Ending (date)_____

Account Number	Account Name		
Owner of the Account	Reconciliation prepared by		
Reconciliation Status Circle one **A)** Balanced with no outstanding explanations **B)** Balanced with known adjustments to be taken **C)** Not balanced with investigative actions to be taken	**Actions** 1) _____ _____ 2) _____ _____ 3) _____ _____		
Reviewer's signature			Date
Second-level signature			Date

Balance per Subledgers or Supporting Schedule			**$xxx,xxx**
Reconciling Items (add or subtract known adjustments)	Month	$xx,xxx	
Total known adjustments to be taken			$xx,xxx
Unreconciled balance (aged and investigated)			**$xx,xxx**
Balance per General Ledger			**$xxx,xxx**

In accordance with the Policy, forward to corporate accounting with summary of supporting documentation.

Internal Use Only

QUARTERLY SUBCERTIFICATION PROGRAM

The quarterly subcertification program demonstrates completion of the governance journey by linking big G Governance requirements of the Sarbanes-Oxley Act and the Securities and Exchange Commission (SEC) requirements to this little g governance program. Even if you are not required to prepare quarterly submissions to the SEC, this program is a powerful way to confirm that all parts of the organization are aligned, covered and prepared for internal control testing.

OVERVIEW

The purpose of the quarterly subcertification program is to support the policy that all disclosures made by the company be accurate, complete, and fairly present the company's financial condition and results of operations in compliance with applicable laws and stock exchange requirements. Since the chief executive officer (CEO) and chief financial officer (CFO) do not have intimate knowledge of all business processes, information presented in the financial statements and related SEC filings, the purpose of the quarterly subcertification process is to ensure that the information required to be disclosed for external financial reporting purposes is accumulated and communicated to the company's management, as appropriate, to allow timely decisions regarding required disclosure.

The following is taken from the Sarbanes-Oxley Act of 2002 (SOX) section 302, which requires a public company's principal executive officer (CEO) and the principal financial officer (CFO), to personally certify with each 10-Q and 10-K filing:

(1) the signing officer has reviewed the report;

(2) based on the officer's knowledge, the report does not contain any untrue statement of a material fact or omit to state a material fact necessary in order to make the statements made, in light of the circumstances under which such statements were made, not misleading;

(3) based on such officer's knowledge, the financial statements, and other financial information included in the report, fairly present in all material respects the financial condition and results of operations of the issuer as of, and for, the periods presented in the report;

(4) the signing officers:

    (A) are responsible for establishing and maintaining internal controls;

    (B) have designed such internal controls to ensure that material information relating to the issuer and its consolidated subsidiaries is made known to such officers by others within those entities, particularly during the period in which the periodic reports are being prepared;

    (C) have evaluated the effectiveness of the issuer's internal controls as of a date within 90 days prior to the report; and

    (D) have presented in the report their conclusions about the effectiveness of their internal controls based on their evaluation as of that date;

(5) the signing officers have disclosed to the issuer's auditors and the audit committee of the board of directors (or persons fulfilling the equivalent function):

    (A) all significant deficiencies in the design or operation of internal controls which could adversely affect the issuer's ability to record, process, summarize, and report financial data and have identified for the issuer's auditors any material weaknesses in internal controls; and

    (B) any fraud, whether or not material, that involves management or other employees who have a significant role in the issuer's internal controls; and

(6) *the signing officers have indicated in the report whether or not there were significant changes in internal controls or in other factors that could significantly affect internal controls subsequent to the date of their evaluation, including any corrective actions with regard to significant deficiencies and material weaknesses.*

This program was developed to assist the CEO and CFO with their certification. Since the CEO and CFO do not have intimate knowledge of all business processes, data, and information presented in the financial statements and related SEC filings, the CEO and CFO invite select employees to subcertify that the data and information provided by their areas of responsibility is in accordance with the SOX and SEC governance requirements. The Quarterly subcertification program is established to oversee this process.

MATRIX AND LETTER

There are two major inputs to the quarterly subcertification program:

1) The process owner matrix (matrix) identifying the positions and individuals that are required to certify to the quarterly subcertification letter. The objective is to identify those who are responsible for knowing details required for certification.

2) The management representation letter and its various components (letter) indicating the certification statements.

Note to reader:
The examples or organization structure and description of functional responsibility will vary from company to company.

---

1) Matrix

The matrix is a list of the company's processes and identifies an executive owner, process owner, and the process owner's financial and legal counterparts. If the processes are not centralized with a global owner, then regional process owners and their support must also be listed.

The first part of the matrix is the list of processes. It is important that someone versed in organizational development and process management review this list to ensure that the company is organized in an effective and efficient manner. Processes are generally grouped according to a process hierarchy, with the matrix containing the list of all relevant processes.

For a company that has not thought about its process flow, this is an important exercise that will highlight how the various functions interact with each other. When I visit a company for the first time, I ask them to tell me about themselves. How they respond tells me a lot about what is important and how they are organized. Process-driven companies begin by telling me how they produce and deliver goods and services to customers.

When preparing this matrix for the first time, it is not unusual to find that there are:

* Processes listed that do not belong as separate and distinct but rather should be organized within a different functional group; for example, the shipping of product for sales may be organized under operations and perhaps would be better suited within supply chain management.

Function or Process	Executive Sponsor	Business / Process Owner	Financial Controller / Designate	Legal Support
Product Management				
Sales				
Marketing				
Administration/Operartions				
Human Resources				
Information Technology/Information Systems				
Accounting and Finance				
Compliance				
Legal				

- Processes may be missing from the list; for example, goods receipting might be handled by the facilities function and would be better represented as a stand-alone process or included within inventory management.

As the matrix is prepared, it should become obvious where there are operational risks and opportunities due to the way the company is organized. These observations become opportunities for improvement.

The next step is to identify owners for each of the cells within the matrix. The process ownership role is essential in defining and running the company with purpose. A process owner is someone who has extensive knowledge in executing and managing the operational tasks. Remember that you are looking to name someone who has intimate knowledge of the process, data, and information as it will ultimately appear in reporting documents.

In my experience, first-time preparers of the matrix are often surprised that:

- They can't fill in names for the positions, meaning there are gaps in process coverage.

- There is a mismatch of talent to process, meaning that process owners must have the appropriate level of subject matter expertise and authority.

- One person is responsible for multiple processes, meaning that a working process owner needs to be assigned or recognized.

When filling in the names of process owners, ownership must also be identified for their accounting and legal support. We highlight accounting and legal areas because these functions should have detailed knowledge of the process, regulations, and results in order to advise the CEO and CFO as to certification. Some organizations may want to expand the matrix to include human resources and information technology support.

Ensure that the rank of the process-within-the-process hierarchy has an employee of commensurate rank as process owner and support. In other words, you don't want to have a junior manager in charge of a process that is critical to the success of the company.

Process owners must have the authority and accountability to implement and execute a process with effectiveness and efficiency in order to satisfy company goals and objectives. Process owners may have specific responsibility to:

- Provide strategic, tactical, and operational direction for an effective and efficient set of related tasks.

- Use data, information, and competitive comparisons to improve process performance.

- Provide leadership in managing functional and cross-functional teams, ensuring that individuals have the appropriate level of knowledge, skill, and authority required to perform the job.

- Communicate and report results upstream to senior management and downstream to team.

Because of the nature of the SOX certification, a process owner's accounting and legal support are also called upon to render an opinion on the state of the process. Note that within accounting, finance and legal functions, there are processes that also require a business process owner, accounting finance representative, and a legal designate.

Each quarter, the matrix is updated to reflect changes in position, organizational structure, and responsibility. Since the CEO and CFO must certify, senior management may request that additional employees be included if they have or may have data and information which is in scope to the subcertification process.

Steps to Customize the Matrix

The process list will vary based on such considerations as the type of industry you are in or the grouping of processes by your organizational structure. To customize the matrix:

- Determine the processes and subprocesses that define your business.

- Identify the executive sponsor and business or functional operational process owner by name. List in the detail where individual process owners have authority, accountability to execute, and implement process management.

  - For each process, identify their accounting and finance support.

  - For each process, identify their legal support.

Add columns if process owner responsibilities differ by geographic region.

Following are examples of subprocesses that support the functional areas listed.

Product Management	Information Technology/Information Systems
• Research and Development	• Master Data
• Engineering	• Information Handling
• Manufacturing	• Access
• Production	• Privacy
• Inventory Management/Supply Chain	• Network Management
• Distribution/Logistics	**Accounting and Finance**
• Intellectual Property	• Accounts Payable
• Royalty	• Accounts Receivable

• Quality Assurance	• Consolidation
• Strategic Integration and Business Development	• Equity Compensation
Sales	• Financial or External Reporting
• Sales Administration	• Financial Planning and Analysis
• Sales Operations	• Fixed Assets, Property, Plant and Equipment, Long-Lived Assets
• Commissions	• General Ledger
• Presales Support	• Payroll
• Postsales Technical Support	• Tax
Marketing	• Treasury
• Branding, Trademarks	**Compliance**
• Competitive Intelligence	• Business Continuity
• Product Marketing	• Insurance and Risk Management
• Field Marketing	• Internal Audit
• Promotions, Trade Shows, Events, Sponsorships	• Internal Controls
• Contributions, Donations	• Investor Relations
• Communication	• Records Information Management
Administration/Operations	**Legal**
• Procurement	• Contracts
• Corporate Communication	• Government and Public Relations
• Import/Export	• Litigation
• Occupational and Environmental Health and Safety	
• Real Estate and Facilities	
Human Resources	
• Recruiting, Hiring	
• Compensation	
• Benefits, Tuition Reimbursement, Leaves	
• Assignments	
• Postretirement	
• Learning, Education, and Training	
• Employee/Internal Communication	

The matrix is used to identify who should receive the letter.

2) Letter

The letter is a combination of various components used to collect information and comments from selected employees. This information is used to satisfy and support statements submitted to big G Governance. The submission and related statements apply to internal control over financial reporting (ICOFR) regulations. The objective of the letter is to hold those closest to the process accountable for the management of that process, including the data, information, and disclosures about transactional processing, control environment, and current and potential risks.

Attached to the invitation from the CEO/CFO to participate in the quarterly subcertification process, the letter contains the following sections:

A) Management letter that supports the financial data and operational processes. All invitees are asked to complete this section of the letter.

B) Specifically for 302 (financial) subcertification. Section B is required to be completed by those responsible for approving transactions that are ultimately reflected within the financial statements and those who contribute to management discussion and analysis (MD&A) or provide input for disclosure statements.

C) Specifically for 404 (internal control) subcertification. Section C is required to be completed by those responsible for designing, implementing, or overseeing the process; once completed, it must be forwarded as part of the response.

Depending on their role and participation in the company's operational and financial processes, individuals may have to complete some or all sections. For ease in following up with respondents, there should be three separate distribution lists (those who are required to complete sections A, B, and C; A and B only; and A and C only).

Each quarter, the letter is updated to reflect changes in the scope for responding to big G Governance requirements, organizational structure, and responsibility. A sample letter with all of its attachments follows. Highlighted areas must be completed by the person certifying to the quarterly subcertification.

Schedule

The timeline for completing the required tasks begins with the end date (i.e., the date for submission to the SEC). Working backward, other tasks include reviews of the 10K/10Q and the related certifications with the board of directors, audit committee, executive team, and the financial reporting team. After each of these reviews, there may be additional comments that require resolution.

In order to prepare for these reviews, the Internal Controls function must address *all* comments received by either resolving that they have already been reflected in the financial statements and/or MD&A or are included within other disclosures.

A suggested timeline for completing the required tasks might include the following. Business day 0 represents the date that the submission to the SEC for the 10Q/10K is planned.

Tasks	Business Days
Submission to the SEC	0
Review with the board of directors	−2
Review with the audit committee	−3
Review with internal control over financial reporting (ICOFR) committee or team	−4

Responses due from those completing sections A, B, and C and A and B of the letter	−7
Distribute draft 10Q/10K to subcertifiers	−10
Responses due from those completing sections A and C	−14
Training for first-time subcertifiers	−18
Invitation from CFO with letter and matrix sent to subcertifiers	−20
Approved matrix and letter finalized	−20

Once the matrix and the letter are prepared, representatives from internal controls, financial reporting, legal, compliance, and senior management review and approve the package to be distributed and the response timeline. These representatives are also known as the ICOFR committee or team.

It's important to note that the letter is a personal certification and to assist preparers with understanding what that means, they are asked to attend training. A training presentation is included as part of this program. Customize and deliver it for all first-time subcertifiers and those who want to learn more about the subcertification process.

Following is a suggested process flow for completing the matrix and letter, sending the package to each of the executive sponsors, program owners, accounting, and legal staff identified on the matrix.

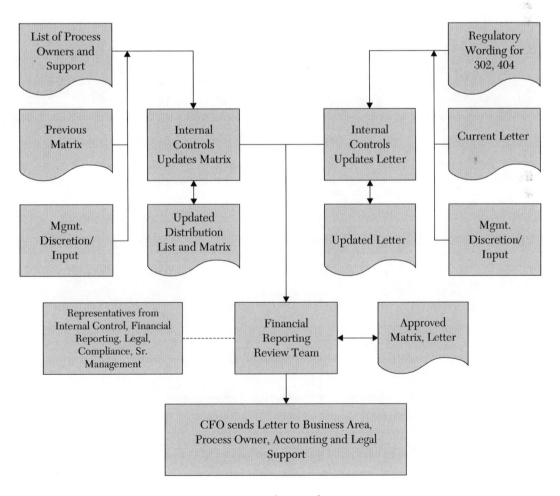

Once the letter and the package are received by the process owner, accounting, and legal support, they conduct a level of due diligence that provides them with enough comfort to address the certification statements. In well-run companies, the level of due diligence occurs throughout the quarter and is not just a quarter-end exercise. Since the process owners are responsible for managing their processes, presumably, there are no surprises.

Process owners may decide to retain a running list of financial reporting and internal control weaknesses and opportunities that they remediate throughout the quarter. Not everything on this list is material enough to be listed as a comment within the letter; however, everything on the list should be worked on. If the process owner or others are in doubt as to what to report or not report in the letter, they should be encouraged to contact their internal controls and/or financial reporting representative.

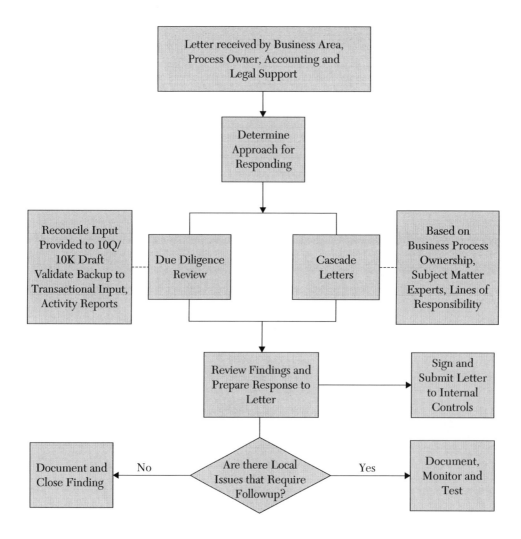

As internal controls receives input from the process owners and their support, they must respond to every comment to ensure the comments have been reflected in the financial statements and/or disclosed. Depending on the volume and type of comments received, internal controls may decide to keep track of the comments manually, within an Excel spreadsheet, or as part of the internal controls software application that tracks controls and compliance-related issues.

Unresolved comments received from section A may require either remediation or an immediate change to the financial statements; comments from section C require remediation; while unresolved comments received from Section B require an immediate change to the financial statements and/or disclosure before the 10Q/10K can be filed.

As deadlines are reached, the internal controls program manager prepares a status report and distributes it to the ICOFR team for action. Since time is of the essence, it is helpful if each of the groups decide ahead of time what types of comments they will follow up with.

The status report may include details segmented by process, region, or type of issue. The types of issues may be classified as a) adequately disclosed and closed, b) there is no ICOFR impact and closed, c) remains open and requires additional investigation or review to determine ICOFR impact, and, d) an "other" category. For those items that remain open, the type and amount of the potential impact to the financial statements for the quarter must be estimated.

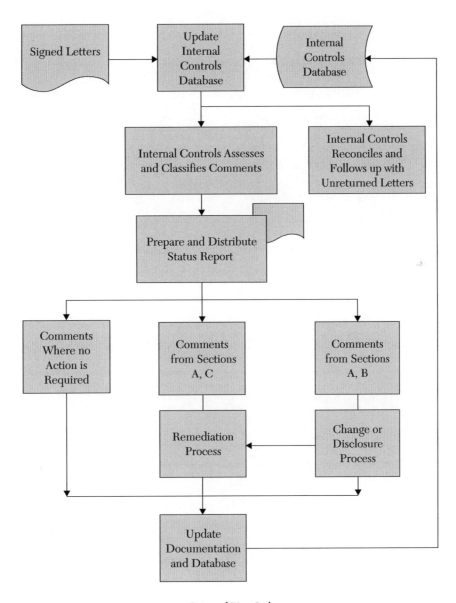

The remediation process is discussed elsewhere in this manual; process items identified must be considered as part of the risk assessment and part of the internal control posture. Material weaknesses and significant deficiencies unresolved prior to quarter-end must be disclosed with the submission to the SEC. Once all the comments have been addressed, internal controls submits the internal control posture statements for inclusion in the 10Q/10K and submits its report to the CFO, CEO, and external auditors.

In order to improve the internal control process effectiveness and efficiency, after the 10Q/10K is filed, the internal controls program manager assesses and evaluates the program for process improvements, remembering to ask for feedback from those who provided input to preparing the matrix, letter, and comments as well as those who had to remediate open comments prior to SEC submissions.

The quarterly subcertification program and process is a commanding tool and technique used to bring together the elements of governance, risk, oversight, documentation, and internal control.

Following is the letter and the section C questionnaire.

Date:
To: Distribution List
From: Chief Financial Officer

Subject: **Quarterly Subcertification Letter:**

In accordance with Securities and Exchange Commission (SEC) regulations, the chief executive officer (CEO) and the chief financial officer (CFO) are required to sign the quarterly certification letter (letter). Since they do not have intimate knowledge of all business processes, information presented in the financial statements and related SEC filings, selected employees who have knowledge of financial and business issues across the company are asked to certify that the information provided from their areas of responsibility is complete, accurate and conforms to the company's code of conduct, policies, procedures, and internal controls. You have been identified as one of these selected employees based on line of sight, which refers to those individuals with sufficient authority and line of sight to the operational or functional area and coverage for all business areas.

You are asked to review, comment, and sign the following letter. Based on your line of sight, you are asked to attest to some or all of the sections. The letter contains three sections:

A)   Management representation letter

B)   Sarbanes-Oxley 302 disclosure subcertification

C)   Sarbanes-Oxley 404 subcertification

To assist, attached are:

- Matrix and distribution list identifying the A, B, C sections that apply to you

- 404 Questionnaire—for those asked to complete section C. This must be returned whether the internal control posture has changed or not.

For those who have to respond to section B, as the draft 10Q/10K is available, it will be forwarded to enable you to complete the section.

Training is available for first-time subcertifiers and those who want to learn more about the subcertification process.

In order to complete your response, you must perform a level of due diligence that is appropriate. Suggested approaches include: internal control reviews and testing, monitoring and analyzing process performance, and internal control data and/or further cascading the letter through your organization.

Fill in the highlighted areas; add comments where appropriate; sign and handwrite the date. Fax or scan a copy of the letter and then e-mail both the scanned copy of the letter and the completed 404 questionnaire to Internal Controls *<insert address>*. If you are unavailable during this time, you must have written delegation of authority to an appropriate level employee forwarded to internal controls prior to the return date.

Please submit the signed letter no later than *<insert date and time>*. You may contact the internal controls team for additional information or questions.

We expect 100 percent compliance. I appreciate your urgent attention to this matter.

Thank you for your cooperation and assistance.

<Insert CFO name>

Chief Financial Officer

\<Date\>

Re: Quarterly subcertification letter for the quarter period ending **\<insert quarter end date\>**

I confirm to the best of my knowledge and in the acting capacity of my responsibilities the following representations regarding the financial information provided to the company as of **<u>\<date for the submission of this letter\></u>** and for the quarter period ending as stated above.

My representations are based on the execution of standard disclosure controls and procedures, review for adequacy of internal controls over financial reporting and appropriate documentation supporting significant or unusual items and accounting adjustments, inquiry of key operating and financial personnel, and other evaluation procedures I consider necessary to collect and disclose, in a timely manner, information required to be recorded or disclosed in our financial information.

To the best of my knowledge and belief, I **\<Name and title\>** representing **\<Area of Responsibility\>** confirm the following:

A) Representation of Financial Data and Business Practices

1. In accordance with the company's code of conduct and in my role, the financial data provided to the accounting and finance departments and our external auditors is inclusive of all relevant information, is true and accurate, and is prepared in conformity with U.S. generally accepted accounting principles (U.S. GAAP) and the company's policies and procedures. The data fairly presents in all material respects the financial position, results of operations, and cash flows of my area of responsibility.

2. I am not aware of any accounts, transactions, or agreements not authorized or properly recorded in the financial records underlying the financial information provided or that is not in accordance with the company's policies in all material respects.

3. I have no knowledge of any violations of laws or regulations with regard to the company's business practices and specifically those defined in the United States Foreign Corrupt Practices Act (FCPA) of 1977 or the company's anti-bribery policy. I am not aware of (a) any fraud as defined in Note 1 (below) involving management or employees, (b) any violations of laws or regulations whose effects have not been considered for disclosure in the financial information provided or as a basis of recording a loss contingency, (c) any communications from regulatory agencies concerning noncompliance with or deficiencies in financial information provided, or (d) any failure to comply with contractual agreements where such failure would have a material effect on the financial information provided.

4. We have not entered into any agreements not in the ordinary course of business, nor have any other matters or occurrences come to my attention up to the present time that would materially affect the interim financial information provided for the period covered.

5. I understand that, although I am not expected to have knowledge in relation to areas for which I am not responsible, this certification relates to any knowledge that I in fact have about the company.

6. I am aware of no other liabilities, loss contingencies or guarantees, whether written or oral, that have not been accrued. All accrued balances are appropriately supported.

7. I am aware of no material transactions that have not been properly recorded in the accounting records. Furthermore, no material events have occurred subsequent to the period covered in this representation letter that have not been appropriately disclosed but prior to the release of the company's 10Q/10K. With respect to the period between the date of this letter and the date the Form 10Q/10K is filed, communication of any material changes since the date of this representation letter must be provided to the CFO's office immediately.

8. To the best of my knowledge, the company has satisfactory title to all owned assets, there are no liens or encumbrances on such assets, nor has any asset been pledged as collateral and the carrying amounts of all material assets will be recoverable.

9. Accounts receivable represent valid claims against debtors for sales or other charges arising on or before the last day of the month and appropriate provisions have been made for losses that may be sustained on uncollectible receivables.

10. All sales agreements recorded are final and there are no side letters or concessions which would alter the original terms of the contract. Revenue recognized has been modified to the extent appropriate when right of return, price protection, or other significant future obligations exist under the terms of the sales arrangements.

11. If I manage inventory, provisions have been made, where necessary, for losses sustained in the fulfillment or inability to fulfill any sales commitments, losses resulting from purchase commitments for inventory, or losses resulting from reduction of inventory values.

12. If I manage investments, provisions have been made, where necessary, for losses sustained as a result of other-than-temporary declines in the fair value of investments.

13. I sign this certification without qualification, except as may be indicated below:

Note 1. The term *fraud* includes misstatements arising from fraudulent financial reporting and misstatements arising from misappropriation of assets. Misstatements arising from fraudulent financial reporting are intentional misstatements, or omissions of amounts or disclosures in financial statements to deceive financial statement users. Misstatements arising from misappropriation of assets involve the theft of an entity's assets where the effect of the theft causes the entity's financial statement not to be fairly presented.

B) For Financial Statement Subcertifiers (302 Disclosure Subcertification)

14. I have reviewed the relevant sections of the draft quarterly report on Form 10Q/10K for the quarter ended (the quarterly report) that is to be filed with the SEC based on my area of responsibility and any other materials I believe to be relevant in providing this certification. In connection with preparation and/or review of the quarterly report, I have provided or caused to be provided for consideration for inclusion in the quarterly report all information that I believe may be material for purposes of disclosure in the quarterly report. To the best of my knowledge, the quarterly report does not contain any material misrepresentations or omit a material fact necessary to make the statements in the quarterly report not misleading.

15. I understand that should any material events that could change the representations made above occur between the date of this letter and the date that the quarterly report is filed with the SEC, it is my responsibility to notify the CFO and internal controls, in writing, of the nature of such events immediately.

16. I understand that the CEO, CFO, and the company's officers shall rely on this certification to support their evaluation concerning the effectiveness of the company's disclosure controls and procedures.

17. I sign this certification without qualification, except as may be indicated below:

C) 404 Subcertification

18. I am responsible for establishing and maintaining adequate internal controls in my area of responsibility (as defined above) to provide reasonable assurance regarding the reliability of financial reporting and the preparation of financial statements for external purposes in accordance with generally accepted accounting principles. The assertions made in this subcertification are to report changes to internal controls that have occurred during the quarter.

19. In connection with the overall maintenance of internal control over financial reporting, and monitoring of changes in internal controls therein, I assert that, I have completed, or reviewed the completed *404 Internal Control Questionnaire* (Questionnaire) for my area of responsibility.

20. I, along with the Company's senior management, continue to communicate to employees, management's ownership for internal controls and to reinforce the company's commitment at all levels to the ongoing maintenance of an appropriately controlled environment.

21. I have received satisfactory answers to any questions I have raised (or have knowledge that were raised) that could have a potential financial statement impact or that could require disclosure in the financial statements except as noted below:

_____
_____
_____

22. I sign this subcertification without qualification, except as indicated below:

_____
_____
_____

Quarterly Subcertification

I **<Name and Title>** have reviewed the following sections (identify the sections that refer to you with a checkmark) with due diligence as these sections relate to **<Area of Responsibility>** and unless otherwise noted in the specified item numbers, I confirm that to the best of my knowledge I am in compliance.

❑   A) Representation of Financial Data and Business Practices

❑   B) Financial Statement Subcertifiers (302 disclosure)

❑   C) Internal Control Subcertification (404 certification)

I understand that the CEO and CFO will rely on this subcertification to support the company's disclosure requirement to report material changes to the company's internal control over financial reporting for the quarter ended.

Signature:

_____   _____

Print   Signature

_____   _____

Title   Date of Representation (handwrite date)

QUARTERLY SUBCERTIFICATION
SECTION 404 QUESTIONNAIRE

For all those required to complete section C of the quarterly subcertification, complete this questionnaire and forward to internal controls as part of the certification letter submission.

I **<insert name>**, am responsible for establishing and maintaining adequate internal controls over financial reporting in my process area of responsibility **< insert process>**.

To the best of my knowledge, I confirm the following:

Question	Yes/No	Comments
1. Have there been any new or significant changes to information technology systems for the area?		
2. Has there been any significant modification to processes (e.g., reengineering)?		
3. Were there any significant changes to roles and responsibilities within the area (e.g., changes to key management, staffing, turnovers)?		
4. Has the company acquired an entity or integrated a process that would affect the internal control environment or activities?		
5. Has the company divested an entity in whole or part, or outsourced a process in whole or part?		
6. Have new business risks and/or changes to existing business risks been identified that would affect the internal control environment or activities?		
7. Have there been any process changes resulting from implementing new policies or procedures within the area?		
8. Have there been any regulatory changes that have had or will have an impact on the internal control status?		
9. Have there been any changes to customer, employee, or vendor contracts that would have or will have an impact on the internal control status?		
10. Has there been or are you expecting any changes or potential changes that could have an impact on the internal control status, not otherwise addressed within this questionnaire?		

If you respond "yes" to any of the above questions, provide a detailed description of the change and indicate whether the change has been reviewed, tested, and approved by internal controls.

Policy and Procedure		
Procedure No. B06a	Section: Corporate	Page 1 of 2
	Quarterly Subcertification	
Department Ownership	Issue/Effective Date:	Replaces previously issued

Prepared by: Approved by: Authorized by:
Date   Date   Date

Scope

The document applies to all IDÆAL LLP's legal entities, subsidiaries and business units.

Policy

It is IDÆAL, LLP's (company) policy that selected business area managers and process owners as well as their financial and legal counterparts are responsible for providing a subcertification to the chief executive officer (CEO) and chief financial officer (CFO) on a quarterly basis. The subcertification asks individuals to certify that the information provided from their areas of responsibility is complete, accurate and conforms to the company's code of conduct, policies, procedures, and internal controls.

Representatives from the company's internal controls, financial reporting, legal, and compliance departments oversee this policy, and approve the details of this program including and not limited to the distribution list (also known as the matrix), the preparation of the letter (also known as the quarterly subcertification letter). The internal controls department is responsible for the execution, monitoring, and tracking the components of this program.

Procedure

Each quarter, the internal controls program manager updates the process owner matrix (matrix), which produces the distribution list of those who are required to subcertify the various sections of the quarterly subcertification letter (letter).

The letter is reviewed and updated according to changes in regulations or management emphasis.

The letter is made up of three sections:

A) Management letter that supports the financial data and operational processes. All invitees are asked to complete this section of the letter.

B) Specifically for 302 (financial) subcertification. Section B is required to be completed by those responsible for approving transactions which are ultimately reflected within the financial statements, those who contribute to management discussion and analysis (MD&A), or provide input for disclosure statements.

C) Specifically for 404 (internal control) subcertification. Section C is required to be completed by those responsible for designing, implementing, or overseeing the process; once completed, it must be forwarded as part of the response.

	Policy and Procedure	
Procedure No. B06a	Section: Corporate	Page 2 of 2
	Quarterly Subcertification	
Department Ownership	Issue/Effective Date:	Replaces previously issued

The quarterly subcertification package includes the invitation from the chief financial officer to participate, matrix, letter, and the 404 questionnaire.

The recipients of the letter shall conduct due diligence reviews or further cascade the letter through their organizational area of responsibility. They must document the approach they use to subcertify and they must retain related documentation to support their comments and certification.

Recipients shall conduct reviews to a degree that will satisfy the claims to be made within the Letter (e.g., accurate and complete). Exceptions or deviations (also called issues or findings) from the representations must be identified within the space provided within the letter.

Once received, the issues or findings are evaluated and assessed to determine: (1) if they are immaterial and considered a local issue to remediate, (2) if they are cross-referenced to other issues or findings previously identified and currently under remediation, (3) if they are new to the issue and findings list. Once categorized, the issues/findings are logged into the internal control database for monitoring and tracking.

All issues and findings are evaluated and assessed as to whether they require a change to and/or disclosure to the current quarter 10Q or 10K submission.

Findings and issues are reviewed with internal controls, financial reporting, legal, and compliance prior to review with senior management, the audit committee, and the board of directors.

Control/Areas of Responsibility

- Compliance with this policy is the responsibility of each functional area's executive manager and controller. Business areas or processes that have comments and/or have identified areas with weak internal controls must be investigated, monitored, and resolved.

- Internal control monitors the timely submission of the letters and will follow up on all open items.

- Internal controls, financial reporting, legal, and compliance review the comments and outstanding items to determine the completeness and accuracy of the financial statement presentation and SEC filings. Business areas or processes that have comments and/or have identified areas with weak internal controls must be investigated, monitored, and resolved prior to submission to the SEC.

Contact

Internal Control Program Manager

Chief Financial Officer

QUARTERLY SUBCERTIFICATION - MATRIX

Instruction

The first part of the matrix is the list of processes. It is important that someone versed in organizational development and process management review this list to ensure the company is organized in an effective and efficient manner. Processes are generally grouped according to a process hierarchy; with the matrix containing the list of all relevant processes.

For a company that has not thought about its process flow, this is an important exercise which will highlight how the various functions interact with each other. When I visit a company for the first time, I ask them to tell me about themselves. How they respond tells me a lot about what is important and how they are organized. Process driven companies begin by telling me how they produce and deliver goods and services to customers.

When preparing this matrix for the first time, it is not unusual to find that there are:

- processes listed which do not belong as separate and distinct but rather should be organized within a different functional group, for example, the shipping of product for sales may be organized under Operations and perhaps would be better suited within supply chain management.

- processes may be missing from the list (e.g., goods receipting) might be handled by the facilities function and would be better represented as a stand alone process or included within inventory management.

As the matrix is prepared, it should become obvious where there are operational risks and opportunities due to the way the company is organized. These observations become opportunities for improvement.

The next step is to identify owners for each of the cells within the matrix. The process ownership role is essential in defining and running the company with purpose. A process owner is someone who has extensive knowledge in executing and managing the operational tasks. Remember that you are looking to name someone who has the intimate knowledge of the process, data and information as it will ultimately appear in reporting documents. In my experience, first time preparers of the matrix are often surprised that:

- They can't fill in names for the positions; meaning there are gaps in process coverage.

- There is a mismatch of talent to process; meaning that process owners must have the appropriate level of subject matter expertise and authority.

- One person is responsible for multiple processes; meaning that a working process owner needs to be assigned or recognized.

When filling in the names of process owners, ownership must also be identified for their accounting and legal support. We highlight accounting and legal areas because these functions should have the detail knowledge of the process, regulations and results in order to advise the CEO and CFO as to certification. For some organizations, you may want to expand the matrix to include human resources and information technology support.

Ensure that the rank of the process within the process hierarchy has an employee of commensurate rank as process owner and support. In other words, you don't want to have a junior manager in charge of a process which is critical to the success of the company.

Process owners must have the authority and accountability to implement and execute a process with effectiveness and efficiency in order to satisfy company goals and objectives. Process owners may have specific responsibility to:

- Provide strategic, tactical and operational direction for an effective and efficient set of related tasks.

- Use data, information, and competitive comparisons to improve process performance.

- Provide leadership in managing functional and cross functional teams, ensuring individuals have the appropriate level of knowledge, skill and authority required to perform the job.

- Communicate and report results upstream to senior management and downstream to team.

Because of the nature of the SOX certification, a process owner's accounting and legal support are also called upon to render an opinion on the state of the process. Note that within accounting, finance and legal functions there are processes which also require a business process owner, accounting finance representative as well as a legal designate.

Each quarter the matrix is updated to reflect changes in position, organizational structure and responsibility. Since the CEO and CFO must certify, senior management may request additional employees be included if they have or may have data and information which is in-scope to the sub-certification process.

QUARTERLY FINANCIAL SUBCERTIFICATION TRAINING
FOR FIRST-TIME SUBCERTIFIERS

Note to Readers and Presenters:

PowerPoint slides may be downloaded via the URL.

Following are the slides and notes for presenters to conduct awareness training for first time quarterly subcertifiers. Notes for presenters are advice on how to present the slide or additional information in support of the bullets identified on the slide. The presenter must be thoroughly familiar with the quarterly subcertification process and what is required. It is often wise to have representatives from internal controls, legal and finance as well as others from the internal control over financial reporting team.

Slide: **Agenda**

- Overview

  - Certification

  - Process

- Letter is made up of sections:

- Representation of Financial Data and Business Practices

- 302 Disclosure Subcertification

- 404 Internal Control Subcertification

- Deadlines and applying the rules

  - Materiality

  - Due diligence

Slide: **Program Objectives**

- The effort is focused on designing and implementing a company-wide, integrated, bottom-up approach to these processes.

- **Objectives:**

  - Cover all types of disclosures (i.e., operational, financial, regulatory) across all business units and geographic areas.

  - Develop the **tools** necessary to identify, track, and elevate disclosure issues.

  - Create a **calendar** for the primary disclosure vehicles.

  - **Institutionalize** the disclosure process to provide consistency across disclosure cycles.

Note for Presenters:

In response to the new requirements enacted by Congress and the Securities and Exchange Commission (SEC), the company is enhancing the disclosure and certification processes. The effort is focused on designing and implementing a company-wide, integrated, bottom-up approach to these processes.

Objectives:

Design, document and implement **a company-wide, integrated, bottom-up approach to the disclosure process**, leveraging current internal efforts already underway and incorporating existing disclosure processes already in place.

Clarify **roles and responsibilities** in the disclosure and **subcertification processes**, and **accountabilities** to cover all types of disclosures (i.e., operational, financial, regulatory) across all business units and geographic areas.

Develop the **tools** necessary to identify, track, and elevate disclosure issues, such as checklists of key considerations for subcertifiers and disclosure guidelines.

Create a **calendar** for the primary disclosure vehicles (10Q, 10K, press releases, etc.) to identify timing and ownership of discrete processes.

Institutionalize the disclosure process to provide consistency across disclosure cycles.

Slide: **Certification Summary**

As a public company, IDÆAL, LLP, operates under the scrutiny of numerous regulatory bodies. Regulations are designed to **strengthen corporate governance and restore investor confidence.**

Certification is made for the following:

A) Representation of Financial Data and Business Practices ensures that financial data is complete and accurate.

B) Section 302 of the Sarbanes-Oxley Act makes the CEO and CFO **personally responsible** for the disclosures made in filings.

C) Section 404 of the Sarbanes-Oxley Act assigns ownership to the CEO and CFO to define ongoing oversight.

Slide: **Subcertification Summary**

- Since the CEO/CFO do not have intimate knowledge of all business processes and in order to assign responsibility and accountability and have comfort that the information presented in the financial statements and SEC filings is complete and accurate, they require selected employees to also sign/attest.

- Individuals invited to subcertify are chosen based on:

  - **Line of Sight**

  - **Provide Oversight**

  - **Coverage**

Note for Presenters:

Line of Sight: Subcertifiers should be individuals with sufficient authority and line of sight to the operational or functional area.

Provide Oversight: Subcertifiers should be individuals who provide oversight for control activities at their operational and/or geographic area of responsibility and who have reporting staff with direct internal control over financial reporting responsibilities.

Coverage: Complete coverage of all business areas.

Slide: **Assigning Ownership for Subcertification**

Methodology:

Cascading approach based on line of command and process ownership:

- Review of organization chart to identify the executive and process owners and their designated support team
- Include global and geographic process owners
- Match the owners to their financial and legal counterparts

Notes for Presenters:

The internal controls function is responsible for the design, implementation, and execution of the subcertification process. The program is made up of two elements: the matrix that identifies process owners and their accounting and finance support and the letter and its various components used to encompass the areas which require CEO/CFO certification.

The methodology used to assign ownership of the processes and their support team is based on a cascading approach based on line of command and process ownership and reading the four steps.

Slide: **Subcertification Matrix**

- Assigns subcertification responsibility based on process
- Processes are defined by internal controls and others to ensure all processes ae captured.

Function or Process	Executive Sponsor	Business / Process Owner	Financial Controller / Designate	Legal Support
Product Management				
Sales				
Marketing				
Administration / Operartions				
Human Resources				
Information Technology / Information Systems				
Accounting and Finance				
Compliance				
Legal				

Note for Presenters:

Refer to the matrix as distributed in the package; have them review it for accuracy and concur.

Slide: **Subcertification Process Flow**

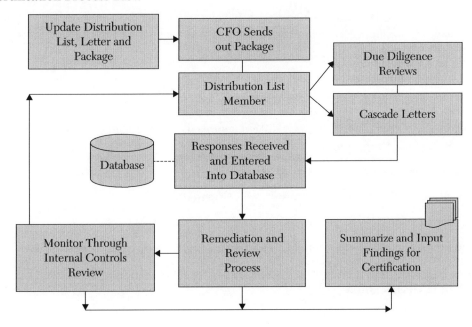

Note for Presenters:

Describe the steps of the process flow.

Slide: **Framework and Process**

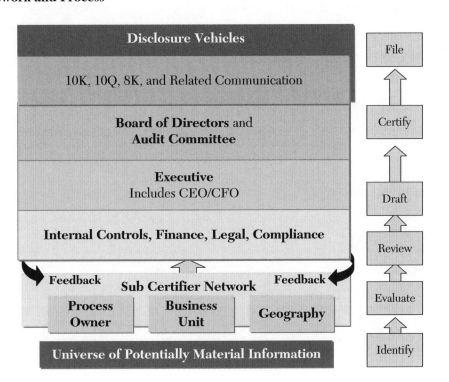

Note for Presenters:

Reading the chart from the bottom up, identify those who have or should have intimate knowledge of the processes, operations, and business transactions that ultimately are reflected within the company's financial statements and areas for disclosure.

Using the comments from the letter as input, internal controls oversees that each comment is evaluated, investigated, and addressed **prior** to submitting results to executive management. Once the comments have been addressed and reflected in the financial statements and/or areas for disclosure a draft of the various SEC reports and related external communications is reviewed and approved by the executive, board of directors, and audit committee **prior** to filing the release.

Slide: **Section A: Management Letter of Representation**

Slide: **Representation of Financial Data and Business Practices**

Note for Presenters:

Over the next several charts copy the statements as they appear in the quarterly subcertification letter and read through them.

Slide: **Section B: 302 Certification**

Slide: **302 Subcertifier Responsibilities**

- The CEO and CFO rely on subcertifiers for assurance that filings are **accurate, complete,** without omission, and not misleading.

- Responsibilities:

  - **Review draft 10K/10Q** for potentially material information.

  - **Conduct due diligence** and resolve any outstanding issues related to potential disclosure.

  - **Elevate potentially material items** so that fully informed decisions on materiality can be reached.

  - **Sign the 302 subcertification form** attesting to due diligence in reviewing information for potential disclosure.

  - At any time, inform internal controls, financial reporting, and/or compliance of any possible misstatements or omissions **of a potentially "material event"** that has occurred or is likely to occur.

Note for Presenters:

Read through the slide.

Slide: **Section B: 302 Certification**

Note for Presenters

Copy the statements as they appear in the quarterly subcertification letter and read through them.

Slide: **Section C: 404 Certification**

Internal Control over Financial Reporting (ICOFR) is:

A process designed to provide reasonable assurance regarding the **reliability of financial reporting and the preparation of financial statements** for external purposes in accordance with generally accepted accounting principles.

ICOFR includes those policies and procedures that provide reasonable assurance that:

- **Records** are maintained.

- **Transactions** are recorded.

- **Receipts and expenditures** are authorized.

Note for Presenters:

The SEC and the Public Company Accounting Oversight Board (PCAOB) have defined internal control over financial reporting (ICOFR) as:

A process designed to provide reasonable assurance regarding the **reliability of financial reporting and the preparation of financial statements** for external purposes in accordance with generally accepted accounting principles.

ICOFR includes those policies and procedures that provide reasonable assurance that:

- **Records** are maintained.

- **Transactions** are recorded.

- **Receipts and expenditures** are authorized.

- **Unauthorized acquisition, use, or disposition of assets** that could have a **material effect** are prevented or detected.

Slide: **Management's Role and Responsibility**

On an **annual** basis, management must:

- Assess the effectiveness of the ICOFR.

- Support its evaluation.

- Accept responsibility.

- Identify and disclose material or potentially material changes.

- Present a written assessment and certification.

On a **quarterly** basis, management must:

- Report on the status of significant deficiencies and/or material weaknesses.

- Identify and disclose material or potentially material changes.

Note for Presenters:

To support management's assertions regarding the effectiveness of internal control over financial reporting:

On an *annual* basis, management must:

Assess the effectiveness of the company's internal control over financial reporting using suitable criteria. The objective of such assessment is to obtain reasonable assurance as to whether any material weaknesses exist.

Support its evaluation with sufficient evidence, including documentation.

Accept responsibility for the effectiveness of the company's internal control over financial reporting, identify and disclose **material or potentially material changes to the company's internal control over financial reporting** and **present a written assessment and certification** concerning the effectiveness of the company's internal control over financial reporting.

On a *quarterly* basis, management must:

Report on the status of significant deficiencies and/or material weaknesses to the audit committee.

Identify and disclose **material or potentially material changes to the company's internal control over financial reporting.**

Slide: **Section C: 404 Certification**

Note for Presenters

Copy the statements as they appear in the quarterly subcertification letter and read through them.

Slide: **Certification**

Slide: **Quarterly Subcertification**

I *<Name and Title>* have reviewed the following sections (identify the sections that refer to you with a checkmark) with due diligence as these sections relate to *<Area of Responsibility>* and unless otherwise noted in the specified item numbers, I confirm that to the best of my knowledge, I am in compliance.

      ❑ A) Representation of Financial Data and Business Practices

      ❑ B) Financial Statement Subcertifiers (302 disclosure)

      ❑ C) Internal Control Subcertification (404 certification)

I understand that the CEO and CFO will rely on this subcertification to support the company's disclosure requirement to report material changes to the company's internal control over financial reporting for the quarter ended.

Note for Presenters:

Read the certification statement and remind the certifiers to sign, date, and submit the form to internal controls.

Slide: **Certification: Next Steps**

- Remediate open items that require action, including those that you deemed immaterial, to be reported.

- Embed the internal controls principles (e.g., accuracy, completeness, authority) into your regular reviews.

- Plan and incorporate internal control testing into processes and monitor results for continuous process improvement.

Note for Presenters:

Comments and process items identified in the letter must be considered as part of the risk assessment and part of the internal control posture. Material weaknesses and significant deficiencies unresolved prior to quarter-end must be disclosed with the submission to the SEC. Once all the comments have been addressed, internal controls submits the internal control posture statements for inclusion in the 10Q/10K and submits its report to the CFO, CEO, and external auditors.

Slide: **References**

- For additional information on Sarbanes-Oxley, visit:

- www.sec.gov/spotlight/sarbanes-oxley.htm

- http://thecaq.aicpa.org/Resources/Sarbanes+Oxley/

- For internal support, contact your internal controls department.

- For program information, contact

- ID&AL via Policyguru via www.idealpolicy.com

Note for Presenters:

Encourage first-time certifiers to visit these sites to learn more about their responsibilities, the regulations, and the process.

CONTROL ACTIVITY
PROGRAM TESTING GUIDES

CONTROL ACTIVITY PROGRAM

The first unit of the manual describes the governance journey from big G Governance to little g governance, using risk assessment and an oversight strategy to identify the scope of what needs to be covered within the internal control program. Presented are concepts, models, and a general discussion about the broader aspects of governance. From the first unit, by following the exercises you should have prepared and ranked a list of processes and accounts where there is control risk. These are the processes and accounts where you will want to focus on control activity first.

The second unit of the manual describes the internal control program and dives deeper into specific control environment policies, procedures and processes to complete the governance journey. In addition to the internal control program itself are specifically chosen policies and programs that are universally recommended for all companies regardless of the type of industry. To be effective in your company, the programs and processes presented *must be customized;* however, to serve as an effective control, the strategic intent and concepts presented must remain the same.

The exercises presented in the internal control program should assist you in identifying control objectives and activities which would be suitable for addressing the risks identified from the first unit. This third unit should aid in putting the rest of the program together including testing, monitoring, and reporting.

This third unit of the manual uses the basic structure of the internal control program presented in the second unit to build specific internal control activity plans. Within this unit are finished product testing guides with an accompanying excel worksheet (available via the URL download) ready for you to conduct the control activities, monitor, and track remediation efforts. For most companies these testing guides will be too generic to serve the purpose of providing complete control activity coverage.

Therefore, rather than just present a series of flowcharts, questions, and activities to perform, it is better to first provide instruction as to how to build your own set of testing guides. Following this chapter are the templates and forms referenced in this introduction and following those forms are actual testing guides for you to customize.

Instruction for Building Your Testing Guide

The testing guides should be made available to anyone who wants to review them and use them as interim readiness or preparation checklists. These guides must change as the result of risk assessment change, as actual control activities are performed and findings are discovered or as the internal control professional deems necessary.

The sample of test guides issued within this unit has assumed risk assessed processes and subprocesses have identified the focus areas. The internal control representatives have decided on a level of testing commensurate with the level of risk. Use these as a guide or point of reference for developing your own internal control activity testing plans and guides.

Testing guides are prepared by the internal control department and may contain input from internal audit, compliance, and the process manager. Since the internal control department has prepared, reviewed, and approved the use of the guide.

The testing guide template used as the control activity plan serves as the cover sheet to the evidence collected. The guide and the summary evidence is then attached to the Result of Control Activity Testing form, otherwise known as the findings report.

The header of this form contains information required for the classification and administration of this document. The procedure number should follow the same "smart numbering" criteria used to classify and group the company's policies and procedures. The section name refers to the functional area or business unit responsible for the process. Process refers to the department or functional area that oversees this process. The issue date refers to this version of the testing guide and for tracking purposes; you may want to reference the document date that this guide replaces.

The rest of the heading refers to this testing cycle and indicates the name of the process owner and the physical location where the control activities are tested. The internal control representative conducts or oversees the testing and the date the tests begin and end.

Reference those policies and procedures that apply to this process or that influence this process's control environment.

Flowchart refers to including a high-level flowchart or list of procedure steps to be followed. The intent is to summarize the process flow so that anyone picking up the document would understand the scope of the process under review.

If developing flowcharts for the first time, unless you are an engineering company where everyone understands how to read and use flowcharts, I strongly recommend keeping flowcharts simple. Ask what input is required to start the process then continue to ask "then what" until the output has been identified. At decision points, ask about the criteria for decision making, who reviews the information prior to the decision, and who is authorized to make those decisions. When flowcharting decisions make sure the "Yes" and "No" response have output boxes.

Hint: Make sure lines go into and out of every box, don't get caught in loops.

Use the standard flowchart symbols and connect them with lines and arrows showing the direction of the process flow.

- *Process symbol*—describes what has to be done. Hint: begin with a verb where possible.

- *Database symbol*—identifies stored data. The process may call for data to be accessed, changed, and replaced.

- *Decision symbol*—identifies a point where a decision is required. Ensure the likely outcomes of the decision; for example, "yes", "no" responses are indicated on the flow.

- *Document symbol*—identifies the point within the process where a hard or soft copy document is produced or referenced. Document symbols are often attached to process box symbols.

A popular alternative and substitute to simple process flowcharts are swim lane process flows, emphasizing roles and responsibilities.

Control objectives and activities are selected to address the specific risk identified. The Internal Control representative will be testing for the existence of the control objective which if present would eliminate or mitigate the risk. Specific control activities are selected or designed to ensure those objectives are met. Evidence is collected to support the fact that an appropriate level of due diligence has occurred. Findings and areas of improvement are identified on the Result of Control Activity Testing form.

Control Objectives

As defined in previous chapters, generally accepted control objectives are:

- Compliance with laws and regulations

- Compliance with company policies, procedures

- Compliance with contract terms and conditions

- Authorization and approval

- Internal controls over financial reporting (ICOFR) includes control objectives to address that:

  - Payments are paid, recorded, and reflect authorized transactions.

  - Payments are received, recorded, and reflect authorized transactions.

  - Transactions are recorded in a timely manner.

  - Disclosures provide transparency to the transaction.

  - Operational and financial reviews are conducted as due diligence

- Reconciliations

- Integrity is made up of accuracy, completeness, and timeliness.

- Segregation of duties

- Safeguarding assets

Control Activities

When considering approaches to collect and evaluate evidence consider cost versus benefit. Some common types of control activities are described.

- Direct or sample testing, ordinarily performed on a periodic basis by individuals with a high degree of objectivity relative to the controls being tested. Because this type of control testing requires time and resources, not only from internal control professionals but from the process stream, this is a disruptive and costly control activity that should be used in high-risk areas. In the first year or early years of an internal control program, more direct testing may need to be done in order to establish a baseline of controllable activities.

- Checklists are generally used when there are a lot of steps and/or decisions which may require alternate processing streams. You may want to design into the process description peer or management reviews for selected transactions over a pre-defined threshold limit. For example, sales orders over $100,000 require peer-to-peer review, and sales orders over $500,000 require management review of the checklist.

- Peer-to-peer reviews is a useful tool when (1) training new employees or (2) validating that the process is being followed. Peers may review the output of the process or observe the entire process to ensure that each process step and especially control steps are not bypassed. Having current and management approved desk procedures are useful when peer-to-peer or checklists are used as control activities.

- Control self-assessments tools generally mirror audit working plan and ask that the process owner take responsibility for being prepared for an audit or internal control testing. The use of a control self assessment by a process owner may not be accurate in that they know the "intended" approach and may not be objective or diligent to observe the actual approach. It is recommended that self-assessments be facilitated by an objective, independent third party who understands the process and control environment. The facilitator must not only challenge the process owner about following the defined described steps but also note and include suspected areas of control weaknesses and deficiencies. A truly knowledgeable facilitator will also be able to recommend process improvements.

- Observation controls are similar to peer-to-peer reviews of the process; however, like self-assessments, these are undertaken by objective, independent facilitators. This approach is mostly used when there is little or no documentation to support the process. The observer walks the process from beginning to end and prepares notes as to the steps performed, highlighting areas that need additional control or process improvement. The comments and notes the observer makes assist the process manager in formally producing documented procedures.

- Ongoing monitoring and tracking of key performance indicators is a normal management activity for recurring activities. These are generally automated controls mapped across time with acceptable control variances determined ahead of time. Periodically, test the thresholds of control variances to ensure that the limits are established appropriately. This type of testing is appropriate for high-volume, low-risk areas.

It is not enough to simply perform these control activities; it is vital that the approach and the results be documented. Regardless of the approach used, it is important to document the type of activities performed and in support of those activities collect evidence to prove the status of the control effectiveness.

Readiness checklist is used as a preparation guide for the process owner. The answers to these questions and evidence to support the answers should be made available to the internal control representative prior to the testing. However, if this is not completed before, then the internal control representative could use this as a prelude to the actual control activities.

The readiness checklist is designed to:

- Identify audit readiness or self-assessment questions. These questions should be answered as "Yes" or "No," with the "No" responses indicating a control weakness.

- There is a similarity of questions from process to process because these readiness questions are generally aimed at ensuring the basic requirements exist.

- Regardless of whether detailed control activities are scheduled for a process, the process owner should review their responses to the readiness checklist at least annually.

- Each business area and/or process owner must have sufficient documentation and evidence to support their readiness checklist or self-assessment responses.

Key measures are intended to demonstrate that the process is measured, monitored, and tracked. List key or likely operational indicators and/or measures that may be monitored to ensure control objectives and activities are met. These should be recurring measures that the process owner uses to oversee the effectiveness (refers to defects and efficiency; refers to cycle time of the process). List key financial indicators that would be used for decision making and reporting purposes.

Instruction for Completing the Result of Control Activity Testing Form

The Internal Controls—Result of Control Activity Testing form is presented at the end of this chapter and can be used as an aid when documenting, ranking, and consolidating the control activities.

To complete the form, identify the following information as part of the header:

- Company refers to the company, functional business area, or process being tested.

- Location refers to the geographic location where the test is executed.

- Financial period refers to the financial period or transaction period under review.

- Date refers to the date the test is conducted or use a start and end date if the testing period is over a significant amount of time.

- Prepared by refers to the person or team leader conducting the internal control test.

- Reviewed by refers to the person or team leader overseeing and reviewing the test and findings.

Purpose: Identify the purpose of the testing as:

- *Self-assessment*—conducted or overseen by the process manager. Results of self-assessments should be shared with the internal control representative or may be submitted directly to the internal control program manager.

- *Interim control activity assessment*—conducted by an internal control representative as an "off-cycle" assessment that could be a surprise spot assessment or a remedial assessment.

- *Control activity assessment*—conducted by the internal control representative as part of the planned internal control testing plan.

Scope or process description: The intent is not to duplicate existing documentation but to reference the procedure in existence at the time of the testing. Reference to the in-scope process documentation may include policy and procedures, instructions, and forms.

Result of Control Activities Tested:

- Number and identify each control objective and activity being tested. Follow or create a cross-reference to the control objectives and activities as listed on the test guide.

- Result of the control activity should identify the size of the sample criteria used for sampling and the finding; reference findings as (E) controls were found to be in existence, (CT) controls were found to be executed completely and in a timely fashion, (VA) controls were found to be valid and accurate. Include other assertion levels as appropriate to your test plans.

- Assessment refers to your evaluation as to whether the control is working as it should be. **Rate as 1 to 4, with each rating defined as 1 as a significant deficiency, 2 as a material weakness, 3 as a reportable condition, or 4 as an effective control.**

Evaluation: is the place where you can offer an overall evaluation as to whether internal control objectives are being met or not. Include an overall rating of 1, 2, 3, or 4.

Signatures are required from those who prepared or led the control team conducting the review and those who reviewed and approved the findings and results.

Process owners may use this form to identify control activities they perform on a regular or ongoing basis. In this case, I recommend completing the form once a quarter and attaching the results from each review, noting the timing, extent, and result of the control activity.

Following is a list of the most common result of control activity testing comments and identified areas for improvement.

- *Inadequate knowledge of company policies, procedures, or governing regulations.* Employees generally feel very comfortable executing their duties in order to "get the job done," and for the most part, these instructions should not pose internal control issues. As we all know, employees often encounter roadblocks and have to find another route or bypass and this is where the control issues are hidden. Employees may not be aware that there are overarching policies and procedures that address unique situations. Ensure that there is periodic training and review of all policies and procedures.

- *Inappropriate access to assets.* Employees often have a level of trust that might compromise the safeguarding of assets through such activities as sharing passwords, leaving keys in the open or offices unlocked, and access to cash and/or checks not fully secured.

- *Form over substance.* Having this type of control exposure refers to when employees really don't understand the full extent of their responsibility; for example, *review and approve* has a different connotation than *approve*. Employees must ensure that not only the control directive is followed but also its intent.

Having the best internal controls in place may still be hampered by a soft control environment where managers or others may exercise "control override" for the sake of "getting the job done" or excusing mistakes and errors as "human errors."

Other types of internal control missteps indicative of a weak control environment include:

- Lack of adequate management oversight and accountability and failure to develop a strong awareness of internal environment which respects internal controls.

- Inadequate assessment of the risk of certain activities. Unfortunately, this is often skill and/or experience related with the risk mitigated by building controls into the process and ensuring employees follow the process.

- The absence or failure of key control activities, such as segregation of duties, approvals, verifications, reconciliations and reviews of operating performance.

- Inadequate communication of information between levels of management, especially in the upward communication of problems.

- Inadequate or ineffective internal control program and other monitoring activities.

Once the form is complete, attach the test guide and supporting evidence and forward to the internal controls program manager. These forms are consolidated and used to follow up on remediation plans for items rated 1 or 2 and to determine the overall status of the company's internal control environment.

Monitoring and Tracking

Monitoring refers to the assessment of internal control performance over time. It is accomplished by collecting key performance indicators, results from the various types of testing approaches and of course by direct testing. The purpose of monitoring is to determine whether internal controls are adequate to detect and prevent exposures and unnecessary risk.

Monitoring could be the same as a control objective and/or activity. For example, authorizing documentation is a control objective with the evidence of that authorization serving as support of the authorization activity. Performed sporadically, it is a control objective and activity; performed with each qualifying event, it is a monitoring activity.

To the extent practicable, build in standardized consistent control activities that can function as both control and monitoring activities.

Because the internal control program is a process, its effectiveness is an assessment of the condition of the process at more than one point in time. Just as control activities help to ensure that actions to manage risks are carried out, monitoring is the part of the process that ensures that control activities and other planned activities are carried out properly and in a timely manner and that the actionable items that are identified as a result of the testing process are tracked to ensure the timely, complete, and accurate correction of findings and areas for improvement.

The effectiveness of monitoring depends on the persuasiveness of the information obtained and whether or not operational improvements have occurred as a result. Persuasiveness is measured not by the volume of measures but on the quality of the measures and how well they are aligned to the control objective. For example, to measure whether accrual journal entries are posted in the accounting system on time, test the beginning-of-the-month journal entry activity to determine if the data and information was known and should have been accrued at the end of the previous month. Monitor and track the number and dollar volume of the errant journal entries. Correcting the problem is then considered part of remediation.

A clear indication that monitoring is effective is when the appropriate control measures are used to better understand the process and drive process effectiveness (i.e., less defects and efficiencies, i.e., less time and resources) and therefore increase bottom line profitability. Effective monitoring shall be designed to identify and correct weaknesses before those weaknesses could manifest and adversely impact achieving the company's objectives.

Remember that the internal control program and process also requires testing, monitoring and tracking. Control objectives and activities must be established to ensure that this program is working as designed.

Remediation

Remediation refers to the investigation and correction of control deficiencies or opportunities for process improvement. Remediation follows closely to monitoring and tracking in that necessary actions must be taken in between collecting data and information for follow-up. The purpose of remediation and corrective action is to mitigate and reduce the number of internal control findings producing a better-controlled environment.

The remediation efforts begin by identifying and classifying opportunities to improve the company's control posture. These opportunities are collected from the Result of Control Activity Testing form.

- These opportunities are analyzed by process to discover the overall control status of the process and also analyzed across processes where similar deficiencies may point to a centralized solution (e.g., improve access controls).
- Classify and prioritize the items which are to be monitored establishing a qualitative or quantitative indicator for process owners to report.
- Work with the process owner to provide corrective action.
- Collect indicators and analyze trends over the period in between testing.
- Schedule testing more frequently for those areas that have high volume or high risk or are stalled (i.e., no real progress has been made).
- Retain open communication between process owners and senior executives.
- Facilitate and mediate to close the process gaps.

Since decisions to remediate will depend on the diagnosis, accurate assessment of the root cause is crucial. Investigative and correction techniques vary and may include such analytical and decision-making aids as fishbone diagrams, cause-and-effect diagrams, and process value chains. The objective is to identify the root cause of the control issue and design controls into the process that will correct the control deficiency or at least mitigate it.

In the quest to identify and implement the most "elegant" remediation solution, be careful not to overdesign the correction, remember to conduct a cost-versus-benefit analysis and risk assess it before it is implemented. It is expensive, in time and resources, to reengineer a process and the consequences are felt up- and downstream.

The completion and implementation of the corrective action can be tedious with potential for ineffectiveness within the correction process itself. Although the findings have been identified and the detailed plans have been identified, there is a point within correction where scope creep comes into play (i.e., "while we are at it, let's also try to correct this") and boredom sets in (i.e., "is this project still around"). Use the remediation phase to stay focused on the task or divide the remediation effort into milestone stages so that successes can be readily achieved and momentum is not lost.

Measure the results of the remediation efforts and once implemented, conduct a detailed test of the control objectives that were to be remediated. If the control weakness is a high volume and high risk, consider running and testing the old and new control activities in parallel before closing the control issue.

Reporting

As we've previously identified, information and communication are essential to effecting the control environment. Reliable and relevant data and information flowing from the top down, bottom up and across functions are required for an effective program; reporting falls into this category. Open lines of communication must occur between all the stakeholders with reports adapted to address their focus areas. The focus for process owners and participants is at the detail level, while for senior executives it has to do with identifying opportunities and weaknesses which will affect meeting company goals and objectives and for the audit committee of the board of directors and external auditors, it is about transparency and compliance with regulations.

Developing an internal control scorecard to identify the key findings, items to be remediated and the status of that remediation is important for communication. The use of standardized communication reports and vehicles requires up-front planning and ensures that busy executives will likely take the time to review it. Following is a scorecard based on the Internal Control—Results from Control Activity Testing.

Instructions to Complete the Internal Controls–Reporting Scorecard

The Internal Controls–Reporting Scorecard is presented at the end of this chapter and is one way to easily report and communicate on the company's internal control status.

The heading is composed of the following information which is the same as what is required on the Result of Control Activity Testing form. The Reporting Scorecard consolidates the results from the testing form and presents the information at a higher level.

The report should be distributed to those who need to know including and not necessarily limited to: chief executive officer, chief financial officer, executive team, and process owners.

The *purpose* of this report is to consolidate the findings from the Result of Control Activity Testing and report on the progress made to remediate open issues.

The *goal,* of course, is to achieve zero material weaknesses and zero significant deficiencies, as these have been determined to be unacceptable levels of risk. The Reporting Scorecard is required because it is recognized that resolution for these issues may take time and resources to resolve. In the meantime, workaround controls must be implemented to reduce the level of risk and exposure.

Since exposures and risks are identified via the internal control testing process, we have to also identify how well the testing process is going and whether the internal control testing plan is being executed as designed; therefore, a statement is included as part of the goal to indicate that the internal control testing plan is current as of a specific date.

The *findings* table is completed by listing the processes at a consolidated high level such as sales, manufacturing, inventory management, distribution, real estate, occupational health and safety, legal, human resources, finance and compliance. The high-level processes must be comparable to the risk assessments. There could be additional processes identified; however, the processes previously identified as having a high or medium risk level must be included on this list.

In order to prepare the consolidated view, a bottom up build of the processes and subprocesses identified in the Results of the Control Activity Testing forms must be grouped and combined as reports are communicated along the line of command. Supporting reports may or may not need to be distributed based on the volume of issues with unacceptable ratings.

The list of processes must be consolidated at a high level with detail available to drill down when necessary. If this is a report that is distributed to executive leaders, group the processes by functional area with a senior manager. Drilldown of backup charts should be made available upon request and must tie into the data and information collected from the control activities.

Total number of controls refers to the number of control activities that were executed. This is intended to demonstrate internal control due diligence as compared to process risk.

Aggregate the number of activities by the rating they achieved. The ratings must be consistent with the Results of Control Activity Testing forms. Ratings are 1 to 4 defined as 1 for a significant deficiency, 2 as a material weakness, or 3 as a reportable condition Those activities rated as a 4, effective control, do not have to be reported on this table. However, they should be counted in the number of control activities from the first column.

Subtotal the columns, noting that the columns will not add across before of the activities rated as effective. Be careful not to play a numbers game, as more is not necessarily better. It is strategically better to target the control objective and the control activity to get to the data and information required to prove that the control objective exists.

The *action* table brings attention to those items rated 1 (SD) and 2 (MW), representing processes and subprocesses that must be part of everyone's radar screen and require additional information. If you want to get fancy, you can highlight those remediation plans that are past their expected completion date.

The process may be a subprocess of one mentioned above. If the consolidated process was generally found to be acceptable, however, one area or subprocess requires remediation, highlight that one area; example: Accounts Payable—Check Disbursement.

Each subprocess with a 1 or 2 rating must be listed.

The process owner or the person responsible for remediating the exposure is named as is the long- and short-term remediation actions and the expected completion date.

For example:

Actions:

Process	Process Owner	Remediation Actions	Expected Completion Date
Accounts Payable—Check Disbursement	Jane Doe	Acquire a lockbox to store signature plates.	April 1, 2XXX

The final section of this report provides room for internal controls to enter comments about the process including those areas:

- Where additional or potential risk has been discovered

- Which require attention even though the rating has not reached unacceptable levels (i.e., 1 or 2)

- Which are ready for retesting and to eliminate them from the Reporting Scorecard

- Where a solution may be replicated for use in other processes

Internal Control Planning, Testing, and Remediation Worksheet

As described in the second unit the Internal Control Planning, Testing and Remediation Worksheet serves as the database to log findings, monitor, and track improvements and report on progress.

As a planning tool, this worksheet the processes and subprocesses identified in the risk assessment are listed. The potential risks and/or control objectives that must be present in the process are identified and the specific activity to prove the existence of the control objective is identified and planned.

An example of a completed worksheet:

Process/Account	Control Objective or Risk	Control Activity or Test
Accounts Payable	Accurate	There is a chart of accounts and instruction for assigning account distribution for accuracy in recording transactions and classifying expenses. Daily, peer to peer reviews are established. Test a sample of transactions for account coding accuracy.
A/R – Collections	Reconciliation	Review reconciliations of customer A/R balances between the sub ledger and general ledger. Review and reconcile the aging report to the general ledger.
Revenue	Compliance with Contract Terms	All customers have a valid and approved contract. Customers requesting non-standard contract terms and conditions require additional financial and legal approval. Review exception report for customs without valid contracts and remediate for resolution.

As a testing tool, the internal control representative records the details of the testing activities and identifies the supporting evidence collected.

An example of a completed worksheet:

Control Objective or Risk	Sample size and results of Testing	Control in Place (Y/N) if No type of exposure
Accurate	Verified that there are instructions and a valid Chart of Accounts available for coding transactions, however there were errors. Sample size of 50 transactions from all levels of transaction dollar thresholds. A checklist was available for peer to peer reviews. There were lapses in the peer to peer reviews with the most material transaction not fully reviewed. Errors were minor and did not affect financial reporting data or information.	Yes, 3. The control is generally in place, however there is opportunity for improvement.
Reconciliation	Reviewed and analyzed the reconciliations prepared each month of the quarter. Further analysis on unrecognized amounts included a recurring condition where reductions to price were routinely granted to customers who were not satisfied with the product's performance. These reductions were not reflected as an adjustment to revenue but rather recognized within the Allowance for Doubtful Accounts.	No, 2. although the reconciliations were prepared, they were not appropriately analyzed, documented or approved. Revenue is not appropriately recognized.
Compliance with Contract Terms	Sample size 100% of all customer contracts over $100,000, 50% random sample for those contracts between $50,000 and $100,000 and 10% for those contracts less than $50,000. Customer signs standard terms and conditions, however side agreements are present indicating that if the customer is "not happy" the Customer may return the product or accept an adjustment to the amount owed the company.	No, 1. This is a significant deficiency. There are unapproved side agreements with acceptance clauses and revenue is improperly recognized because the price is not fixed nor determinable.

As a remediation tool, those items rated as 1, significant deficiency (SD); 2, material weakness (MW); and 3, reportable condition (RC) require action. Because of the risk of noncompliance exposures, significant deficiencies and material weaknesses require immediate action. Reportable conditions also require action or at least comment as they may be tracking toward an unacceptable level of risk.

An example of a completed worksheet:

Process / Account	Process Owner	Remediation Actions	Next Follow up / Due Date
Accounts Payable	Jamie Doe	1) Automate expense coding into the A/P system. 2) Prepare thresholds for peer to peer reviews including all transactions over a certain size (e.g., $20,000) and 50% randomly selected sample for transactions between $5,000 and $20,000 and 20% review sample size for those less than $5,000. Rather than daily reviews, consider implementing peer to peer reviews once a week and covering the weekly activity. Management to select a sample from each category to review.	1) Investement anlaysis and change request analysis for A/P system in 5 days 2) 5 days to review and update the peer to peer checklist and immediately thereafter re-instate the peer to peer reviews with management sign off.
A/R – Collections	Terry Doe	Review the Company's policies and procedures to ensure that the following is included: appropriate financial and legal approval is required for any and all post contract changes. Ensure the Allowance is only used for Bad Debt expenses, where the customer is unable to pay debts owed to the Company.	Weekly reviews until this issue is resolved, the policies and procedures are clear. Follow up with training for A/R staff.
Revenue	Mike Doe	Review the Revenue Recognition policies and procedures to ensure this topic is adequately addressed. Those not in compliance with company policy may be terminated. Assess current contracts to determine the extent of this issue. Prior period restatement and disclosure to the SEC may be required. Institute a process for monitoring contracts and side agreements, training sales force, sales administration, legal and finance as to revenue recognition issues and consequences.	Within 2 days, assess contracts with this clause. Within 5 days, develop a remediation plan and action.

	Internal Control	
Procedure No. C01a	Section: Accounting and Finance	Page 1 of 1
	\<Template – Insert process name\>	
Process Name	Issue Date:	Replaces previously issued

Reference Policies and Procedures

- List the policies and procedures that apply to this process

Readiness Checklist

- Identify audit readiness or self-assessment questions. These questions should be answered as "Yes" or "No" with the "No" responses indicating a control weakness.

- There is a similarity of questions from process to process because these readiness questions are generally aimed at ensuring the basic requirements exist.

- Regardless of whether detailed control activities are scheduled for a process, the process owner should review their responses to the readiness checklist at least annually.

- Each business area and/or process owner must have sufficient documentation and evidence to support their readiness checklist or self assessment responses.

Flowchart

Insert a high-level process flowchart.

Control Objectives and Activities

- Based on the type of risk identified, identify the control objectives that, if present, would eliminate or mitigate the risk.

- Specific control activities must be designed to ensure those objectives are met. Evidence is collected to support the fact that an appropriate level of due diligence has occurred. Findings and areas of improvement are identified on the Result of Control Activity Testing form.

Key Measures

- List key or likely operational indicators and/or measures that may be monitored to ensure control objectives and activities are met. These should be recurring measures that the process owner uses to oversee the effectiveness (i.e., refers to defects and efficiency; i.e., refers to cycle time of the process).

- List key financial indicators that would be used for decision-making and reporting purposes.

This test guide is used as the internal control activity for:

Process Owner:	
Located at:	
Control Activities conducted by:	
Date:	

Internal Controls		
Procedure No. C01b	Section: Accounting and Finance	Page 1 of 1
	Result of Control Activity Testing	
Company	Location Financial Period Date	Prepared by: Reviewed by:

Purpose:

This form is to be used as a template to document the results of the control testing activities. Identify the purpose and timing of the testing e.g., quarterly SOX review.

Scope or Process Description:

Policy and Procedure references

Result of Control Activities Tested

- Number and identify each control objective and activity being tested. Follow or create a cross-reference to the control objectives and activities as listed on the test guide.

- Result of the control activity should identify the size of the sample, criteria used for sampling and the finding; reference findings as (E) controls were found to be in existence, (CT) controls were found to be executed completely and in a timely fashion, (VA) controls were found to be valid and accurate. Include other assertion levels as appropriate to your test plans.

- Assessment refers to your evaluation as to whether the control is working as it should be. **Ratings are 1 to 4 defined as 1 for a significant deficiency, 2 as a material weakness, 3 as a reportable condition, or 4 as an effective control.**

	Description of Control Objective / Activity tested	Result of Control Activity	Assessment 1, 2, 3, 4
1.			
2.			
3.			
4.			
5.			
6.			

Evaluation: In my opinion, the overall control assessment for the process described above is rated as *< insert rating 1, 2, 3, 4 >* and *<describe why you reached this conclusion>*.

Prepared by: _____	Date _____
Reviewed and approved by: _____	Date _____

Once complete, attach the test guide as a cover sheet to the supporting evidence and forward to internal controls.

Internal Use Only

INTERNAL CONTROL—PLANNING, TESTING, AND REMEDIATION WORKSHEET

Available in the URL download is an excel worksheet with the following columns. For your convenience, the download is prepopulated with process/account, control objectives, and control activities as described in the internal control testing guides from of this manual.

Process/Account

- Using a top-down assessment approach, list the significant processes and/or accounts that require testing.

- After the risk assessment has been performed and the risks shall be classified and prioritized with owners and next step actions identified.

Control Objective/Risk

- Identify the control objective or risk element that must be documented or tested.

- Designate your own control objectives or use the ones identified and defined within testing guides presented in the manual.

Control Activity

- Identify the planned control activity that must be documented or tested.

- Design your own control activities, or use the ones identified and defined within testing guides presented in the manual.

- Remember that the control activity must demonstrate that the internal control representative has defined a substantive activity that will produce sufficient evidence that the control is working. Supporting evidence shall be included or referenced on the Internal Control—Result of Testing form.

Sample Size and Results of Testing

- Describe the approach used to determine the sample size, identify the sample size, and describe the findings that result.

- Reference the Internal Control—Results of testing checklist and the supporting evidence collected.

- Remember to note where the control objective is working as designed and there are no findings.

- Even if not an immediate control exposure, remember to include areas of concern which may lead to control exposures or where process effectiveness and efficiency opportunities may exist.

Control in Place

- Identify "Yes" or "No" as to whether the control objective is in place and proved by the control activity.

- If "No," then describe the issue and rate the control as: assessment refers to your evaluation as to whether the control is working as it should be. Rate 1 as a significant deficiency, 2 as a material weakness, 3 as a reportable condition, and 4 as an effective control.

Remediation Actions

- If remediation actions are required, identify the immediate next steps and corrective action plans.

- Remediation actions and next steps should be developed in cooperation with the process manager.

Next Follow-up Date or Due Date

- A follow-up date is required for those issues that cannot be readily corrected. This date should not be more than two weeks from the date of the testing to ensure a timely response from the process manager. If the corrective action requires significant process re-engineering plan on periodic meetings to ensure that the reengineering design corrects the control issues.

- A due date is preferable as the date the issue is corrected and ready for retesting.

- Allow time for the correction to be implemented and performance indicators prove that the correction has been deployed; then follow with a retest of the control objective.

Available with the URL download, this worksheet is populated with the processes, control objectives and activities described in the test guides that follow.

<table>
<tr><td colspan="3" align="center">**Internal Control**</td></tr>
</table>

Procedure No. C01d	**Internal Control**	Page 1 of 2
	Section: Accounting and Finance	
	Reporting Scorecard	
Company	Location	Financial Period	Prepared by:
		Date	Reviewed by:

Distributed to:

Chief executive officer, chief financial officer, executive team, and process owners

Purpose: Consolidate the findings from the Result of Control Activity Testing and report on the progress made to remediate open issues.

Goal: Zero material weaknesses and zero significant deficiencies

Testing is current as of **<u>*<insert date matching to the internal control testing schedule>*</u>**

Findings:

Process	Total # Controls	Rating 1 SD	Rating 2 MW	Rating 3 RC
Total				

Ratings are 1 to 4 defined as 1 for a significant deficiency (SD), 2 as a material weakness (MW), or 3 as a reportable condition (RC).

Actions:

Process	Process Owner	Remediation Actions	Expected Completion Date

	Internal Control	
Procedure No. C01d	Section: Accounting and Finance	Page 2 of 2
	Reporting Scorecard	
Company	Location	Financial Period	Prepared by:
		Date	Reviewed by:

Internal control comments or observations

_____

_____

_____

	Internal Controls	
Procedure No. C02	Section: Accounting and Finance	Page 1 of 5
	Accounts Payable – Disbursements Request Payment to Third Party Vendors	
Department Ownership	Issue/Effective Date:	Replaces previously issued

Reference Policies and Procedures

- Accounts Payable—Request Payment to Third-Party Vendors
- Journal Entry
- Accrual
- Procurement
- Escheat

Flowchart

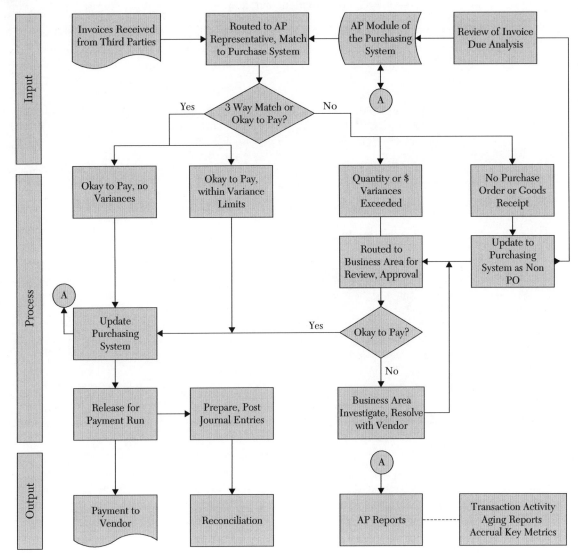

Internal Controls		
Procedure No. C02	Section: Accounting and Finance	Page 2 of 5
Accounts Payable – Disbursements Request Payment to Third Party Vendors		
Department Ownership	Issue/Effective Date:	Replaces previously issued

Readiness Checklist

- Are there documented policies and procedures? Have employees been trained as to the rules, regulations and information technology (IT) systems regarding the accounts payable (A/P) module within the procurement system?

- Is supporting documentation in the form of purchase orders, invoices, receiving reports available to A/P representatives?

- Have samples of the three-way match input been traced back to the source documents and verified as complete and accurate? Is there a strategy for collecting, reviewing the samples, and documenting the remediation plans and actions?

- Have samples of the activity that does not qualify as three-way match been traced to source documents and verified as complete, accurate and authorized for payment? Is there a strategy for collecting, reviewing the samples, and documenting the remediation plans and actions?

- Are there system-related IIT controls embedded into the design of the feeds from Procurement and to/from the payment distribution system? Are the results of the reviews documented?

- Are vendor invoices reviewed for correctness including quantity, price, tax, terms, and calculations prior to processing it for payment?

- Are there controls to ensure an invoice is not paid twice?

- Are debit balances detected and resolved on a timely basis?

- Are the roles and responsibilities segregated from those who establish or approve vendors, order products and/or services, receive products and/or services, receive and approve invoices for payment, and those who reconcile the activity?

- If A/P is outsourced, is there a valid SAS 70 on file with the A/P department? Has the company conducted test sampling to ensure that controls, reviews and audits are performed at the outsourced location where the company's A/P payments are processed? Are the results documented?

Control Objectives and Activities

Complete

- Only to those invoices and check requests that have been posted are included within the payment run. Transactions are authorized and released for the payment run by the A/P manager. Review and observe the process.

<table>
<tr><td colspan="3" align="center">**Internal Controls**</td></tr>
<tr><td>Procedure No. C02</td><td align="center">Section: Accounting and Finance</td><td align="right">Page 3 of 5</td></tr>
<tr><td colspan="3" align="center">**Accounts Payable – Disbursements Request Payment to Third Party Vendors**</td></tr>
<tr><td>Department Ownership</td><td align="center">Issue/Effective Date:</td><td align="right">Replaces previously issued</td></tr>
</table>

Accurate

- There is a chart of accounts and instruction for assigning account distribution for accuracy in recording transactions and classifying expenses. Daily, peer-to-peer reviews are established. Test a sample of transactions for account coding accuracy.

- Vendors are paid in accordance with agreed terms and conditions. Select payments and confirm with vendor payment terms. Peer-to-peer tests are performed and documented.

Authorized

- Payments may only be made to preapproved vendors established within the vendor master database. Review variance and exception reports for remediation plans.

- All disbursements are reviewed and authorized as witnessed by signature and date. Reviewers and authorizers are as identified within the delegation of authority. Review signatory list to ensure that they have appropriate levels of delegation.

Disbursement of Funds

- For manual checks and wire transfers, only approved vendor invoices as identified within the A/P system can be processed as a manual payment. A self-assessment checklist is completed for each wire transfer. Select a sample and trace payment back to source documentation.

Reconciliation

- The A/P representative prepares a reconciliation of the monthly open payables report/subledger to the general ledger A/P account and any variances are resolved in a timely manner. The A/P manager evidences the review and approval of the reconciliation by dated sign-off. Select a sample and review the supporting documentation and approval levels.

- Unmatched items or items that have been flagged as partial receipt/payment are identified and investigated. Review and observe how these are resolved; document control issues.

Safeguarding Assets

- Assets used for processing payments (i.e., check stock, signing plates, wire transfer terminals, check signing machines) are stored in a physically secure area with restricted access to authorized personnel only. Review, observe, and document the safeguarding of assets.

Segregation-of-duties tests are performed by observing roles and responsibilities and reviewing documented flowcharts and/or procedures. Segregation of duties exists between employees who have access to:

- Vendor master data and maintenance (owned by procurement department) and employees who have access to process vendor invoices (A/P department)

- Create and maintain purchase orders (POs) (owned by procurement department) and employees who have access to process vendor invoices

- PO approval (performed by business area requesting the goods and/or services) and employees who have access to process vendor invoices

- Process vendor invoices and employees who have access to goods receipt on a PO (performed by the receiving department or business area requesting the goods and/or services)

- Process vendor invoices and employees who have access to A/P payments

- Bank reconciliation (performed by treasury) and employees who have access to process vendor invoices

- Enter invoices into the A/P IT system and personnel authorized to sign checks and electronic funds transfers

Information Technology Controls

- The A/P system is configured to automatically process for invoice payment with a price tolerance limit of plus or minus 10% or $100 over the PO amount, whichever is less. Quantity must not exceed the total quantity of the PO. Variances in quantity or in price tolerance are blocked for payment in the system.

- In accordance with company policy and procedure, the IT system is configured to perform three-way matches.

- On a quarterly basis, the file share owner(s) perform a documented review of the A/P IT system and file share access to ensure access is restricted to authorized personnel:

  - Process invoices against POs including ability to input, edit, or cancel invoices.

  - Process invoices and payment requests that do not have a PO and/or goods receipt including the ability to input, edit, or cancel invoices.

  - Release invoices for payment.

  - Have access to enter manual payments.

  - Unblock invoices that have been automatically blocked for payment.

- Additional A/P IT systems are designed with controls that:

  - Do not allow processing of duplicate invoice numbers for the same vendor.

  - Will not process payables transactions for inactive vendors.

  - Track the remaining balance of blanket POs with recurring payments and closes the PO when the balance becomes zero.

- Controls are in place to ensure that recurring vendor payments are processed in according with contract terms.

	Internal Controls	
Procedure No. C02	Section: Accounting and Finance	Page 1 of 5
	Accounts Payable – Disbursements Request Payment to Third Party Vendors	
Department Ownership	Issue/Effective Date:	Replaces previously issued

Key Measures

- Transaction analysis and exception reports to monitor and track the number of exceptions

- A/P aging reports to measure and monitor the days' payable outstanding (DPO) metric

- Transactional reconciliation reports to monitor and track the number of invoices received and payments processed

- Bank reconciliation reports to monitor and track cash disbursements and outstanding checks

This test guide is used as the internal control activity for:

Process owner:	
Located at:	
Control activities conducted by:	
Date:	

Internal Controls		
Procedure No. C02a	Section: Accounting and Finance	Page 1 of 4
Accounts Receivable – Allowance for Doubtful Accounts		
Department Ownership	Issue/Effective Date:	Replaces previously issued

Reference Policies and Procedures

- Accounts receivable—Allowance for doubtful accounts
- Journal Entries
- Account reconciliation

Flowchart

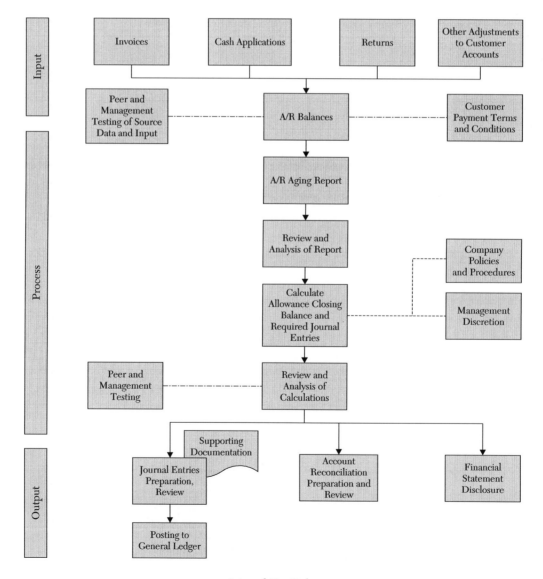

	Internal Controls	
Procedure No. C02a	Section: Accounting and Finance	Page 2 of 4
	Accounts Receivable – Allowance for Doubtful Accounts	
Department Ownership	Issue/Effective Date:	Replaces previously issued

Readiness Checklist

- Are there documented policies and procedures? Has there been a change to the external rules and regulations regarding this topic?

- Have samples of the input been traced to source documents and verified as complete and accurate? Has the process been analyzed and updated for noncompliance issues?

- Has there been a change to the calculation methodology for the allowance? If so, has the change been approved by the chief accounting officer (CAO) and communicated to external reporting?

- Is there documentation for the review and analysis of account receivable balances to determine valuation for the allowance and to identify those account balances that should be written off?

- Have the formulas within reports and/or spreadsheets been verified as complete and accurate?

- Are peer reviews established to sample and validate that the calculation is complete and accurate? Are the results of the reviews documented?

- Are there management reviews and approvals for the output? Is the final output signed by management?

- If end-user computing (EUC) spreadsheets are used, are they in compliance with EUC review and approval procedures?

Control Objectives and Activities

Complete

- A month-end accounts receivable (A/R) aging report is used to determine the month-end allowance for doubtful account balance and that customer A/R activity is current and complete.

  - Review the efficiency, that is, timeliness for updating customer A/R balances and input to the A/R aging report; measure the time from when sales orders have been shipped to updating the A/R balance and from when confirmation that cash has been received to updating the A/R balance.

  - Review the effectiveness, that is, defects of the information provided within the A/R aging report. Confirm and reconcile company A/R balances with the customer's A/P records.

Accurate

- The allowance for doubtful accounts is appropriately calculated and presented in compliance with company policy, procedures, and accounting guidance. Establish management oversight, review and approval for data used, calculation, and reporting.

	Internal Controls	
Procedure No. C02a	Section: Accounting and Finance	Page 3 of 4
	Accounts Receivable – Allowance for Doubtful Accounts	
Department Ownership	Issue/Effective Date:	Replaces previously issued

- Validate that the most current A/R aging report is used to calculate the allowance.

- Validate the use of an approved template/spreadsheet to gather the input and test calculations.

- Validate that all relevant account balances, including those identified by management discretion, have been included within the allowance calculation.

Reconciliation

- Review the monthly A/R reconciliation for completeness, accuracy, and to ensure that unreconciled items are promptly investigated and resolved. Ensure that reconciliations have been reviewed and approved by management.

Authorize

- The allowance is correctly and accurately authorized and recorded in the general ledger.

  - Review that the analysis and approval for the account reconciliation, journal entries, and supporting documentation have been properly authorized.

  - The finance manager verifies that the allowance for doubtful accounts is correctly recorded by comparing the balance in the general ledger to the approved calculation.

- The allowance is reviewed for compliance with and consistent application of company methodology. The VP Finance or corporate controller, reviews, signs, and dates the detailed schedules and financial disclosures. Review the input for financial disclosure and supporting documentation.

Information Technology Controls

- Verify that system controls are designed into the programs and that they are executing as designed. System controls may include matching: the customer's A/R input to other company information such as invoices; returns accepted by the company must equal the amount of returns posted to customer A/R accounts; cash application totals must equal cash applied to outstanding customer A/R balances.

Key Measures

Key financial indicators:

- Allowance balance as a percent of net A/R

- Bad debt expense as a percent of net credit sales

Process efficiency indicators, that is, the time it takes to:

- Collect the input

- Calculate the allowance

- Gain appropriate reviews and approvals

	Internal Controls	
Procedure No. C02a	Section: Accounting and Finance	Page 4 of 4
	Accounts Receivable – Allowance for Doubtful Accounts	
Department Ownership	Issue/Effective Date:	Replaces previously issued

Process effectiveness indicators:

- Number of defects or times it takes to redo the allowance calculation before it is acceptable

- Bad debt expense and allowance for doubtful account forecast accuracy

This test guide is used as the internal control activity for:

Process owner:	
Located at:	
Control activities conducted by:	
Date:	

	Internal Controls	
Procedure No. C02b	Section: Accounting and Finance	Page 1 of 4
	Accounts Receivable – Cash Applications	
Department Ownership	Issue/Effective Date:	Replaces previously issued

Reference Policies and Procedures

- Accounts receivable
- Journal Entries
- Account reconciliation
- Escheat

Flowchart

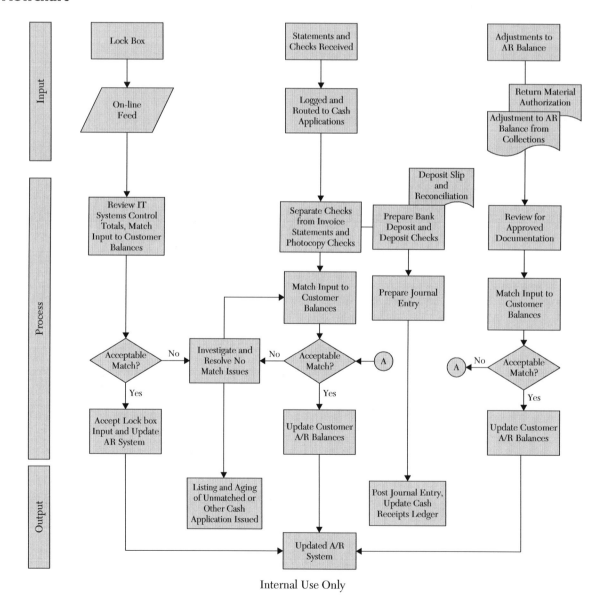

Internal Use Only

	Internal Controls	
Procedure No. C02b	Section: Accounting and Finance	Page 2 of 4
	Accounts Receivable – Cash Applications	
Department Ownership	Issue/Effective Date:	Replaces previously issued

Readiness Checklist

- Are there documented policies and procedures? Have employees been trained as to the rules, regulations, and information technology (IT) systems regarding this topic?

- Have samples of the input been traced to the source documents and verified as complete and accurate? Is there a strategy for collecting and reviewing the samples? Are improvement and remediation actions and plans documented?

- Has there been a change to the methodology regarding the application of cash? If so, has the change been approved by the corporate controller and/or chief accounting officer (CAO)?

- Are peer reviews established to perform sample testing and validate that the input to the customer's accounts receivable (A/R) balance is complete, accurate, and up to date? Are the results of the reviews documented?

- Are the cash application roles and responsibilities segregated from those who (1) establish or approve credit limits, (2) phone the customer to solicit collections, (3) collect payments and (4) reconcile customer A/R account balances?

- Are unapplied cash applications and unapplied adjustments treated as reconciling items, investigated, monitored, and resolved on a timely basis?

- Are cash application employees organized and rotated so that from time to time they are given a different set of customer accounts to oversee?

Control Objectives and Activities

Compliance with Laws and Regulations

- The unmatched list is aged with a list of outstanding items more than 90 days old and the supporting documentation forwarded to the escheat manager to be included in escheat analysis. Review selected transactions within the escheat list.

Complete

- For lockbox transactions, daily cash receipts are completely and accurately recorded in the appropriate period. The bank provides a service where they have access to the company's A/R accounts and clears checks received with outstanding customer invoices. They are instructed to clear only those items that are matched exactly. Items that do not match exactly are directed to a clearing account; with resolution to be provided by the company's cash applications team. Select samples and test by following cash applied back to the source documents (i.e., invoices and customer payment).

- For customer mail-in payments, daily checks are promptly deposited and cash is applied to the customer's A/R outstanding invoices completely and accurately recorded in the appropriate

	Internal Controls	
Procedure No. C02b	Section: Accounting and Finance	Page 3 of 4
	Accounts Receivable – Cash Applications	
Department Ownership	Issue/Effective Date:	Replaces previously issued

period. Select samples and test by following cash applied back to the source documents (i.e., invoices and customer payment).

- The treasury analyst prepares and gains approval for the journal entry to record the cash deposited into the cash ledger. Review journal entries for appropriate supporting documentation, account coding, and approvals.

- There are documented rules (i.e., methodology) for applying cash by invoice number and dollar amount and these rules are communicated to cash application employees. Sample testing occurs to ensure the accuracy of the rule deployment.

- For cash register receipts, cash is recorded and deposited daily. Cash register programming is validated for accurate charging of discounts, sales and usage taxes and other cash register calculation functions. Cash register readings are reviewed and tested to ensure accuracy.

Accurate

- For return merchandise adjustments, walk through and observe the request to return merchandise process and document control issues. Select a sample of return adjustments and trace them back to the request and physical return of merchandise.

- For all other adjustments to A/R balances, walk through and observe the process. Select a sample of adjustments and validate that they are in compliance with company policy, appropriately approved, and processed.

- Review peer review checklists. Review, observe, and document findings for applying cash completely and accurately and document findings.

Authorize

- Only authorized personnel may enter cash receipts. On a monthly basis, the A/R system access employee confirms the list of those who should have access to cash applications with the cash applications manager.

Reconciliation

- On a daily basis, the treasury analyst validates and reconciles the import of the electronic bank statements (EBS) as complete and accurate by comparing the before and after bank account balances. Review sample reconciliations by the treasury analyst.

- Daily, the cash applications manager prepares a reconciliation of the source documents received and the cash applied via the lockbox transactions, mail-in transactions, and the adjustments. Review sample reconciliations.

Segregation-of-duties tests are performed by observing roles and responsibilities and reviewing documented flowcharts and/or procedures. Segregation of duties exists between employees who:

- Prepare the bank reconciliation and personnel who can post cash or the general ledger or subledgers.

<table>
<tr><td colspan="3" align="center">**Internal Controls**</td></tr>
<tr><td>Procedure No. C02b</td><td align="center">Section: Accounting and Finance</td><td align="right">Page 4 of 4</td></tr>
<tr><td colspan="3" align="center">**Accounts Payable – Cash Applications**</td></tr>
<tr><td>Department Ownership</td><td align="center">Issue/Effective Date:</td><td align="right">Replaces previously issued</td></tr>
</table>

- Authorize customers to return products and/or materials, validate that the products and/or materials have been received, and those who apply cash or adjustment to the customer's outstanding A/R balance.

- Provide authorization to adjust customer A/R balances and those who apply those adjustments to the customer's outstanding A/R balance.

- Deposit cash receipts (must not have withdrawal privileges).

Information Technology Controls

- IT and system controls are verified to ensure complete and accurate processing of data and information. Review exception reports for the types of issues and resolutions.

- IT has implemented access controls to ensure that only authorized individuals may update a customer's A/R balances.

Key Measures

Process efficiency indicators:

- Number of transactions or dollar value of transactions posted by each employee

- Number of transactions or dollar value of transactions processed via the lockbox versus the amount of the lockbox service

- Number of days or number of phone calls to the customer it takes to resolve unmatched or open issues

Process effectiveness indicators:

- Number of transactions or dollar value of unmatched transactions

- Number of transactions or dollar amount of transactions held in the clearing account

- Unmatched and unapplied items requiring resolution with the customer

This test guide is used as the internal control activity for:

Process owner:	
Located at:	
Control activities conducted by:	
Date:	

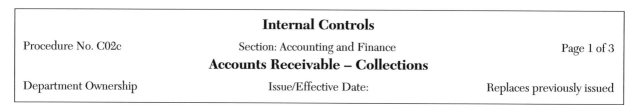

Internal Controls

Procedure No. C02c	Section: Accounting and Finance	Page 1 of 3
	Accounts Receivable – Collections	
Department Ownership	Issue/Effective Date:	Replaces previously issued

Reference Policies and Procedures

- Accounts Receivable—credit, collection, and cash applications

- Allowance for Doubtful Accounts

Flowchart

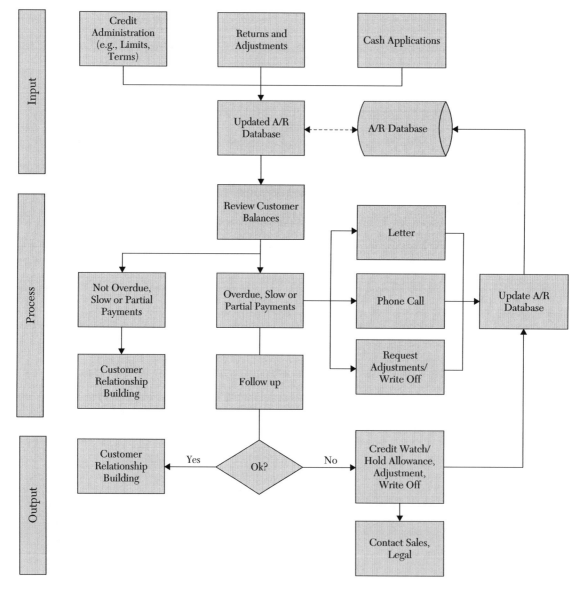

	Internal Controls	
Procedure No. C02c	Section: Accounting and Finance **Accounts Receivable – Collections**	Page 2 of 3
Department Ownership	Issue/Effective Date:	Replaces previously issued

Readiness Checklist

- Are there documented policies and procedures? Is there a list of graduated alternatives and scripts given to collectors to solicit payments from customers?

- Has there been a change to the external rules and regulations regarding this topic?

- Have all collection employees undergone education and training as to the company's policies and procedures and techniques for dealing with customers?

- Are peer reviews established to sample and validate collection techniques taken and updates to the accounts receivable (A/R) collection database? Are the results of the reviews documented?

- Are management reviews performed for requests for customer write offs or adjustments? Is management approval documented when customer write offs or adjustments are taken?

- If end-user computing (EUC) spreadsheets are used, are they in compliance with EUC review and approval procedures?

Control Objectives and Activities

Complete

- The A/R database is the single source of customer account receivable information containing customer contact information, customer A/R credit limits, terms and conditions, buying history, collection history, payment history, and allowing for comments to be added each time the company's A/R representative reaches out to the customer's A/P representative. Observe to ensure that no other database or interim recording files are used to record A/R transactions.

Accurate

- A/R collection problems are documented within the collections database (i.e., one central database). Select samples to validate that customer A/R balances are correct as reported in the A/R database and aging report.

Authorize

- Select samples to verify that A/R management reviewed, authorized, and communicated adjustment to customer A/R balances in accordance with the company's policies and procedures.

Reconciliation

- Review reconciliations of customer A/R balances between the subledger and general ledger. Review and reconcile the aging report to the general ledger.

	Internal Controls	
Procedure No. C02c	Section: Accounting and Finance	Page 3 of 3
	Accounts Receivable – Collections	
Department Ownership	Issue/Effective Date:	Replaces previously issued

Segregation-of-duties tests are performed by observing roles and responsibilities, reviewing documented flowcharts and/or procedures. Segregation of duties exists between employees who have access to:

- The subsidiary records and those who have cash receipts and general ledger control account responsibilities.

- Authorize credit limits and A/R terms, with those who authorize adjustments to A/R account balances.

- Seek collection of payments and those who receive and/or post the cash application of payments and those who reconcile A/R balances.

Information Technology Controls

- The A/R database has access restrictions, which support the company's segregation of duty roles and responsibilities.

- The A/R database is updated frequently to allow for collectors to have timely status reports.

- The A/R database contains system controls to identify a change in customer status and control totals to ensure accuracy of recording.

Key Measures

- Days' sales outstanding—representing the amount of time it takes to collect outstanding A/R

- A/R turnover—representing the amount of times A/R turns over during the year

This test guide is used as the internal control activity for:

Process owner:	
Located at:	
Control activities conducted by:	
Date:	

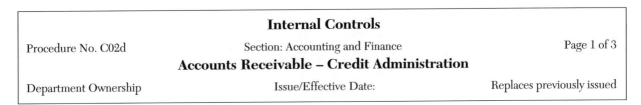

	Internal Controls	
Procedure No. C02d	Section: Accounting and Finance	Page 1 of 3
	Accounts Receivable – Credit Administration	
Department Ownership	Issue/Effective Date:	Replaces previously issued

Reference Policies and Procedures

- Accounts Receivable—credit, collection, and cash applications

- Allowance for Doubtful Accounts

Flowchart

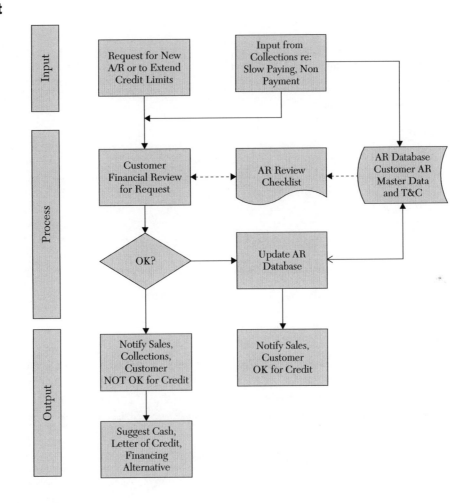

Readiness Checklist

- Are there documented policies and procedures? Have employees been trained as to the rules, regulations, and information technology (IT) systems regarding this topic?

- Is there a checklist for credit administration employee to perform a financial analysis and develop a customer accounts receivable (A/R) profile? Has the checklist been aligned with

Internal Controls		
Procedure No. C02d	Section: Accounting and Finance	Page 2 of 3
Accounts Receivable – Credit Administration		
Department Ownership	Issue/Effective Date:	Replaces previously issued

company sales and cash requirement goals and objectives? Has the checklist been approved by senior executives from sales, treasury, and finance?

- Are peer reviews established to sample and validate that the appropriate level of source documentation, analysis, and decisions has been made regarding extending customer credit and completing customer profiles? Are the results of the reviews documented?

- Does the credit manager review monthly aging schedules or listings of past due customer accounts and investigate unusual items on a timely basis?

- Are management reviews performed for when there are requests to place a customer on credit hold or extend credit beyond approved limits?

Control Objectives and Activities

Complete

- Financial analysis performed to match customer A/R credit limits, terms, and conditions with customer financial profile. If not, provide alternatives to the customer in the form of a letter of credit and/or financing arrangements. Update the A/R customer credit terms and conditions in the A/R database.

- When contacted by collections, financial analysis performed on slow-paying customers to place on credit watch, provide for them as part of the allowance for doubtful accounts and/or write off. Update the A/R customer credit terms and conditions in the A/R database.

- Analyze the customer database to inactivate those customers' credit limits where they have not had sales activity for one year or more.

Authorize

- Only authorized personnel may review and approve a customer's financial profile for A/R credit limits, terms, and conditions. At least on a quarterly basis the role owner reviews the list of employees who have access to the A/R database system to ensure that only authorized individuals have access and that appropriate segregation of duties exists within A/R functional areas.

Segregation of Duties

- Segregation of duties exists between employees who review a customer's A/R profile, establish A/R credit limits, and grant A/R terms, and those A/R employees who perform collection and/or cash application.

Key Measures

- A/R turnover measured as total sales on credit divided by average accounts receivable

- Percent of credit versus cash sales

	Internal Controls	
Procedure No. C02d	Section: Accounting and Finance	Page 3 of 3
	Accounts Receivable – Credit Administration	
Department Ownership	Issue/Effective Date:	Replaces previously issued

- A list comparing existing customer credit limits granted compared to outstanding customer sales and allowance for doubtful accounts

- A root-cause analysis between the credit analysis performed and those customers whose A/R balances are provided for within the allowance for doubtful accounts and/or where customer A/R balances have been written off.

This test guide is used as the internal control activity for:

Process owner:	
Located at:	
Control activities conducted by:	
Date:	

	Internal Controls	
Procedure No. C02e	Section: Accounting and Finance	Page 1 of 4
	Cash and Marketable Securities	
Department Ownership	Issue/Effective Date:	Replaces previously issued

Reference Policies and Procedures

- Cash and Banking
- Cash and Marketable Securities
- Journal Entries
- Account Reconciliation

Flowchart

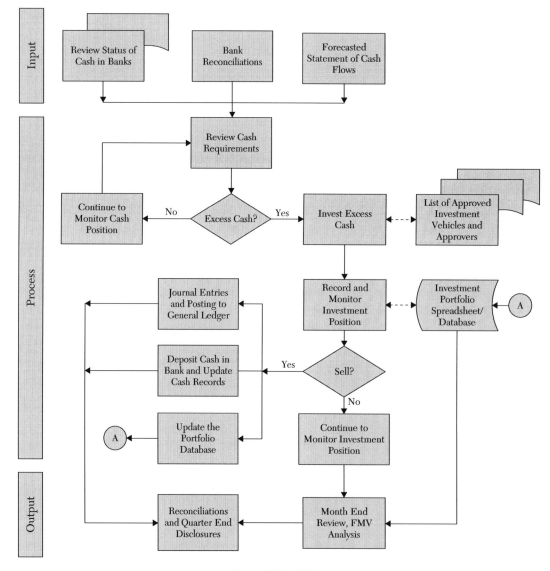

	Internal Controls	
Procedure No. C02e	Section: Accounting and Finance **Cash and Marketable Securities**	Page 2 of 4
Department Ownership	Issue/Effective Date:	Replaces previously issued

Readiness Checklist

- Are there defined cash and banking, investment and marketable securities policies and procedures? Are employees trained on cash and banking, investment and marketable securities policies and procedures?

- Is there clear delegation of authority from the treasurer to those who have authority to invest, monitor and dispose of excess cash? Are the banks given a list of authorized signatories and are promptly notified when the list changes? Are there separate signatory lists for the deposit and withdrawal of funds? Are the banks instructed not to cash checks or other instruments from unauthorized individuals?

- Is there an authorized, defined, and documented database for the recording and monitoring of excess cash and marketable securities?

- Are there separate general ledger accounts or subaccounts for each bank account?

- Are bank accounts and marketable securities reconciled monthly? Are the differences in the reconciliation investigated and corrected on a timely basis? Are the reconciliations reviewed and approved by the appropriate level?

- If end-user computing (EUC) spreadsheets are used, are they in compliance with EUC review and approval procedures?

Control Objectives and Activities

Complete

- The investment portfolio spreadsheet monitors investment, changes in fair market value, movement of currency from one type of security to another, and disposal of investment. Observe the maintenance and use of the investment portfolio.

- All investments are recorded, monitored and tracked in the investment portfolio spreadsheet. Observe to ensure there are no side databases or repositories. Select a sample set of transactions to trace back to source documentation.

Accurate

- At least monthly, the current fair market value of the investment portfolio is monitored and reviewed to ensure that decisions regarding changes in fair market value are made on a timely basis. Review findings of peer reviews of the self-assessment checklists.

- Formula accuracy within the investment portfolio spreadsheet is validated each month as confirmed with peer-to-peer reviews. Select the quarter-end spreadsheets for review and compliance with the end-user computing review and approval process.

	Internal Controls	
Procedure No. C02e	Section: Accounting and Finance	Page 3 of 4
	Cash and Marketable Securities	
Department Ownership	Issue/Effective Date:	Replaces previously issued

- Financial information is appropriately presented and all information that is necessary for fair presentation and compliance with generally accepted accounting principles (GAAP) including disclosure for realized and unrealized gains/losses, liquidation, and impaired marketable securities. Review the treasury policies and procedures to ensure they are complete, accurate, approved and communicated.

Authorize

- Investments are authorized and are within established limits as defined by the delegation of authority. Excess cash is invested based on the limits as defined by cash and marketable securities policy and procedures. Review monthly financial reports and select a grave-to-cradle sample for review and audit.

- Once approved, delegated individuals may transfer excess cash to authorized marketable security accounts. All transactions must be authorized and documented. Review checklists for complete, accurate, and authorized transactions.

- The treasurer reviews and approves all investment-related journal entries and supporting documentation, including transfers, purchases, sales, interest income, realized gains and losses, and unrealized gains and losses and the associated tax effect, evidenced by a signature and date. Review journal entries for accurate account coding, supporting documentation and timely processing.

- The treasurer reviews and approves the quarterly disclosures provided to external reporting for submission to the company's 10Q and 10K. Review the quarter-end submission, supporting documentation, and audit trail.

Reconciliation

- Monthly, the movement of cash between bank accounts and marketable security accounts is reconciled. Monthly, the investment portfolio account balance is reconciled to the transactional activity that occurred during the month. Select reconciliations to ensure appropriate analysis, supporting documentation, review, and approval signatures.

- At least on a quarterly basis, the treasurer reviews the investment portfolio, including money market funds, to ensure that it continues to comply with the investment limits as defined within the cash and marketable securities policy and procedure.

Key Measures

- List and aging summary of the types of investments held by the company, country, and currency of the investment

- Return on investment for the portfolio and each investment

	Internal Controls	
Procedure No. C02e	Section: Accounting and Finance	Page 4 of 4
	Cash and Marketable Securities	
Department Ownership	Issue/Effective Date:	Replaces previously issued

- Fair market value realized and unrealized gains and losses

- Gain and/or losses on disposal or movement of cash within marketable investments

This test guide is used as the internal control activity for:

Process owner:	
Located at:	
Control activities conducted by:	
Date:	

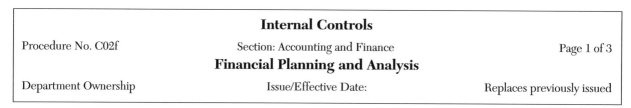

	Internal Controls	
Procedure No. C02f	Section: Accounting and Finance	Page 1 of 3
	Financial Planning and Analysis	
Department Ownership	Issue/Effective Date:	Replaces previously issued

Reference Policies and Procedures

- Financial Planning and Analysis
- Key Financial Indicators

Flowchart

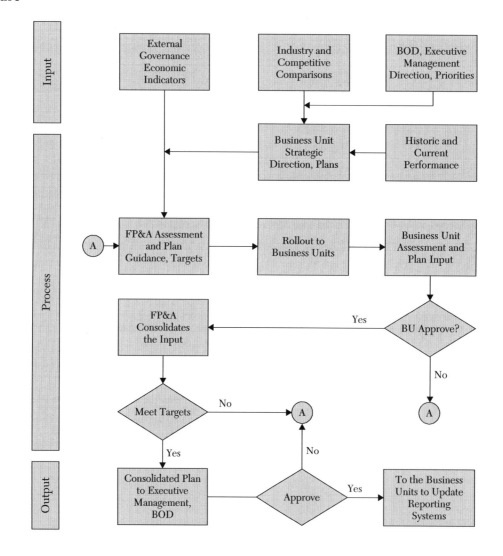

	Internal Controls	
Procedure No. C02f	Section: Accounting and Finance **Financial Planning and Analysis**	Page 2 of 3
Department Ownership	Issue/Effective Date:	Replaces previously issued

Readiness Checklist

- Are there documented policies and procedures for determining the plan guidance, instructions, and targets? Have employees been trained as to the rules, regulations, and information technology (IT) systems regarding this topic?

- Is there a budget schedule with enough time allotted for adequate assessment and reviews before the plan has to be finalized?

- Are periodic meetings held to discuss the methodology and calculations to be used in establishing departmental budgets and procedures for measuring performance? Are these meetings documented with an agenda, minutes, and action items?

- Are accounts properly categorized and classified so that the summary of the details is consistent with financial statements reporting?

- If end-user computing (EUC) spreadsheets are used, are they in compliance with EUC review and approval procedures?

Control Objectives and Activities

Complete

- Review process checklists to ensure that all business units, functional departments, and operational business activities have submitted budget input.

- Account classification and budget reports are consistent with other financial statements and reports. Review variance analysis and sample selected accounts.

- Compare a list of approved capital project requests, whether in progress or not yet started, to ensure that they are included and properly classified within the budget process.

Accurate

- Review the budget instruction and guidance to ensure that it advises compliance with generally accepted accounting principles (GAAP), period-over-period consistency, and use of current and historic performance and is normalized for one-time events. Monitor the effectiveness of budget and forecast accuracy, noting how feedback is used to improve the budget process.

- Review actual to plan variance analysis for reasonable explanations. Select sample variances to determine the accuracy of the explanations.

Authorize

- Review business unit input to financial planning and analysis to ensure that the business unit manager and his/her financial controller have reviewed and approved the input prior to

	Internal Controls	
Procedure No. C02f	Section: Accounting and Finance **Financial Planning and Analysis**	Page 3 of 3
Department Ownership	Issue/Effective Date:	Replaces previously issued

submission. Review the agendas, minutes, and memos of budget-related meetings to ensure an appropriate level of due diligence has been applied.

- To ensure that an appropriate level of due diligence has been applied before the budget is submitted to the board of directors for final approval, review senior management agendas, minutes, and memos related to internal review and approval of the annual budget and quarterly forecasts.

Information Technology Controls

- Within the budgeting application, system control totals are used to ensure complete and accurate processing of budgeting input. Review the design of the application and match to the control totals.

Key Measures

- Variance to plan and forecast accuracy by line item
- Achievement of budgeted performance and key performance indicators

This test guide is used as the internal control activity for:

Process owner:	
Located at:	
Control activities conducted by:	
Date:	

Internal Controls		
Procedure No. C02g	Section: Accounting and Finance	Page 1 of 4
Fixed Assets, Long Lived Assets, Property, Plant and Equipment Capitalized Assets		
Department Ownership	Issue/Effective Date:	Replaces previously issued

Reference Policies and Procedures

- Fixed Assets; Long-Lived Assets; Property, Plant and Equipment
- Physical Inventory
- Journal Entry
- Account Reconciliation

Flowchart

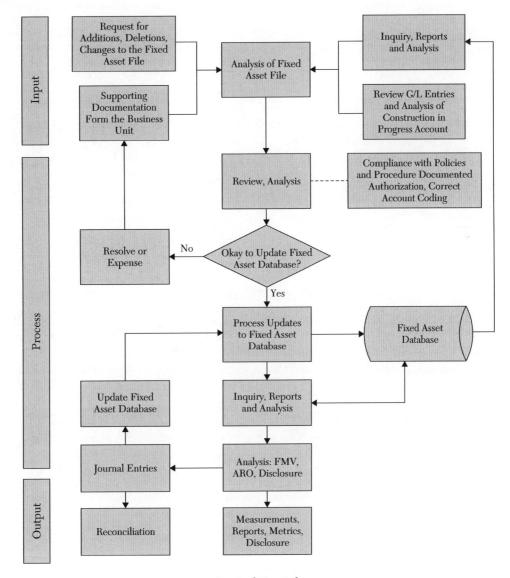

<table>
<tr><td colspan="3" align="center">**Internal Controls**</td></tr>
<tr><td>Procedure No. C02g</td><td align="center">Section: Accounting and Finance</td><td align="right">Page 2 of 4</td></tr>
<tr><td colspan="3" align="center">**Fixed Assets, Long Lived Assets, Property, Plant and Equipment Capitalized Assets**</td></tr>
<tr><td>Department Ownership</td><td align="center">Issue/Effective Date:</td><td align="right">Replaces previously issued</td></tr>
</table>

Readiness Checklist

- Are there documented company policies and procedures? Have differences between local jurisdictions and the company policy and procedure (e.g., differences due to generally accepted accounting principles [GAAP] and/or tax regulations) been documented, approved, monitored, and tracked?

- Since fixed-asset recording affects all areas of the business, is there education and training for business unit representatives as well as accounting and finance employees?

- Are there approved forms for the addition, movement, and disposal of fixed assets?

- Are peer reviews established to sample and validate collection techniques taken and updates to the fixed-asset database? Are the results of the reviews documented?

- Is there a fixed-asset physical inventory schedule to validate the existence of fixed assets?

- Are management reviews and approvals performed for write-offs or adjustments?

- If end-user computing (EUC) spreadsheets are used, are they in compliance with EUC review and approval procedures?

Control Objectives and Activities

Complete

- To capture unrecorded fixed assets, the fixed-asset manager or designee reviews activity posted to specific general ledger expense accounts (e.g., office, information technology [IT], and repair and maintenance) to identify activity that meets or exceeds local capitalization thresholds. The review is documented through a monthly signed journal entry with support of items that need to be capitalized.

- The fixed-asset manager or designee reviews the construction in progress (CIP) and/or clearing account to determine whether purchase should be capitalized or expensed. Review the balance in the CIP account and the policy and procedure for capitalization versus expense.

Accurate

- All transactions posted to the fixed-assets subledger are valid, accurate and are reconciled to the general ledger. Peer-to-peer review of self-assessment checklists prepared by the fixed-asset analyst to record additions, changes, and deletions from the fixed-asset database. Select a sample of checklists to review for completeness, accuracy, and authorization.

- Capitalized amounts for fixed assets are consistent with company-approved capitalization limits and policies. Review the company policy and procedure for fixed assets for period-over-period comparison and compliance with GAAP. Review for consistency of application between geographic areas.

Internal Controls		
Procedure No. C02g	Section: Accounting and Finance	Page 3 of 4
Fixed Assets, Long Lived Assets, Property, Plant and Equipment Capitalized Assets		
Department Ownership	Issue/Effective Date:	Replaces previously issued

- Fixed assets are coded to the appropriate asset classification account, and depreciation begins when the asset is in service. Review asset categories and the types of assets coded to the account. Review the depreciation schedule and compare it to company policy.

Authorize

- The fixed-asset department forwards a list of all CIP to the respective business unit areas (e.g., real estate, facilities, IT), which respond with a confirmation of completed and placed in service. The review is evidenced by the fixed-asset manager's approval signature. Trace the responses received to the preparation and posting of journal entry reclassification of assets. Select a grave-to-cradle sample set of transactions to trace back to source documentation.

- The fixed-asset manager reviews and approves as evidenced by signing and dating the journal entries, which is used for posting depreciation entries to the general ledger.

- The fixed-asset manager reviews and approves the quarterly disclosures provided to external reporting for submission to the company's 10Q and 10K. Review the quarter-end submission, supporting documentation, and audit trail.

Reconciliation

- Fixed-asset records include details as to description and identification of the asset, location, acquisition date, vendor, date placed into service, cost of asset, depreciable life, tax depreciable life (if different), salvage or end-of-life value and appropriate general ledger accounts. Items that are incomplete are flagged as reconciling items. Review the fixed-asset database to ensure the complete and accurate recording of data.

- The fixed-asset manager reviews, approves, signs, and dates the reconciliation of general ledger balances to the accumulated depreciation subledger on a monthly basis. Review reconciliations for accuracy, timeliness, and resolution of unreconciled items.

- Review the reconciliation of the CIP and/or clearing account. Select recently completed projects and trace the transactional activity into CIP and from CIP to its final account classification.

Safeguard Assets

- A physical inventory count process is documented, planned, communicated, and executed. Review the plan and results of the physical inventory. Sample test the physical inventory count.

- Fixed assets are reviewed for existence and valuation to reconcile book balances to the physical asset balances.

    - The fixed-asset manager or designee conducts a periodic physical inventory count of fixed assets and reconciles their findings to the fixed-asset subledger. Variances, if any, are researched, reviewed, approved, signed, and dated appropriately.

	Internal Controls	
Procedure No. C02g	Section: Accounting and Finance	Page 4 of 4
Fixed Assets, Long Lived Assets, Property, Plant and Equipment Capitalized Assets		
Department Ownership	Issue/Effective Date:	Replaces previously issued

- The fixed-asset manager or designee reviews and approves as evidenced by signing and dating the journal entries, which are used to record adjustments to the general ledger due to variances identified during the physical inventory.

Segregation of duties exists and is maintained between employees who have update or maintenance access to the fixed-asset database and those employees who:

- Have access to process vendor invoices (i.e., accounts payable).

- Post goods receipts against the purchase order (i.e., receiving department, procurement, or the business area).

Information Technology Controls

- Access is restricted to authorized personnel via a system feed from the human resource database, identifying those active employees who require access based on their job responsibilities and others as per management approval. Review the process to ensure that current HR database files are used. Validate and test the criteria used to assign responsibility and grant fixed-asset database access.

Key Measures

- Fixed assets aging file

- Fixed-asset rollover analysis identifying additions, deletions, depreciation, and adjustments to the fixed-asset database

- Return on assets, return on investment

This test guide is used as the internal control activity for:

Process owner:	
Located at:	
Control activities conducted by:	
Date:	

	Internal Controls	
Procedure No. C02h	Section: Accounting and Finance	Page 1 of 4
	Intercompany Transactions – Cross Charges	
Department Ownership	Issue/Effective Date:	Replaces previously issued

Reference Policies and Procedures

- Intercompany Transactions
- Journal Entries
- Account Reconciliation

Flowchart

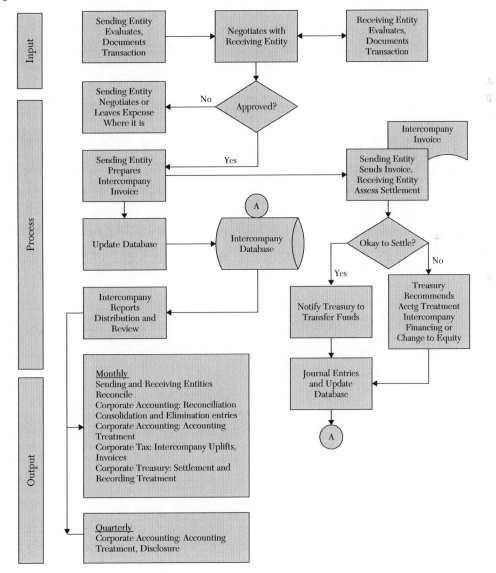

	Internal Controls	
Procedure No. C02h	Section: Accounting and Finance	Page 2 of 4
	Intercompany Transactions – Cross Charges	
Department Ownership	Issue/Effective Date:	Replaces previously issued

Readiness Checklist

- Are policies and procedures prepared, communicated, and tested for compliance? Are employees trained on the policies and procedures?

- Have corporate tax and corporate treasury reviewed and approved the intercompany policy, procedure, and guidance? Are transfer pricing uplifts included where and as necessary?

- Are intercompany invoices prepared for all intercompany transactions?

- Are the intercompany balances cleared as part of the closing process?

- Are intercompany charges settled promptly?

- Are withholding taxes and foreign exchange differences processed in accordance with company policies and procedures?

Control Objectives and Activities

Compliance with Laws and Regulations

- Review and validate that intercompany agreements are established, reviewed, and approved where and as necessary with local laws and regulations.

- Review and analyze the Intercompany policy, procedure and instruction to ensure compliance with local laws, regulations and generally accepted accounting principles (GAAP). Validate cross-border treatment with corporate tax and import/export departments. Validate instruction with corporate treasury.

Complete

- Review and analyze the intercompany account general ledger activity for the types and treatment of charges. Review corresponding business area activity to ensure the complete, accurate, and timely recognition of the intercompany account receivable and payable within both business entities.

- Local country controllers review account activity to ensure that items eligible for intercompany cross-charges are properly documented, reviewed, and approved prior to processing as an Intercompany transaction. Observe the local country controller procedure and review approval process.

- Review the instruction and checklist for transaction processing cutoffs, consolidation, and intercompany elimination entry processing. Observe and comment on the process.

Internal Controls		
Procedure No. C02h	Section: Accounting and Finance	Page 3 of 4
	Intercompany Transactions – Cross Charges	
Department Ownership	Issue/Effective Date:	Replaces previously issued

Accurate

- Review the process for and a select a sample of transactions to ensure that there are approvals and acceptance from the receiving entity prior to the charges being sent. Intercompany invoices are prepared by the entity sending the charge (i.e., the entity holding the intercompany accounts receivable) and submitted to the entity receiving the charge (i.e., the entity obligated for settling the intercompany accounts payable). Verify that information contained on invoices would satisfy custom and tax audit requirements.

- Review the instruction and observe the practice of clearing intercompany balances.

- Review the calculation and accounting treatment for withholding taxes and/or foreign exchange differences.

Authorized

- Prior to posting intercompany journal entries or sending the intercompany invoice, the entity sending the charge must gain approval from the entity receiving the charge. Authorization is witnessed by signatures and dates.

- The various types of intercompany cross-charges and their related accounting and tax treatment are reviewed, including a source data check, integrity testing, and an output data check by the corporate tax, corporate treasury, corporate accounting, and financial reporting. Review the agendas, minutes from meetings, and remedial action items for policy and procedures.

- The intercompany activity is reviewed for compliance with and consistent application of company methodology. The corporate controller reviews, signs, and dates the detailed schedules and financial disclosures. Review the input for financial disclosure and supporting documentation.

Reconciliation

- Review intercompany account reconciliations to ensure account balances are correct with no residual effects due to uplift charges, foreign exchange, or other charges. Follow to ensure that disputes are resolved in a timely manner and adjustments are documented, approved, and signed.

Information Technology Control

- As a system check, the intercompany database matches the details of the journal entries to ensure that both the sending and receiving entities use the same account classification.

- Intercompany database access is restricted to authorized personnel. On a quarterly basis, the role owner reviews access to ensure that only authorized individuals have access to the intercompany database.

	Internal Controls	
Procedure No. C02h	Section: Accounting and Finance	Page 4 of 4
	Intercompany Transactions – Cross Charges	
Department Ownership	Issue/Effective Date:	Replaces previously issued

Key Measures

- Number and amount of intercompany transactions processed per period
- Number and aging of unreconciled or disputed items
- Time to reconcile adjustments or resolve disputes
- Time to settle and type of settlement (e.g., cash, financing, equity)

This test guide is used as the internal control activity for:

Process owner:	
Located at:	
Control activities conducted by:	
Date:	

Internal Controls		
Procedure No. C02i	Section: Accounting and Finance	Page 1 of 7
Raw Materials and Inventory Receipt, Movement, Shipping		
Department Ownership	Issue/Effective Date:	Replaces previously issued

Reference Policies and Procedures

- Raw Materials and Inventory
- Physical Count of Inventory
- Journal Entry
- Account Reconciliation

Flowchart

Receipt

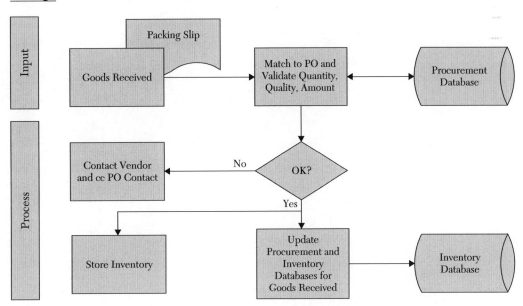

Internal Controls		
Procedure No. C02i	Section: Accounting and Finance	Page 2 of 7
Raw Materials and Inventory Receipt, Movement, Shipping		
Department Ownership	Issue/Effective Date:	Replaces previously issued

Movement

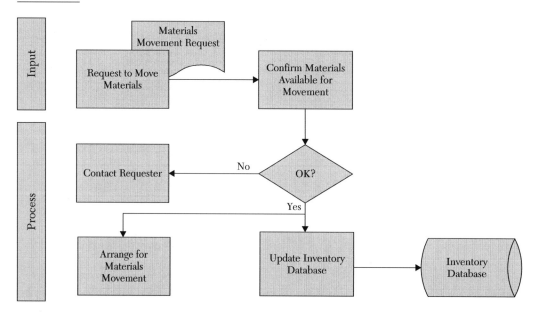

Shipping

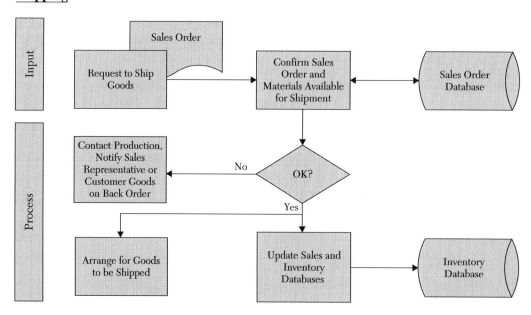

	Internal Controls	
Procedure No. C02i	Section: Accounting and Finance	Page 3 of 7
	Raw Materials and Inventory Receipt, Movement, Shipping	
Department Ownership	Issue/Effective Date:	Replaces previously issued

Physical Count

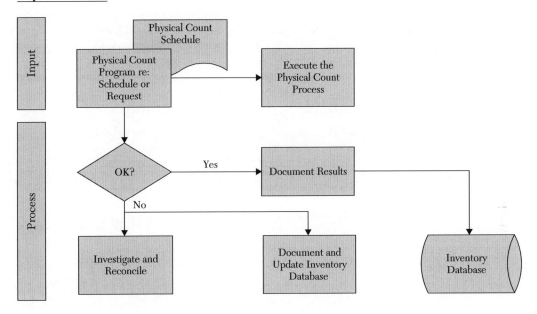

Disposition

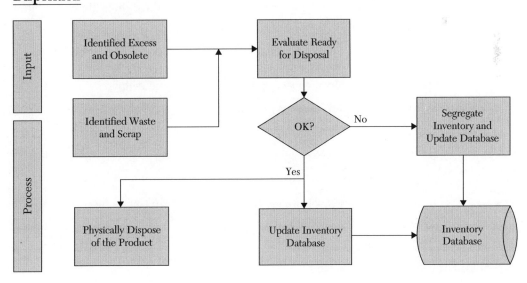

<table>
<tr><td colspan="3" align="center">**Internal Controls**</td></tr>
<tr><td>Procedure No. C02i</td><td align="center">Section: Accounting and Finance</td><td align="right">Page 4 of 7</td></tr>
<tr><td colspan="3" align="center">**Raw Materials and Inventory Receipt, Movement, Shipping**</td></tr>
<tr><td>Department Ownership</td><td align="center">Issue/Effective Date:</td><td align="right">Replaces previously issued</td></tr>
</table>

Readiness Checklist

- Are there documented company policies and procedures that address the purchase of raw materials and inventory, maintaining materials and inventory, material and inventory movement, material and inventory disposition? Are related personnel appropriately trained as to their roles and responsibilities?

- If end-user computing (EUC) spreadsheets are used, are they in compliance with EUC review and approval procedures?

- Are only approved employees allowed access to the inventory database?

- Do all materials and inventory received have an approved purchase order? When materials and inventory is received, is it reviewed for quality, quantity, and accuracy with the purchase order?

- Is the materials and inventory database promptly updated to reflect receipt and storage location?

- Are nonconforming materials and Inventory rejected for receipt or returned to the vendor as soon as practicable?

- Is material and inventory movement through the production and distribution cycles accurately and promptly recorded?

- Are physical counts of the inventory conducted throughout the year and in accordance with company procedures?

- Do all goods shipped have an approved shipping order? Prior to materials and inventory being shipped, is it reviewed for quality, quantity, and accuracy with the shipping order? Is the materials and inventory database updated to reflect goods shipped?

- Are defective, excess, and obsolete materials and inventory properly segregated prior to disposal? Is the materials and inventory database updated promptly?

- Is the inventory management process evaluated for effectiveness and efficiency of operations?

- Are certificates of destruction retained for material and inventory disposal?

- Are peer or self-assessment checklists used for inspecting and receiving materials and inventory, and for shipping and outgoing materials and inventory?

Control Objectives and Activities

Complete

- Review inspection reports for completeness, accuracy, and timely processing of goods received. Review peer-to-peer checklists for the review and acceptance of incoming products.

	Internal Controls	
Procedure No. C02i	Section: Accounting and Finance	Page 5 of 7
	Raw Materials and Inventory Receipt, Movement, Shipping	
Department Ownership	Issue/Effective Date:	Replaces previously issued

- Review and observe the treatment of non-company-owned inventory, e.g., materials and inventory held on consignment or on behalf of a customer is recorded.

- Review and observe that materials and inventory identified for waste or scrap is segregated and recorded.

- Outgoing inventory must be inspected for quality and consistency with the sales order/shipping request prior to shipment. Review peer-to-peer checklists for the review of outgoing products.

- Review certificates of destruction or disposal and confirm that the inventory has been relieved from the inventory records in accordance with approved procedures.

Accurate

- Review the accuracy and completeness of inventory records to trace inventory movement from cradle to grave. Inventory records shall include the product or identifying number, product name or description, vendor, date received, purchase order reference, quantity, price per unit, identifier of the person receiving the inventory and warehouse location where the inventory is stored. Within the materials movement module of the inventory database information is collected about who requests the move, the date and the new location of the product. Within the outgoing module of the inventory database, each inventory record is updated to reflect the customer name and/or customer number, date quantity shipped, shipping carrier, or reference number and sales order reference.

Timeliness

- Observe the use of bar code scanning equipment, to collect and record information within the inventory database.

- Review and observe that inventory received by the company at the end of the accounting cycle and not recorded in the inventory database is accrued according to the company's accrual policy and procedure. Sample test-end and beginning-of-the-month materials and inventory receipts to ensure appropriate period recognition and timing.

Information Technology Controls

- Access to the inventory database is controlled.

- Control totals are used to ensure complete recording of transactions. Ensure that the instruction for and the actual use of control totals are incorporated at appropriate control points and serve as appropriate control indicators.

- Increases and decreases to inventory volumes and values trigger reports used in journal entry preparation. Where and as possible, there is an automated process to record incoming and outgoing inventory tracking. Where and as possible, there is an automated process to record materials and inventory movement through the production cycle. Select a sample to review, trace, and match materials and inventory movement through data processing and journal entry reports.

Reconciliation

- Review and analyze reconciliations of inventory identifying incoming, movement, disposition, and shipment by product class and amount.

- Review and analyze reconciliations between cost of goods sold (i.e., inventory database) and the shipment of inventory (i.e., sales order database).

- Review and analyze reconciliations between incoming packing slips (i.e., goods receipt in the procurement database) and inventory received and recorded in the inventory database and with approved and completed purchase orders.

- Review and analyze reconciliations between (1) outgoing shipping reports and inventory shipped and (2) inventory recorded in the inventory database and approved sales orders.

Segregation-of-duties tests are performed by observing roles and responsibilities and reviewing documented flowcharts and/or procedures. Segregation of duties exists between employees who:

- Authorize the acquisition of materials and inventory and those who receive it, have custody over it

- Receive and have custody over materials and inventory and those who authorize the acquisition, movement, or disposal of it

- Have physical custody of materials and inventory and those who are responsible for the accounting, record keeping, and reconciling of it

Safeguarding Assets

- Observe the designated receiving area and process to ensure the complete and accurate recording of the transaction into the appropriate databases.

- Observe the designated shipping area and process to ensure the complete and accurate recording of the transaction into the appropriate databases.

- Review and observe the physical and accounting treatment for materials and inventory as they are: received as incoming, moved between departments or warehouses, released for shipment or outgoing.

- Observe the physical counting of inventory and sample check the counts.

- Confirm that materials and inventory is properly insured by the company and that materials and inventory held on behalf of vendors and/or customers is included within the company's insurance.

- Observe and confirm that access to the warehouse is secure. Confirm that the inventory is properly protected against damage, theft, and misappropriation.

	Internal Controls	
Procedure No. C02i	Section: Accounting and Finance	Page 7 of 7
	Raw Materials and Inventory Receipt, Movement, Shipping	
Department Ownership	Issue/Effective Date:	Replaces previously issued

Key Measures

- Inventory aging and status reports

- Inventory movement compared with sales forecast

- Shipped not billed

- Billed not shipped

- Reserve and actual units and amounts assigned to excess and obsolete materials and inventory

- Reserve and actual units and amounts assigned to scrap and waste materials and inventory

This test guide is used as the internal control activity for:

Process owner:	
Located at:	
Control activities conducted by:	
Date:	

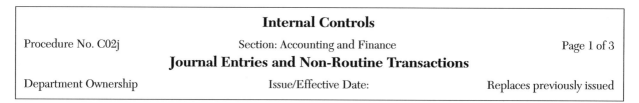

Internal Controls

Procedure No. C02j   Section: Accounting and Finance   Page 1 of 3

Journal Entries and Non-Routine Transactions

Department Ownership   Issue/Effective Date: Replaces previously issued

Reference Policies and Procedures

- Journal Entries and Nonroutine Transactions
- Account Reconciliation

Flowchart

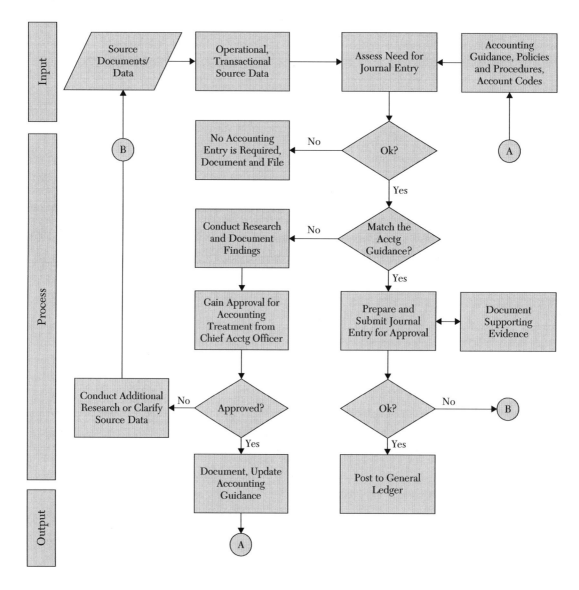

	Internal Controls	
Procedure No. C02j	Section: Accounting and Finance	Page 2 of 3
	Journal Entries and Non-Routine Transactions	
Department Ownership	Issue/Effective Date:	Replaces previously issued

Readiness Checklist

- Are there documented policies and procedures? Have employees been trained as to the rules, regulations, and information technology (IT) systems regarding this topic?

- Does the company have a chart of accounts with definitions and instructional guidance as to accounting treatment for each account?

- Does the company map accounts at the detail level to classification and presentation within the financial statements?

- Is there review and approval control over the establishment, change, and withdrawal of accounts?

- Is the accounting guidance, including a chart of account and account codes, made available to employees who have to assess, prepare, review, and/or approve journal entries?

- If end-user computing (EUC) spreadsheets are used, are they in compliance with EUC review and approval procedures?

- Do all journal entries include review, approval, and supporting documentation?

Control Objectives and Activities

Complete

- The completion, existence, and accuracy of journal entries, including standard and nonstandard journal entries and other adjustments, are accurate. Select a sample of journal entries and review them for completeness and accuracy, including the attachment or reference to supporting documentation. Review peer-to-peer documented reviews of selected journal entries.

- Management shall ensure that these journal entries are initiated, authorized, recorded, and processed appropriately in the general ledger. Select a sample of journal entries and review them for management review and authorization.

- Selected sample of account balances are traced back (i.e., grave-to-cradle sampling), to the source documentation to ensure accurate, complete and timely reporting.

- An accounting schedule is communicated to those who have to prepare, review, and approve journal entries. Review accounting instructions and guidance for completeness, accuracy, and compliance with GAAP.

Accurate

- All journal entries are balanced with debits equaling credits. Only valid and authorized account codes are eligible and accessible for use. Select a test sample of journal entries and review to ensure appropriate level of supporting documentation, review, and approval was performed.

	Internal Controls	
Procedure No. C02j	Section: Accounting and Finance	Page 3 of 3
	Journal Entries and Non-Routine Transactions	
Department Ownership	Issue/Effective Date:	Replaces previously issued

- Journal entries are accurate, initiated, authorized, recorded, and processed appropriately in the general ledger.

- Accruals are adequate, accurate, have adequate support and approvals, and are recorded in the appropriate accounting period. Select a sample and review calculations and accounting treatment.

Authorized

- Only authorized employees have access to prepare, review, approve, and/or post journal entries. A list of approved employees is maintained by financial reporting.

Reconciliation

- Accounts are reconciled or analyzed in detail to ensure that account balances are correct and recorded in the proper period.

Information Technology

- If journal entries are prepared using IT applications, there are controls to ensure that only complete, accurate, and timely journal entries are processed for a given period. Select a sample and conduct a walkthrough of transaction through the technology process.

- Ensure that only accurate account codes are used for journal entries. Review and analyze the company's chart of accounts and general ledger.

- Data entry loads or journal entries are accurate, initiated, authorized, recorded, and processed appropriately in the general ledger.

Key Measures

- Control totals are reconciled when the financial statements are prepared. Clearing accounts and suspense accounts are reconciled prior to the closing of the financial statements

- Timing of journal entry recording is compared to the accounting schedule

- Journal entry volumes and amounts are monitored and tracked

- Number of journal entries per authorized preparer and approver

- Volume, amount of standard recurring journal entries, correcting entries

This test guide is used as the internal control Activity for:

Process owner:	
Located at:	
Control activities conducted by:	
Date:	

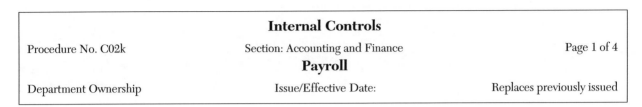

	Internal Controls	
Procedure No. C02k	Section: Accounting and Finance	Page 1 of 4
	Payroll	
Department Ownership	Issue/Effective Date:	Replaces previously issued

Reference Policies and Procedures

- Account Reconciliation
- Bank Reconciliation
- Cash and banking
- Payroll/Salary and Payment Authorization
- Escheat

Flowchart

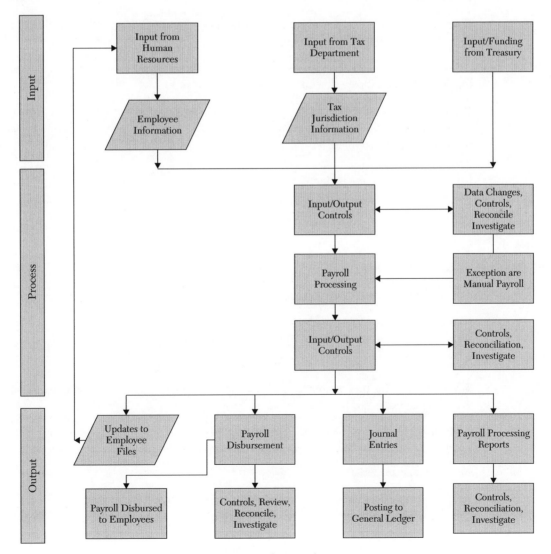

Internal Use Only

	Internal Controls	
Procedure No. C02k	Section: Accounting and Finance	Page 2 of 4
	Payroll	
Department Ownership	Issue/Effective Date:	Replaces previously issued

Readiness Checklist

- Are there documented policies and procedures? Have employees been trained as to the rules, regulations and information technology (IT) systems regarding this topic?

- Have samples of the input been traced back to the source documents and verified as complete and accurate? Is there a strategy for collecting and reviewing the samples and for documenting the remediation plans and actions?

- Are there system-related IT controls embedded into the design of the feeds from human resources and to/from the payroll calculation and payment system? Are the results of the reviews documented?

- If end-user computing (EUC) spreadsheets are used, are they in compliance with EUC review and approval procedures?

- Are the roles and responsibilities segregated from those who (1) establish or approve payroll for those eligible for payroll, and (2) process payments?

- If payroll is outsourced, is there a valid SAS 70 on file with the payroll department? Has the company conducted test sampling to ensure that controls, reviews, and audits are performed at the outsourced location where the company's payroll is processed? Are results documented?

- Are employees asked to verify payroll and banking information at least annually?

- Are employee payroll disputes logged, monitored, and resolved in a timely manner?

Control Objectives and Activities

Compliance with Laws and Regulations

- Review process to ensure appropriate accounting treatment and reporting of those payroll checks required to be segregated for escheat treatment.

- Review accounting treatment and escheat reporting.

- Review processing procedures where local jurisdictional laws and regulations are different than company standard practice.

- Review and reconcile tax and jurisdictional reporting with actual payroll amounts. Ensure the appropriate recording and payment of nonstandard requirements.

Complete, Accurate, and Timely

- Payroll processed or paid is accurate and complete. Payroll calculated based on approved rates and formulas input to the payroll system, including additional pay and deductions.

	Internal Controls	
Procedure No. C02k	Section: Accounting and Finance **Payroll**	Page 3 of 4
Department Ownership	Issue/Effective Date:	Replaces previously issued

Review and analyze period-over-period control totals and variances to planned spending. Select samples and follow the process from time recording to calculation to payroll disbursement.

- Review and analyze the timing of funds transfer between company bank accounts to cover payroll.

- Review employee dispute logs to ensure timely, accurate resolution and root-cause analysis and continuous improvement to the payroll process.

Authorize

- Review and analyze payroll policy, procedures, and instructions for processing payments.

- Manual checks are authorized and approved by two authorized signatories as named within the treasury guidelines. Observe and review the manual check process. Select a sample of checks and validate the calculation, management review, and authorized signatories.

- Review all journal entry methodology including expense, liabilities, and cash produced for payroll processing. Select sample journal entries for review of supporting documentation and processing of the transactions.

Reconciliation

- Bank reconciliation of the payroll processing account is performed after each payroll check run. Select bank reconciliation and review for accuracy, management review, and authorization and appropriate journal entry treatment.

- Review the processing and reconciliation trail by following totals and selected sampling through the transaction, review and approval cycle. For example, review the process which calculates and disburses payroll through to the recording and posting of journal entries and finally the clearing of cashed payroll checks to the bank statements.

Safeguard Assets

- Check paper stock and signature plates are retained in a locked safe with limited access by authorized personnel. Perform a physical inspection of these assets.

Segregation-of-duties tests are performed by observing roles and responsibilities, reviewing documented flowcharts and/or procedures. Segregation of duties exists between employees who:

- Have access to systems and those who process the data

- Have access to employee master data, identifying eligible employees and approved pay rates

- Authorize and input data

- Approve and oversee change data or system maintenance and those who input or process the data

- Review and reconcile reports

	Internal Controls	
Procedure No. C02k	Section: Accounting and Finance	Page 4 of 4
	Payroll	
Department Ownership	Issue/Effective Date:	Replaces previously issued

Information Technology Controls

- Review access controls and the list of authorized employees between the company's payroll system and human resource employee records.

- IT processing and calculation controls are built into the payroll calculation, which identifies amounts in excess of approved thresholds.

- Review and analyze IT control logs. Review and analyze selected system control reports and follow the process to resolve issues on exception reports.

- If any part of the process is outsourced, review the SAS 70 report provided to the company to ensure that the outsource provider has adequate internal controls in place. Select samples to ensure consistent processing of information.

Key Measures

- Establish payroll processing performance measures (e.g., number of payroll checks processed versus number of payroll employees)

- Number of payroll-related processing errors per run

- Number and percent of manual or out-of-process checks issued

This test guide is used as the internal control activity for:

Process owner:	
Located at:	
Control Activities conducted by:	
Date:	

	Internal Controls	
Procedure No. C02l	Section: Accounting and Finance **Procurement**	Page 1 of 4
Department Ownership	Issue/Effective Date:	Replaces previously issued

Reference Policies and Procedures

- Procurement
- Accounts Payable—request payment to third-Party vendors

Flowchart

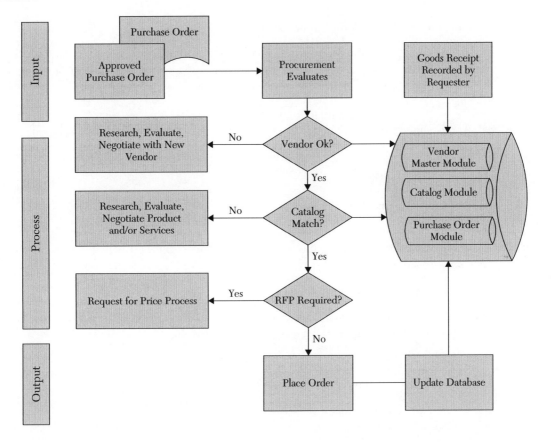

Readiness Checklist

- Are there documented policies and procedures? Have employees been trained as to the rules, regulations, and IT systems regarding the procurement system?

- Are procurement transactions supported by appropriate documentation purchase requisition, purchase order, receiving reports, evidence to support price competition?

Internal Controls		
Procedure No. C02l	Section: Accounting and Finance	Page 2 of 4
	Procurement	
Department Ownership	Issue/Effective Date:	Replaces previously issued

- Do vendors undergo a qualification and review process before being accepted as a company-approved vendor?

- Does the review include a review of their financial position, quality of their product, and/or service performance and approval of the vendor contract terms and conditions, if different than the company's terms and conditions?

- Are there system-related IT controls embedded into the design of system feeds from procurement to/from the payment distribution system? Are the results of the reviews documented?

- Are purchase orders or remaining balances on purchase orders cleared at least annually?

- If procurement activity is outsourced, is there a valid SAS 70 on file? Has the company conducted test sampling to ensure that controls, reviews, and audits are performed at the outsourced location where the company's procurement activity occurs? Are the results documented?

- Are incomplete and unfilled purchase orders (POs) aged and tracked for resolution or closure?

Control Objectives and Activities

Compliance with Laws and Regulations

- Review the process to ensure that vendor qualification requires processing through the government databases to ensure the company may conduct business with and provide payment to the approved vendor.

Compliance with Contract Terms and Conditions

- Review and ensure all vendors have valid procurement contracts and where there are nonstandard terms and conditions, those contracts have additional finance and legal approval.

Complete

- Walk through and observe the purchase requisition to purchase order process. Select a sample of approved POs and review for accuracy, completeness, and timeliness of processing.

- Walk through and observe the goods receipting process and closing of open POs by requesting departments. Select a sample and review for accuracy, completeness, and timeliness of processing.

Accurate

- Review procurement activity reports and performance measures to ensure accurate, complete, timely reporting. Review remediation actions and plans.

- Review the chart of accounts and the application of the account assignment on approved POs.

	Internal Controls	
Procedure No. C02l	Section: Accounting and Finance **Procurement**	Page 3 of 4
Department Ownership	Issue/Effective Date:	Replaces previously issued

- Review exception reports from accounts payable (A/P) signaling quantity and quality differences between the PO and the invoice. Select a sample and review for resolution, remediation, and action plans.

Authorized

- Select a sample of POs and review for completeness, accuracy, and authorization. Review that POs are placed with qualified and approved vendors.

- Select a sample of changes to POs and validate accuracy and preauthorization.

- Review exception reports and remediation plans for POs are placed after the goods and/or services have been received.

- Observe and walk through the vendor qualification process. Review and analyze vendor performance reports, vendor site visit reports, and remediation action plans.

- Review exception reports and remediation plans for POs placed with unqualified vendors or for unauthorized products or services.

Segregation-of-duties tests are performed by observing roles and responsibilities and reviewing documented flowcharts and/or procedures. Segregation of duties exists between employees who have access to:

- Vendor master data and maintenance (owned by procurement department) and employees who have access to process vendor invoices (A/P department)

- Request goods and/or services via a PO (owned by procurement department) and employees who place the order with the vendor

- PO approval (performed by business area requesting the goods and/or services) and employees who have access to process vendor invoices

- The procurement professionals who negotiate the contract terms and conditions with the vendor are separate from the employee who requests the goods and/or services

- Process vendor invoices and employees who have access to goods receipt on a PO (performed by the receiving department or business area requesting the goods and/or services)

Information Technology Controls

- In accordance with company policy and procedure and at least quarterly, the file share owner(s) perform a documented review of the procurement system and file share access to ensure access is restricted to authorized personnel.

- Additional procurement system controls are designed which:

  - Do not allow for changes to the purchase order during the goods receipt process (e.g., changes to products or services orders, quantities, and/or amounts as previously approved).

	Internal Controls	
Procedure No. C02l	Section: Accounting and Finance	Page 4 of 4
	Procurement	
Department Ownership	Issue/Effective Date:	Replaces previously issued

- Tracks the remaining balance of blanket purchase orders with recurring payments and closes the PO when the balance becomes zero.

Key Measures

- Procurement process performance measures
- Number of qualified vendors per purchasing category, including vendor performance measures
- Number and frequency of POs compared to amount per purchase order

This test guide is used as the internal control activity for:

Process owner:	
Located at:	
Control activities conducted by:	
Date:	

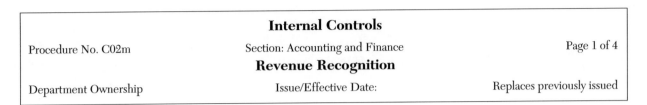

	Internal Controls	
Procedure No. C02m	Section: Accounting and Finance	Page 1 of 4
	Revenue Recognition	
Department Ownership	Issue/Effective Date:	Replaces previously issued

Reference Policies and Procedures

- Revenue Recognition
- Delegation of Authority
- Journal Entry

Flowchart

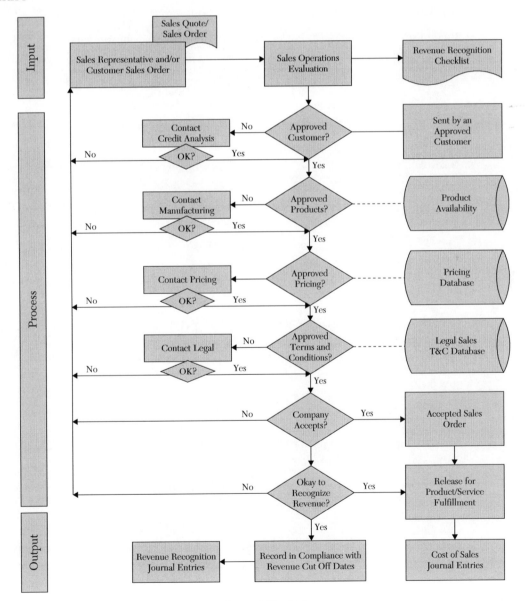

Internal Controls		
Procedure No. C02m	Section: Accounting and Finance	Page 2 of 4
	Revenue Recognition	
Department Ownership	Issue/Effective Date:	Replaces previously issued

Readiness Checklist

- Are there documented policies and procedures? Have employees been trained as to the rules, regulations, and information technology (IT) systems regarding the revenue?

- Has there been a change to the external rules and regulations regarding this topic?

- Are there suitable chart of accounts, standard journal entries, control accounts and subsidiary records for recording, classifying, and summarizing revenues based on product or service classification and geographic location?

- If end-user computing (EUC) spreadsheets are used, are they in compliance with EUC review and approval procedures?

- Is a revenue recognition checklist established to assist with addressing specific revenue recognition concerns?

- Are peer reviews established to validate the application and use of the revenue recognition checklist?

- Is revenue, sales, and cost of sales analysis performed by product and geographic segment?

Control Objectives and Activities

Compliance with Contract Terms

- All customers have a valid and approved contract. Customers requesting nonstandard contract terms and conditions require additional financial and legal approval. Review exception report for customers without valid contracts and remediate for resolution.

- Review customer dissatisfaction and escalation reports to identify the types of issues customers are having with the Company's products and/or services. Analyze how the company investigates the root cause of these issues, improves the process, and resolves the issue with the customer.

Complete

- All sales orders are input to the sales database and once accepted by the company, the sales order is released to distribution for fulfillment. Review exception reports and follow up with remediation plans. Select and sample to test sales orders for complete, accurate, and timely processing.

- Zero-dollar sales orders are reviewed for accuracy of revenue and inventory accounting treatment. Review the zero-dollar sales report and validate the reasons provided for zero-dollar fulfillment. Select a sample and test accuracy of reason classification.

- Completed sales orders are reconciled to the original contract with differences explained, authorized, and documented. Contract and supporting documentation including approvals are retained and maintained with the customer file according to sales order. Review peer-to-peer

	Internal Controls	
Procedure No. C02m	Section: Accounting and Finance **Revenue Recognition**	Page 3 of 4
Department Ownership	Issue/Effective Date:	Replaces previously issued

or self-assessment checklists. Select a sample and verify reconciliation reports and remediation plans.

Timeliness

- Instructions as to revenue cutoff periods are communicated prior to each month-end closing. Review communications and schedules.

Accurate

- Review and analyze the company's policy and procedure for revenue recognition. Select a sample of revenue recognition checklists to ensure that the revenue recognition criteria have been met. For a selected sample of transactions, review and follow cradle-to-grave supporting documentation, including customer contract, sales orders, shipping and fulfillment orders, and customer correspondence.

- Review and analyze estimate and reserve accounts for compliance with company policies and procedures, accuracy of calculation, and timeliness of processing. Recalculate estimate and reserve amounts for accuracy and consistency.

Authorize

- Select a sample of sales orders and review for completeness, accuracy, and authorization prior to processing.

- The revenue segmentation reporting by product and geography is reviewed for compliance with consistent application of company methodology. The finance VP or corporate controller reviews, signs, and dates the detailed schedules and financial disclosures.

Reconciliation

- Account analysis and reconciliation is performed between the:
  - Sales order database and revenue booked and recognized
  - Accounts receivable and recognized revenue
  - Sales and use tax and revenue
  - Intercompany revenue and intercompany receivables
  - Revenue and royalty payable
  - Sales orders, revenue, and incentive compensation

Segregation-of-duties tests are performed by observing roles and responsibilities and reviewing documented flowcharts and/or procedures. Segregation of duties exists between employees who:

- Prepare, enter and fulfill the sales orders and those who record the related accounting transactions

	Internal Controls	
Procedure No. C02m	Section: Accounting and Finance **Revenue Recognition**	Page 4 of 4
Department Ownership	Issue/Effective Date:	Replaces previously issued

- Invoice the customer and those who collect and process customer payment

- Record the accounting transactions and those who reconcile the accounts

Key Measures

- Period-over-period revenue movement

- Vertical income statement analysis with each income statement summary line expressed as a percent of revenue and compared with period-over-period percentages

- Volume and amount of sales orders

    - To be processed (i.e., waiting for company review and acceptance)

    - In backlog (i.e., accepted and not yet filled)

    - Processed (i.e., delivered and recorded for accounting purposes)

- Sales, revenue, and adjustments to revenue by product segment and geographic location

This test guide is used as the internal control activity for:

Process owner:	
Located at:	
Control activities conducted by:	
Date:	

	Internal Controls	
Procedure No. C02n	Section: Accounting and Finance **Retail Sales Orders to Business Partners**	Page 1 of 4
Department Ownership	Issue/Effective Date:	Replaces previously issued

Reference Policies and Procedures

- Distribution and Fulfillment
- Inventory
- Product Pricing
- Revenue Recognition

Flowchart

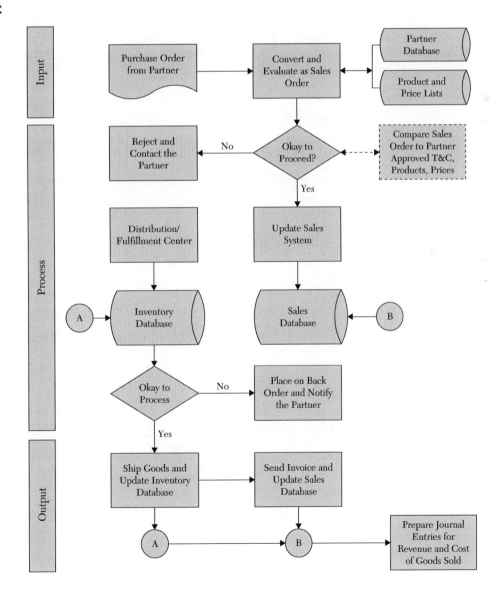

	Internal Controls	
Procedure No. C02n	Section: Accounting and Finance	Page 2 of 4
	Retail Sales Orders to Business Partners	
Department Ownership	Issue/Effective Date:	Replaces previously issued

Readiness Checklist

- Are there documented policies and procedures? Have employees been trained as to the rules, regulations, and information technology (IT) systems regarding this topic?

- Do business partners undergo a qualification and review process before being accepted as a company-approved retail partner?

- Do all business partners have valid and current contracts?

- Are retail sales orders produced from accurate and current product and pricing books?

- Have samples of the input been traced back to the source documents and verified as complete and accurate? Is there a strategy for collecting and reviewing the samples and for documenting remediation plans and actions?

- Are there system-related IT controls embedded into the design of the feeds to/from the sales order system? Are the results of the reviews documented?

- If end-user computing (EUC) spreadsheets are used, are they in compliance with EUC review and approval procedures?

- Are the roles and responsibilities reviewed to ensure appropriate segregation of duties?

Control Objectives and Activities

Compliance with Contract Terms

- Retail partner list is complete and accurate and represents authorized retail partners who have valid master sales agreements with the company. All business partners have a valid and approved contract. Business partners requesting nonstandard contract terms and conditions require additional financial and legal approval.

Complete

- Business partner product and pricing lists are complete and accurate and represent products the company is authorized to sell to retail partners. Review the product and pricing list for authorization, communication, and to reflect these products and prices are included within business partner orders.

- The sales order manager reviews and approves sales orders prior to forwarding the sales order to distribution for fulfillment. Review the completed sales order checklists to ensure that the company may fulfill requested product quantities at quoted prices and validate calculation extensions. Select a sample and test supporting documentation.

<table>
<tr><td></td><td align="center">**Internal Controls**</td><td></td></tr>
<tr><td>Procedure No. C02n</td><td align="center">Section: Accounting and Finance
Retail Sales Orders to Business Partners</td><td align="center">Page 3 of 4</td></tr>
<tr><td>Department Ownership</td><td align="center">Issue/Effective Date:</td><td align="center">Replaces previously issued</td></tr>
</table>

Accurate

- All shipments are recorded accurately, in a timely manner, and in the appropriate period. Review shipping reports and select a sample to review supporting documentation.

- Walk and observe the process from when the company receives and processes the sales order to fulfilling and shipping the order to recording journal entries. Document control issues and findings.

Authorized

- Business partners are qualified and preapproved and undergo credit authorization.

- In accordance with company policy and procedures, as these require additional review and approval, sales order reports are generated to identify those sales orders less than or greater than general sales order volumes and amounts. Review and analyze these reports for additional management review, approval, and supporting documentation.

Reconciliation

- Reconciliations are prepared, reviewed, and approved between sales orders received and orders fulfilled; unreconciled items are aged for resolution. Select reconciliations, review source data, recalculate and validate approvals.

- Reconcile fulfilled sales orders and business partner account receivable data flow. Select a sample; review calculations, approvals, and supporting documentation.

Segregation-of-duties tests are performed by observing roles and responsibilities and reviewing documented flowcharts and/or procedures. Segregation of duties exists between employees who have access to:

- Evaluating and approving business partners and those processing sales orders, shipping product, or accounts receivable processing.

Information Technology Controls

- The system automatically monitors customer credit limits and designates a customer as "hold over credit limit" if the customer purchase order exceeds the approved credit limit in the system.

- Only valid and accurate purchase orders are entered into the systems. Orders are reviewed for accuracy and validity prior to entry into the system as evidenced by sign-off of the purchase order.

Key Measures

- Sales order volumes; quantity by product, contract value segmented by business partner

- Status of sales orders in sales order administration e.g., (inaccurate or incomplete information), customer on credit hold, approved and forwarded to distribution, no charge sales

Internal Controls		
Procedure No. C02n	Section: Accounting and Finance **Retail Sales Orders to Business Partners**	Page 4 of 4
Department Ownership	Issue/Effective Date:	Replaces previously issued

- Status of sales orders in fulfillment (e.g., back order, partially fulfilled, fulfilled)
- Revenue and profit by business partner

This test guide is used as the internal control activity for:

Process owner:	
Located at:	
Control activities conducted by:	
Date:	

	Internal Controls	
Procedure No. C02o	Section: Accounting and Finance **Income Tax**	Page 1 of 4
Department Ownership	Issue/Effective Date:	Replaces previously issued

Reference Policies and Procedures

- Tax Preparation
- Journal Entries
- Account Reconciliation

Flowchart

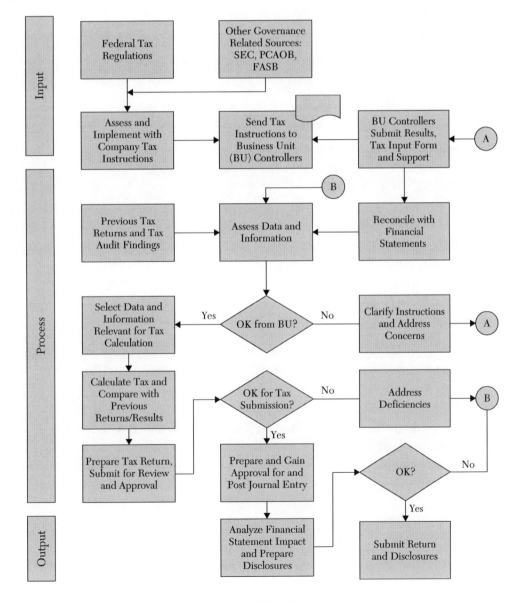

	Internal Controls	
Procedure No. C02o	Section: Accounting and Finance	Page 2 of 4
	Income Tax	
Department Ownership	Issue/Effective Date:	Replaces previously issued

Readiness Checklist

- Are there documented policies and procedures? Have employees been trained as to the rules, regulations and information technology (IT) systems and applications regarding this topic?

- Have instructions been communicated to business unit controllers or designates who provide input to the tax department?

- Are there programs or applications used by the tax department that reconcile business unit input to financial statement input?

- Are accounting records used in tax preparation reconciled with the accounting records used for financial reporting?

- Do income tax calculations comply with taxing authority rules and regulations?

- Are income tax calculations based on actual company transactions and supported by the appropriate source level documentation?

- Is an income tax calculation, preparation, and approval checklist deployed within the tax department? If end-user computing (EUC) spreadsheets are used, are they in compliance with EUC review and approval procedures?

- If tax preparation is outsourced, is there a valid SAS 70 on file with the tax department? Has the company conducted test sampling to ensure that controls, reviews, and audits are performed at the outsourced location where the company's tax obligations are processed? Are results documented?

Control Objectives and Activities

Compliance with Laws and Regulations

- Tax schedules are prepared that represent the company's jurisdictional obligations for income tax preparation and filing. The tax department can demonstrate adherence to the schedule. Review and analyze the list of jurisdictional filings.

- Tax research is documented, identifying company-specific procedures to implement tax requirements into operational and tax processes. Review the list of tax items researched and assessment as to whether the researched item needs to be incorporated into the company's policies and procedures. Senior executives are assured that all available and appropriate tax advantages are included within income tax preparation, tax submissions, and disclosures.

Complete

- There are established lines of communication between the tax function and the functional and geographic business units, providing clear instruction as to required input for income tax preparation. Review policies and procedures for inclusion of tax considerations where and as appropriate.

	Internal Controls	
Procedure No. C02o	Section: Accounting and Finance	Page 3 of 4
	Income Tax	
Department Ownership	Issue/Effective Date:	Replaces previously issued

- The tax management compares the forecasted pretax income with the tax provision work papers. Review peer-to-peer or self-assessment checklists to determine if the work papers are complete. Verify the use of the income tax checklist and supporting documentation.

Accurate

- The tax provision calculation is properly documented, accurately determined, supported, and recorded in the general ledger. Review the assumptions and process used to calculate, review, and approve tax provisions. Select sample calculations for recalculation.

- Sales and use tax liabilities are captured and recorded completely and accurately with payments submitted in a timely manner. Review and analyze sales and use tax work papers and presentation of liabilities.

- Business unit and tax management verify the integrity and completeness of gathered data. The tax function performs timely recalculations to assess the accuracy and reasonableness of computations. Internal controls reviews the data input and tax calculations.

- To serve as a check and balance and for purposes of accuracy, those who prepare income tax computations/work products and those who review and approve tax submissions and those who approve and/or reconcile journal entries. Walk through and observe the process from receiving data input to preparing journal entries and from tax submissions and disbursement of taxes payable.

Authorize

- The tax VP reviews and approves the income tax rate that must be used for budget and forecasting purposes. This rate is reconciled to the actual calculated year-end rate.

- The tax VP reviews and approves the income tax journal entries and classification between current and deferred, short- and long-term obligations.

- The tax VP reviews and approves the blended statutory state income tax rate.

- The chief financial officer (CFO) quarterly reviews and approves the contingency reserve, noting support in accordance with SFAS 5 and the related effects on the tax accounts.

- Company policies and procedures (e.g., intercompany transactions, cross-border and transfer product pricing) are adequately reviewed and approved for income tax implications.

- The income tax provisions, presentations, and disclosure requirements are reviewed for completeness, accuracy, and compliance laws and regulations. The finance VP or corporate controller reviews, signs, and dates the detailed schedules and financial disclosures. Review the disclosure and supporting documentation.

Reconciliation

- Reconciliations are performed between the financial data submitted by the business units and the information submitted to the tax department. Review and analyze selected reconciliations.

Internal Controls		
Procedure No. C02o	Section: Accounting and Finance **Income Tax**	Page 4 of 4
Department Ownership	Issue/Effective Date:	Replaces previously issued

- The tax VP reviews and approves the roll-forward schedule and analysis, which includes current taxes payable, deferred taxes, and the tax provision. Review and analyze selected reconciliations.

- The tax VP reviews the reconciliation of the requested tax entries to the balances reflected on the general ledger to confirm that the information was posted accurately and that the tax accounts are correctly stated. Review and analyze selected reconciliations.

- The accrual for sales and use tax contingencies is reconciled monthly to supporting schedules or general ledger to ensure the accrual is complete and accurate. Review and analyze selected reconciliations.

Key Measures

- Period-over-period and overall and individual business unit tax rates for the profit-and-loss and balance sheet tax accounts

- Company income tax rates compared to the industry leaders

This test guide is used as the internal control activity for:

Process owner:	
Located at:	
Control activities conducted by:	
Date:	

Appendix

This worksheet is an excel based program which has been pre-populated with information from the testing guides so as to serve as a planning, testing, documentation and remediation tool when conducting SOX testing. This section is made up of

- The Worksheet
- Result of the control activity form
- Reporting Scorecard

The Worksheet

Following is a description of each of the columns. There is an example at the beginning of the worksheet, so you can see how it is to be completed.

Internal Control Planning, Testing and Remediation Worksheet
Process/Account
Using a top-down assessment approach, list the significant processes and accounts which require testing.
Control Objective / Risk
Identify the control objective or risk element that must be documented or tested.
Designate your own control objectives, or use the ones identified and defined within Testing Guides presented in the manual.
Control Activity
Identify the planned control activity that must be documented or tested.
Design your own control activities, or use the ones identified and defined within Testing Guides presented in the manual.
Remember that the Control Activity must demonstrate that the internal control representative has defined a substantive activity which will produce sufficient evidence that the control is working. Supporting evidence shall be included or referenced on the Internal Control – Result of Testing form.
Sample Size and Results of Testing
Describe the approach used to determine the sample size, identify the sample size and describe the findings which result.

Reference the Internal Control – Results of testing checklist and the supporting evidence collected.

Remember to note where the control objective is working as designed and when there are no findings.

Even if not an immediate control exposure, remember to include areas of concern which may lead to control exposures or where process effectiveness and efficiency opportunities may exist.

Control in Place

Identify **Yes** or **No** as to whether the control objective is in place and proved by the control activity.

If No, then describe the issue and rate the control as assessment refers to your evaluation as to whether the control is working as it should be. **Rate as 1 to 4** with each rating defined as 1 as a significant deficiency, 2 as a material weakness, 3 as a reportable condition or 4 as an effective control.

Process Owner

Those items rated as 1, 2 or 3 require a process owner to oversee the remediation efforts. This column is to identify the name of the process owner or person responsible for remediation.

Remediation Actions

If remediation actions are required, identify the immediate next steps and corrective action plans.

Remediation actions and next steps should be developed in cooperation with the Process Manager.

Next Follow Up Date or Due Date

A follow up date is required for those issues which cannot be readily corrected. This date should not be more than two weeks from the date of the testing to ensure a timely response from the Process Manager. If the corrective action requires significant process re-engineering plan on periodic meetings to ensure that the re-engineering design corrects the control issues.

A due date is preferable as the date the issue is corrected and ready for re-testing.

Allow time for the correction to be implemented and performance indicators prove that the correction has been deployed; then follow with a retest of the control objective.

Internal Control – Result of Control Activity Testing

As the Internal Control representative tests each control objective, they should keep track of the tests and results by completing the Result of Control Activity form. This form serves as the cover sheet for evidence collected to support the assertion made about the control objective.

The results of each test, whether positive or negative, must be recorded to demonstrate that the internal control representative exercised an appropriate level of due diligence when reviewing the process. In addition, those items which indicate a deficiency need to be identified and classified for remedial action.

Internal Control – Reporting Scorecard

The Internal Controls – Reporting Scorecard is presented at the end of this chapter and is one way to easily report and communicate on the Company's Internal Control status.

Process/Account	Control Objective or Risk	Control Activity or Test	Sample Size and Results of Testing	Control in Place (Y/N) if No Type of Exposure	Process Owner	Remediation Actions	Next Follow up / Due Date
Accounts Payable	Accurate	There is a chart of accounts and instruction for assigning account distribution for accuracy in recording transactions and classifying expenses. Daily, peer-to-peer reviews are established. Test a sample of transactions for account coding accuracy.	Verified that there are instructions and a valid chart of accounts available for coding transactions; however, there were errors. Sample size of 50 transactions from all levels of transaction dollar thresholds. A checklist was available for peer-to-peer reviews. There were lapses in the peer-to-peer reviews with the most material transaction not fully reviewed. Errors were minor and did not affect financial reporting data or information.	Yes, 3. The control is generally in place; however, there is opportunity for improvement.	Jamie Doe	1) Automate expense coding into the A/P system. 2) Prepare thresholds for peer-to-peer reviews including all transactions over a certain size (e.g., $20,000) and 50% randomly selected sample for transactions between $5,000 and $20,000 and 20% review sample size for those less than $5,000. Rather than daily reviews, consider implementing peer-to-peer reviews once a week and covering the weekly activity. Management is to select a sample from each category to review.	1) Investment analysis and change request analysis for A/P system in 5 days; 2) 5 days to review and update the peer-to-peer checklist and immediately thereafter reinstate the peer-to-peer reviews with management sign off.
A/R – Collections	Reconciliation	Review reconciliation of customer A/R balances between the subledger and general ledger. Review and reconcile the aging report to the general ledger.	Reviewed and analyzed the reconciliation prepared each month of the quarter. Further analysis on unrecognized amounts included a recurring condition where reductions to price were routinely granted to customers who were not satisfied with the product's performance. These reductions were not reflected as an adjustment to revenue but rather recognized within the allowance for doubtful accounts.	No, 2. although the reconciliations were prepared, they were not appropriately analyzed, documented or approved. Revenue is not appropriately recognized.	Terry Doe	Review the Company's policies and procedures to ensure that the following is included: appropriate financial and legal approval is required for any and all post contract changes. Ensure the allowance is only used for bad debt expenses, where the customer is unable to pay debts owed to the Company.	Weekly reviews until this issue is resolved, the policies and procedures are clear. Follow up with training for A/R staff.

Process / Account	Control Objective or Risk	Control Activity or Test	Sample Size and Results of Testing	Control in Place (Y/N) if No Type of Exposure	Process Owner	Remediation Actions	Next Follow up / Due Date
Revenue	Compliance with Contract Terms	All customers have a valid and approved contract. Customers requesting non-standard contract terms and conditions require additional financial and legal approval. Review exception report for customs without valid contracts and remediate for resolution.	Sample size 100% of all customer contracts over $100,000, 50% random sample for those contracts between $50,000 and $100,000 and 10% for those contracts less than $50,000. Customer signs standard terms and conditions, however side agreements are present indicating that if the customer is "not happy," the customer may return the product or accept an adjustment to the amount owed the company.	No, 1. This is a significant deficiency. There are unapproved side agreements with acceptance clauses and revenue is improperly recognized because the price is not fixed nor determinable.	Mike Doe	Review the Revenue Recognition policies and procedures to ensure this topic is adequately addressed. Those not in compliance with company policy may be terminated. Assess current contracts to determine the extent of this issue. Prior period restatement and disclosure to the SEC may be required. Institute a process for monitoring contracts and side agreements, training sales force, sales administration, legal and finance as to revenue recognition issues and consequences.	Within 2 days, assess contracts with this clause. Within 5 days, develop a remediation plan and action.
Accounts Payable	Complete	Only to those invoices and check requests that have been posted are included within the payment run. Transactions are authorized and released for the payment run by accounts payable (A/P) manager. Review and observe the process.					
Accounts Payable	Accurate	There is a chart of accounts and instruction for assigning account distribution for accuracy in recording transactions and classifying expenses. Daily, peer-to-peer reviews are established. Test a sample of transactions for account coding accuracy.					

Process	Control Objective	Control Description				
Accounts Payable	Accurate	Vendors are paid in accordance with agreed terms and conditions. Select payments and confirm with vendor payment terms. Peer-to-peer tests are performed and documented.				
Accounts Payable	Authorize	Payments may only be made to pre-approved vendors established within the Vendor Master database. Review variance and exception reports for remediation plans.				
Accounts Payable	Authorize	All disbursements are reviewed and authorized as witnessed by signature and date. Reviewers and authorizers are as identified within the Delegation of Authority. Review signatory list to ensure they have appropriate levels of delegation.				
Accounts Payable	Disbursement of Funds	For manual checks and wire transfers, only approved vendor invoices as identified within the A/P system can be processed as a manual payment. A self-assessment checklist is completed for each wire transfer. Select a sample and trace payment back to source documentation.				
Accounts Payable	Reconciliation	The A/P representative prepares a reconciliation of the monthly open payables report/subledger to the general ledger A/P account and any variances are resolved in a timely manner. The A/P Manager evidences the review and approval of the reconciliation by dated sign-off. Select a sample and review the supporting documentation and approval levels.				
Accounts Payable	Reconciliation	Unmatched items or items which have been flagged as partial receipt/payment are identified and investigated. Review and observe how these are resolved, document control issues.				

Process / Account	Control Objective or Risk	Control Activity or Test	Sample Size and Results of Testing	Control in Place (Y/N) if No Type of Exposure	Process Owner	Remediation Actions	Next Follow up / Due Date
Accounts Payable	Safeguarding Assets	Assets used for processing payments (i.e., check stock, signing plates, wire transfer terminals, check signing machines) are stored in a physically secure area with restricted access to authorized personnel only. Review, observe and document the safeguarding of assets.					
Accounts Payable	Segregation of Duties	Segregation of Duties tests are performed by observing roles and responsibilities, reviewing documented flowcharts and/or procedures. Segregation of Duties exists between employees who have access to:					
Accounts Payable	Segregation of Duties	Vendor master data and maintenance (owned by Procurement department) and employees who have access to process vendor invoices (Accounts Payable department).					
Accounts Payable	Segregation of Duties	Create and maintain Purchase Orders (PO) (owned by Procurement Department) and employees who have access to process vendor invoices.					
Accounts Payable	Segregation of Duties	PO approval (performed by business area requesting the goods and/or services) and employees who have access to process vendor invoices.					
Accounts Payable	Segregation of Duties	Process vendor invoices and employees who have access to Goods Receipt on a PO (performed by the receiving department or business area requesting the goods and/or services).					
Accounts Payable	Segregation of Duties	Process vendor invoices and employees who have access to A/P Payments.					

Accounts Payable	Segregation of Duties	Bank Reconciliation (performed by Treasury) and employees who have access to process vendor invoices					
Accounts Payable	Segregation of Duties	Enter invoices into the A/P IT system and personnel authorized to sign checks and electronic funds transfers					
Accounts Payable	Information Technology Controls	The A/P system is configured to automatically process for invoice payment with a price tolerance limit of plus or minus 10% or $100 over the Purchase Order (PO) amount, whichever is less. Quantity must not exceed the total quantity of the PO. Variances in quantity or in price tolerance are blocked for payment in the system.					
Accounts Payable	Information Technology Controls	In accordance with Company policy and procedure, the IT system is configured to perform 3-way matches.					
Accounts Payable	Information Technology Controls	On a quarterly basis, the file share owners perform a documented review of the A/P IT system and file share access to ensure access is restricted to authorized personnel.					
Accounts Payable	Information Technology Controls	Process invoices against POs including ability to input, edit or cancel invoices.					
Accounts Payable	Information Technology Controls	Process invoices and payment requests that do not have a PO and/or goods receipt including the ability to input, edit or cancel invoices.					
Accounts Payable	Information Technology Controls	Release invoices for payment.					
Accounts Payable	Information Technology Controls	Have access to enter manual payments.					

(Continued)

Process / Account	Control Objective or Risk	Control Activity or Test	Sample Size and Results of Testing	Control in Place (Y/N) if No Type of Exposure	Process Owner	Remediation Actions	Next Follow up / Due Date
Accounts Payable	Information Technology Controls	Unblock invoices that have been automatically blocked for payment.					
Accounts Payable	Information Technology Controls	Additional A/P IT system are designed with controls that:					
Accounts Payable	Information Technology Controls	Do not allow processing of duplicate invoice numbers for the same vendor.					
Accounts Payable	Information Technology Controls	Will not process payable transactions for inactive vendors.					
Accounts Payable	Information Technology Controls	Tracks the remaining balance of blanket purchase orders with recurring payments and closes the PO when the balance becomes zero.					
Accounts Payable	Information Technology Controls	Controls are in place to ensure that recurring vendor payments are processed in according with contract terms.					
A/R – Credit Administration	Complete	Financial analysis performed to match customer A/R credit limits, terms and conditions with customer financial profile. If not, provide alternatives to the customer in the form of a letter of credit, and/or financing arrangements. Update the A/R customer credit terms and conditions in the A/R database.					
A/R – Credit Administration	Complete	When contacted by Collections, financial analysis performed on slow paying customers to place on credit watch, provide for them as part of the allowance for doubtful accounts and/or writeoff. Update the A/R customer credit terms and conditions in the A/R database.					

A/R – Credit Administration	Complete	Analyze the customer database to inactivate those customer's credit limits where they have not had sales activity for one year or more.		
A/R – Credit Administration	Authorize	Only authorized personnel may review and approve a Customer's financial profile for A/R credit limits, terms and conditions. At least on a quarterly basis the role owner reviews the list of employees who have access to Accounts Receivable database system to ensure only authorized individuals have access and that appropriate segregation of duties exist within A/R functional areas.		
A/R – Credit Administration	Segregation of Duties	Segregation of duties exists between employees who review a Customer's A/R profile, establish A/R credit limits and grant A/R terms and those A/R employees who perform collection and/or cash applications.		
A/R – Collections	Complete	The A/R database is the single source of customer account receivable information containing: customer contact information, customer A/R credit limits, terms and conditions, buying history, collection history, payment history, and allowing for comments to be added each time the company's A/R representative reaches out to the customer's A/P representative. Observe to ensure no other database or interim recording files are used to record A/R transactions.		
A/R – Collections	Accurate	Accounts receivable collection problems are documented within the collections database, i.e., one central database. Select samples to validate that customer A/R balances are correct as reported in the A/R database and aging report.		

(Continued)

Process / Account	Control Objective or Risk	Control Activity or Test	Sample Size and Results of Testing	Control in Place (Y/N) if No Type of Exposure	Process Owner	Remediation Actions	Next Follow up / Due Date
A/R – Collections	Authorize	Select samples to verify that A/R management reviewed, authorized and communicated adjustment to customer A/R balances in accordance with the Company's policies and procedures.					
A/R – Collections	Reconciliation	Review reconciliation of customer A/R balances between the subledger and general ledger. Review and reconcile the aging report to the general ledger.					
A/R – Collections	Segregation of Duties	Segregation of Duties tests are performed by observing roles and responsibilities, reviewing documented flowcharts and/or procedures. Segregation of Duties exists between employees who have access to:					
A/R – Collections	Segregation of Duties	The subsidiary records and those who have cash receipts and general ledger control account responsibilities.					
A/R – Collections	Segregation of Duties	Authorize credit limits and A/R terms, with those who authorize adjustments to A/R account balances.					
A/R – Collections	Segregation of Duties	Seek collection of payments and those who receive and/or post the cash application of payments and those who reconcile A/R balances.					
A/R – Collections	Information Technology Controls	The A/R database has access restrictions, which support the company's segregation of duty roles and responsibilities.					
A/R – Collections	Information Technology Controls	The A/R database is updated frequently to allow for collectors to have timely status reports.					
A/R – Collections	Information Technology Controls	The A/R database contains system controls to identify a change in customer status and control totals to ensure accuracy of recording.					

A/R – Cash Applications	Compliance with laws and regulations	The unmatched list is aged with a list of outstanding items more than 90 days old and the supporting documentation forwarded to the escheat manager to be included in escheat analysis. Review selected transactions within the escheat list.	
A/R – Cash Applications	Complete	For lockbox transactions, daily cash receipts are completely and accurately recorded in the appropriate period. The bank provides a service where they have access to the company's A/R accounts and clears checks received with outstanding customer invoices. They are instructed to clear only those items which are matched exactly. Items which do not match exactly are directed to a clearing account; with resolution to be provided by the company's Cash Applications team. Select samples and test by following cash applied back to the source documents (i.e., invoices and customer payment).	
A/R – Cash Applications	Complete	For customer mail-in payments, daily checks are promptly deposited and cash is applied to the customer's A/R outstanding invoices completely and accurately recorded in the appropriate period. Select samples and test by following cash applied back to the source documents (i.e., invoices and customer payment).	
A/R – Cash Applications	Complete	The Treasury analyst prepares and gains approval for the journal entry to record the cash deposited into the cash ledger. Review journal entries for appropriate supporting documentation, account coding and approvals.	

(Continued)

Process / Account	Control Objective or Risk	Control Activity or Test	Sample Size and Results of Testing	Control in Place (Y/N) if No Type of Exposure	Process Owner	Remediation Actions	Next Follow up / Due Date
A/R – Cash Applications	Complete	There are documented rules (i.e., methodology) for applying cash by invoice number and dollar amount and these rules are communicated to cash application employees. Sample testing occurs to ensure the accuracy of the rule deployment.					
A/R – Cash Applications	Complete	For Cash register receipts, cash is recorded and deposited daily. Cash register programming is validated for accurate charging of discounts, sales and usage taxes and other cash register calculation functions. Cash register readings are reviewed and tested to ensure accuracy.					
A/R – Cash Applications	Accurate	For return merchandise adjustments, walk through and observe the request to return merchandise process and document control issues. Select a sample of return adjustments and trace them back to the request and physical return of merchandise.					
A/R – Cash Applications	Accurate	For all other adjustments to A/R balances, walk through and observe the process. Select a sample of adjustments and validate that they are in compliance with company policy, appropriately approved and processed.					
A/R – Cash Applications	Accurate	Review peer review checklists. Review, observe and document findings for applying cash completely and accurately and document findings.					
A/R – Cash Applications	Authorize	Only authorized personnel may enter cash receipts.					

A/R – Cash Applications	Reconciliation	On a daily basis, the Treasury analyst validates and reconciles the import of the electronic bank statements (EBS) as complete and accurate by comparing the before and after bank account balances. Review sample reconciliation by the treasury analyst.						
A/R – Cash Applications	Reconciliation	Daily, the cash applications manager prepares a reconciliation of the source documents received and the cash applied via the lockbox transactions, mail-in transactions, and the adjustments. Review sample reconciliation.						
A/R – Cash Applications	Segregation of Duties	Segregation of duties tests are performed by observing roles and responsibilities, reviewing documented flowcharts and/or procedures. Segregation of duties exists between employees who:						
A/R – Cash Applications	Segregation of Duties	Prepare the bank reconciliation and personnel who can post cash to the general ledger or subledgers.						
A/R – Cash Applications	Segregation of Duties	Authorized customers to returned products and/or materials, validate the products and/or materials have been received and those who apply cash or adjustment to the customer's outstanding A/R balance.						
A/R – Cash Applications	Segregation of Duties	Provide authorization to adjust customer A/R balances and those who apply those adjustments to the customer's outstanding A/R balance.						
A/R – Cash Applications	Segregation of Duties	Deposit cash receipts must not have withdrawal privileges.						
A/R – Cash Applications	Information Technology Controls	IT and system controls are verified to ensure complete and accurate processing of data and information. Review exception reports for the types of issues and resolution.						

(Continued)

Process / Account	Control Objective or Risk	Control Activity or Test	Sample Size and Results of Testing	Control in Place (Y/N) if No Type of Exposure	Process Owner	Remediation Actions	Next Follow up / Due Date
A/R – Cash Applications	Information Technology Controls	IT has implemented access controls to ensure that only authorized individuals may update a customer's A/R balances.					
A/R – Allowance for Doubtful Accounts	Complete	A month end A/R aging report is used to determine the month-end allowance for doubtful account balance and that customer A/R activity is current and complete.					
A/R – Allowance for Doubtful Accounts	Complete	Review the efficiency, that is, timeliness for updating customer A/R balances and input to the A/R aging report; measure the time from when sales orders have been shipped to updating the A/R balance and from when confirmation that cash has been received to updating the A/R balance.					
A/R – Allowance for Doubtful Accounts	Complete	Review the effectiveness, i.e., defects of the information provided within the A/R aging report. Confirm and reconcile company A/R balances with the customer's A/P records.					
A/R – Allowance for Doubtful Accounts	Accurate	The allowance for doubtful accounts is appropriately calculated and presented in compliance with Company policy, procedures and accounting guidance. Establish management oversight, review and approval for data used, calculation and reporting.					
A/R – Allowance for Doubtful Accounts	Accurate	Validate that the most current A/R aging report is used to calculate the allowance.					
A/R – Allowance for Doubtful Accounts	Accurate	Validate the use of an approved template/spreadsheet to gather the input and test calculations.					

A/R – Allowance for Doubtful Accounts	Accurate	Validate that all relevant account balances including those identified by management discretion have been included within the allowance calculation.							
A/R – Allowance for Doubtful Accounts	Reconciliation	Review the monthly accounts receivable reconciliation for completeness and accuracy and to ensure that unreconciled items are promptly investigated and resolved. Ensure that reconciliations have been reviewed and approved by management.							
A/R – Allowance for Doubtful Accounts	Authorize	The allowance is correctly and accurately authorized and recorded in the general ledger.							
A/R – Allowance for Doubtful Accounts	Authorize	Review that the analysis and approval for the account reconciliation, journal entries, and supporting documentation has been properly authorized.							
A/R – Allowance for Doubtful Accounts	Authorize	The finance manager verifies that the allowance for doubtful accounts is correctly recorded by comparing the balance in the general ledger to the approved calculation.							
A/R – Allowance for Doubtful Accounts	Authorize	The allowance is reviewed for compliance with and consistent application of company methodology. The VP of Finance or corporate controller reviews, signs, and dates the detailed schedules and financial disclosures. Review the input for financial disclosure and supporting documentation.							
A/R – Allowance for Doubtful Accounts	Information Technology Controls	Verify that system controls are designed into the programs and that they are executing as designed. System controls may include: matching the customer's A/R input to other company information such as invoices; returns accepted by the company must equal the amount of returns posted to customer A/R accounts; cash application totals must equal cash applied to outstanding customer A/R balances.							

(Continued)

Process / Account	Control Objective or Risk	Control Activity or Test	Sample Size and Results of Testing	Control in Place (Y/N) if No Type of Exposure	Process Owner	Remediation Actions	Next Follow up / Due Date
Cash and Securities	Complete	The investment portfolio spreadsheet monitors investment, changes in fair market value, movement of currency from one type of security to another, and disposal of investment. Observe the maintenance and use of the investment portfolio.					
Cash and Securities	Complete	All investments are recorded, monitored, and tracked in the investment portfolio spreadsheet. Observe to ensure that there are no side databases or repositories. Select a sample set of transactions to trace back to source documentation.					
Cash and Securities	Accurate	At least monthly, the current fair market value of the investment portfolio is monitored and reviewed to ensure that decisions regarding changes in fair market value are made on a timely basis. Review findings of peer reviews of the self-assessment checklists.					
Cash and Securities	Accurate	Formula accuracy within the investment portfolio spreadsheet is validated each month as confirmed with peer-to-peer reviews. Select the quarter end spreadsheets for review and compliance with the End User Computing review and approval process.					
Cash and Securities	Accurate	Financial information is appropriately presented and all information that is necessary for fair presentation and compliance with GAAP including disclosure for realized and unrealized gains/losses, liquidation, and impaired marketable securities. Review the treasury policies and procedures to ensure they are complete, accurate, approved, and communicated.					

Cash and Securities	Authorize	Investments are authorized and are within established limits as defined by the delegation of authority. Excess cash is invested based on the limits as defined by cash and marketable securities policy and procedures. Review monthly financial reports and select a grave-to-cradle sample for review and audit.			
Cash and Securities	Authorize	Once approved, delegated individuals may transfer excess cash to authorized marketable security accounts. All transactions must be authorized and documented. Review checklists for complete, accurate and authorized transactions.			
Cash and Securities	Authorize	The Treasurer reviews and approves all investment related journal entries and supporting documentation including transfers, purchases, sales, interest income, realized gains and losses, and unrealized gains and losses and the associated tax effect, evidenced by a signature and date. Review journal entries for accurate account coding, supporting documentation and timely processing.			
Cash and Securities	Authorize	The Treasurer reviews and approves the quarterly disclosures provided to external reporting for submission to the Company's 10Q and 10K. Review the quarter end submission, supporting documentation and audit trail.			
Cash and Securities	Reconciliation	Monthly, the movement of cash between bank accounts and marketable security accounts is reconciled. Monthly, the investment portfolio account balance is reconciled to the transactional activity which occurred during the month. Select reconciliation to ensure appropriate analysis, supporting documentation, review and approval signatures.			

(Continued)

Process / Account	Control Objective or Risk	Control Activity or Test	Sample Size and Results of Testing	Control in Place (Y/N) if No Type of Exposure	Process Owner	Remediation Actions	Next Follow up / Due Date
Cash and Securities	Reconciliation	At least on a quarterly basis, the Treasurer reviews the investment portfolio, including money market funds, to ensure that it continues to comply with the investment limits as defined within the Cash and Marketable Securities policy and procedure.					
Financial Planning and Analysis	Complete	Review process checklists to ensure that all business units, functional departments and operational business activities have submitted budget input.					
Financial Planning and Analysis	Complete	Account classification and budget reports are consistent with other financial statements and reports. Review variance analysis and sample selected accounts.					
Financial Planning and Analysis	Complete	Compare a list of approved capital project requests whether in progress or not yet started, to ensure they are included and properly classified within the budget process.					
Financial Planning and Analysis	Accurate	Review the budget instruction and guidance to ensure that it advises compliance with GAAP, period over period consistency, use of current and historic performance and is normalized for one time events. Monitor the effectiveness of budget and forecast accuracy, noting how feedback is used to improve the budget process.					
Financial Planning and Analysis	Accurate	Review actual to plan variance analysis for reasonable explanations. Select sample variances to determine the accuracy of the explanations.					

Financial Planning and Analysis	Authorize	Review business unit input to FP&A to ensure that the business unit manager and his/her financial controller have reviewed and approved the input prior to submission. Review the agendas, minutes, and memos of budget-related meetings to ensure that an appropriate level of due diligence has been applied.				
Financial Planning and Analysis	Authorize	To ensure that an appropriate level of due diligence has been applied before the budget is submitted to the board of directors for final approval, review senior management agendas, minutes, and memos related to internal review and approval of the annual budget and quarterly forecasts.				
Financial Planning and Analysis	Information Technology controls	Within the budgeting application, system control totals are used to ensure complete and accurate processing of budgeting input. Review the design of the application and match to the control totals.				
Fixed Assets, Long-Lived Assets	Complete	To capture unrecorded fixed assets, the fixed-asset manager or designee reviews activity posted to specific general ledger expense accounts (e.g., office, IT, and repair and maintenance) to identify activity that meets or exceeds local capitalization thresholds. The review is documented through a monthly signed journal entry with support of items that need to be capitalized.				
Fixed Assets, Long-Lived Assets	Complete	The fixed-asset manager or designee reviews the construction in progress (CIP) and/or clearing account to determine whether purchase should be capitalized or expensed. Review the balance in the CIP account and the policy and procedure for capitalization versus expense.				

(Continued)

Process / Account	Control Objective or Risk	Control Activity or Test	Sample Size and Results of Testing	Control in Place (Y/N) if No Type of Exposure	Process Owner	Remediation Actions	Next Follow up / Due Date
Fixed Assets, Long-Lived Assets	Accurate	All transactions posted to the fixed assets subledger are valid, accurate, and are reconciled to the general ledger. Peer-to-peer review of self-assessment checklists.					
Fixed Assets, Long-Lived Assets	Accurate	Capitalized amounts for fixed assets are consistent with company approved capitalization limits and policies. Review the company policy and procedure for fixed asset for period-over-period comparison and compliance with GAAP. Review for consistency of application between geographic areas.					
Fixed Assets, Long-Lived Assets	Accurate	Fixed assets are coded to the appropriate asset classification account and depreciation begins when the asset is in service. Review asset categories and the types of assets coded to the account. Review depreciation schedule and compare it to company policy.					
Fixed Assets, Long-Lived Assets	Authorize	The Fixed Asset department forwards a list of all Construction in Process to the respective business unit areas (e.g., real estate, facilities, Information Technology) which responses with a confirmation of completed and placed in service. The review is evidenced through by the Fixed Asset Manager approval signature. Trace the responses received to the preparation and posting of journal entry reclassification of assets. Select a grave to cradle sample set of transactions to trace back to source documentation.					
Fixed Assets, Long-Lived Assets	Authorize	The Fixed Asset Manager reviews and approves as evidenced by signing and dating the Journal entries which is used for posting depreciation entries to the General Ledger.					

Fixed Assets, Long-Lived Assets	Authorize	The Fixed Asset Manager reviews and approves the quarterly disclosures provided to external reporting for submission to the Company's 10Q and 10K. Review the quarter end submission, supporting documentation and audit trail.				
Fixed Assets, Long-Lived Assets	Reconciliation	Fixed asset records include details as to: description and identification of the asset, location, acquisition date, vendor, date placed into service, cost of asset, depreciable life, tax depreciable life (if different), salvage or end of life value and appropriate general ledger accounts. Items which are incomplete are flagged as reconciling items. Review the fixed asset database to ensure the complete and accurate recording of data.				
Fixed Assets, Long-Lived Assets	Reconciliation	The Fixed Asset Manager reviews, approves, signs and dates the reconciliation of General Ledger balances to the accumulated depreciation sub-ledger on a monthly basis. Review reconciliation for accuracy, timeliness and resolution of unreconciled items.				
Fixed Assets, Long-Lived Assets	Reconciliation	Review the reconciliation of the Construction in Progress (CIP) and/or clearing account. Select recently completed projects and trace the transactional activity into CIP and from CIP to its final account classification.				
Fixed Assets, Long-Lived Assets	Safeguard Assets	A physical inventory count process is documented, planned, communicated and executed. Review the plan and results of the physical inventory. Sample test the physical inventory count.				
Fixed Assets, Long-Lived Assets	Safeguard Assets	Fixed Assets are reviewed for existence and valuation to reconcile book balances to the physical asset balances.				

(Continued)

Process / Account	Control Objective or Risk	Control Activity or Test	Sample Size and Results of Testing	Control in Place (Y/N) if No Type of Exposure	Process Owner	Remediation Actions	Next Follow up / Due Date
Fixed Assets, Long-Lived Assets	Safeguard Assets	The Fixed Asset Manager or designee conducts a periodic physical inventory count of Fixed Assets and reconciles their findings to the Fixed Assets sub ledger. Variance if any are researched, reviewed, approved, signed and dated appropriately.					
Fixed Assets, Long-Lived Assets	Safeguard Assets	The Fixed Asset Manager or designee reviews and approves as evidenced by signing and dating the Journal entries which are used to record adjustments to the General Ledger due to variances identified during the physical inventory.					
Fixed Assets, Long-Lived Assets	Segregation of Duties	Segregation of duties exists and is maintained between employees who have update or maintenance access to the fixed-asset database and those employees who have access to process vendor invoices (i.e., A/P) post goods receipts against the purchase order (i.e., receiving department, procurement or the business area).					
Fixed Assets, Long-Lived Assets	Information Technology Controls	Access is restricted to authorized personnel via a system feed from the human resource database identifying those active employees who require access based on their job responsibilities and others as per management approval. Review the process to ensure that current HR database files are used. Validate and test the criteria used to assign responsibility and grant fixed-asset database access.					
Intercompany Transactions	Compliance with laws and regulations	Review and validate that Intercompany agreements are established, reviewed and approved where and as necessary with local laws and regulations.					

Intercompany Transactions	Compliance with laws and regulations	Review and analyze the Intercompany policy, procedure and instruction to ensure compliance with local laws, regulations and GAAP. Validate cross border treatment with Corporate Tax and Import / Export departments. Validate instruction with Corporate Treasury.		
Intercompany Transactions	Complete	Review and analyze the Intercompany account general ledger activity for the types and treatment of charges. Review corresponding business area activity to ensure the complete, accurate and timely recognition of the Intercompany account receivable and payable within both business entities.		
Intercompany Transactions	Complete	Local country controllers review account activity to ensure that items eligible for intercompany cross-charges are properly documented, reviewed, and approved prior to processing as an intercompany transaction. Observe local country controller procedure and review approval process.		
Intercompany Transactions	Complete	Review the instruction and checklist for transaction processing cutoffs, consolidation, and intercompany elimination entry processing. Observe and comment on the process.		
Intercompany Transactions	Accurate	Review the process for and a select a sample of transactions to ensure that there are approvals and acceptance from the receiving entity prior to the charge being sent. Intercompany invoices are prepared by the entity sending the charge (i.e., the entity holding the intercompany accounts receivable) and submitted to the entity receiving the charge (i.e., the entity obligated for settling the intercompany accounts payable). Verify that information contained on invoices would satisfy custom and tax audit requirements.		

(Continued)

Process / Account	Control Objective or Risk	Control Activity or Test	Sample Size and Results of Testing	Control in Place (Y/N) if No Type of Exposure	Process Owner	Remediation Actions	Next Follow up / Due Date
Intercompany Transactions	Accurate	Review the instruction and observe the practice of clearing Intercompany balances.					
Intercompany Transactions	Accurate	Review the calculation and accounting treatment for withholding taxes and / or foreign exchange differences.					
Intercompany Transactions	Authorized	Prior to posting Intercompany journal entries or sending the Intercompany invoice, the entity sending the charge must gain approval from the entity receiving the charge. Authorization is witnessed by signatures and dates.					
Intercompany Transactions	Authorized	The various types of intercompany cross-charges and their related accounting and tax treatment are reviewed including a source data check, integrity testing, and an output data check by the corporate tax, corporate treasury, corporate accounting, and financial reporting. Review the agendas, minutes from meetings, and remedial action items for policy and procedures.					
Intercompany Transactions	Authorized	The Intercompany activity is reviewed for compliance with and consistent application of company methodology. The Corporate Controller, reviews, signs and dates the detailed schedules and financial disclosures. Review the input for financial disclosure and supporting documentation.					
Intercompany Transactions	Reconciliation	Review intercompany account reconciliation to ensure account balances are correct with no residual effects due to uplift charges, foreign exchange, or other charges. Follow to ensure that disputes are resolved in a timely manner and adjustments are documented, approved, and signed.					

Category	Type/Status	Description				
Intercompany Transactions	Information Technology Control	As a system check, the Intercompany database matches the details of the journal entries to ensure that both the sending and receiving entities use the same account classification.				
Intercompany Transactions	Information Technology Control	Intercompany database access is restricted to authorized personnel. On a quarterly basis, the role owner reviews access to ensure that only authorized individuals have access to the Intercompany database.				
Raw Materials and Inventory	Complete	Review inspection reports for completeness, accuracy and timely processing of goods received. Review peer-to-peer checklists for the review and acceptance of incoming products.				
Raw Materials and Inventory	Complete	Review and observe the treatment of non-company-owned inventory (e.g., materials and inventory held on consignment or on behalf of a customer) is recorded.				
Raw Materials and Inventory	Complete	Review and observe that materials and inventory identified for waste or scrap is segregated and recorded.				
Raw Materials and Inventory	Complete	Outgoing inventory must be inspected for quality and consistency with the sales order/shipping request prior to shipment. Review peer-to-peer checklists for the review of outgoing products.				
Raw Materials and Inventory	Complete	Review certificates of destruction or disposal and confirm that the inventory has been relieved from the inventory records in accordance with approved procedures.				

(Continued)

Process / Account	Control Objective or Risk	Control Activity or Test	Sample Size and Results of Testing	Control in Place (Y/N) if No Type of Exposure	Process Owner	Remediation Actions	Next Follow up / Due Date
Raw Materials and Inventory	Accuracy	Review the accuracy and completeness of inventory records to trace inventory movement from cradle to grave. Inventory records shall include the product or identifying number, product name or description, vendor, date received, purchase order reference, quantity, price per unit, identifier of the person receiving the inventory and warehouse location where the inventory is stored. Within the materials movement module of the inventory database information is collected about who requests the move, the date and the new location of the product. Within the outgoing module of the inventory database, each inventory record is updated to reflect the customer name and/or customer number, date quantity shipped, shipping carrier or reference number and sales order reference.					
Raw Materials and Inventory	Timeliness	Observe the use of bar code scanning equipment, to collect and record information within the inventory database.					
Raw Materials and Inventory	Timeliness	Review and observe that inventory received by the company at the end of the accounting cycle and not recorded in the inventory database is accrued according to the company's accrual policy and procedure. Sample test-end and beginning-of-the-month materials and inventory receipts to ensure appropriate period recognition and timing.					
Raw Materials and Inventory	Information Technology Controls	Access to the inventory database is controlled.					

Raw Materials and Inventory	Information Technology Controls	Control totals are used to ensure complete recording of transactions. Review the instruction for and the actual use of control totals are incorporated at appropriate control points and serve as appropriate control indicators.				
Raw Materials and Inventory	Information Technology Controls	Increases and decreases to inventory volumes and values trigger reports used in journal entry preparation. Where and as possible there is an automated process to record incoming and outgoing inventory tracking. Where and as possible, there is an automated process to record materials and inventory movement through the production cycle. Select a sample to review, trace and match materials and inventory movement through data processing and journal entry reports.				
Raw Materials and Inventory	Reconciliation	Review and analyze reconciliation of inventory identifying incoming, movement, disposition and shipment by product class and amount.				
Raw Materials and Inventory	Reconciliation	Review and analyze reconciliation between cost of goods sold, i.e., inventory database and the shipment of inventory i.e., sales order database.				
Raw Materials and Inventory	Reconciliation	Review and analyze reconciliation between incoming packing slips, i.e., goods receipt in the procurement database and inventory received and recorded in the inventory database and with approved and completed purchase orders.				
Raw Materials and Inventory	Reconciliation	Review and analyze reconciliation between (a) outgoing shipping reports and inventory shipped and (b) inventory recorded in the inventory database and approved sales orders.				

(Continued)

Process / Account	Control Objective or Risk	Control Activity or Test	Sample Size and Results of Testing	Control in Place (Y/N) if No Type of Exposure	Process Owner	Remediation Actions	Next Follow up / Due Date
Raw Materials and Inventory	Segregation of Duties	Segregation-of-duties tests are performed by observing roles and responsibilities, reviewing documented flowcharts and/or procedures. Segregation of duties exists between employees who have access to:					
Raw Materials and Inventory	Segregation of Duties	Authorizing the acquisition of materials and inventory and those who receive it, have custody over it					
Raw Materials and Inventory	Segregation of Duties	Receive and have custody over materials and inventory and those who authorize the acquisition, movement or disposal of it					
Raw Materials and Inventory	Segregation of Duties	Physical custody of materials and inventory and those who are responsible for the accounting, recordkeeping and reconciling of it					
Raw Materials and Inventory	Safeguarding Assets	Observe the designated receiving area and process to ensure the complete and accurate recording of the transaction into the appropriate databases.					
Raw Materials and Inventory	Safeguarding Assets	Observe the designated shipping area and process to ensure the complete and accurate recording of the transaction into the appropriate databases.					
Raw Materials and Inventory	Safeguarding Assets	Review and observe the physical and accounting treatment for materials and inventory as they are: received as incoming, moved between departments or warehouses, released for shipment or outgoing.					
Raw Materials and Inventory	Safeguarding Assets	Observe the physical counting of inventory and sample check the counts.					

Raw Materials and Inventory	Safeguarding Assets	Confirm that materials and inventory is properly insured by the company and that materials and inventory held on behalf of vendors and/or customers is included within the Company's insurance.				
Raw Materials and Inventory	Safeguarding Assets	Observe and confirm that access to the warehouse is secure. Confirm that the inventory is properly protected against damage, theft, and misappropriation.				
Journal Entries	Complete	The completion, existence, and accuracy of journal entries, including standard and nonstandard journal entries and other adjustments, are accurate. Select a sample of journal entries and review them for completeness and accuracy including the attachment or reference to supporting documentation. Review peer-to-peer documented reviews of selected journal entries.				
Journal Entries	Complete	Management shall ensure that these journal entries are initiated, authorized, recorded and processed appropriately in the general ledger. Select a sample of journal entries and review them for management review and authorization.				
Journal Entries	Complete	Selected sample of account balances are traced back (i.e., grave-to-cradle sampling) to the source documentation to ensure accurate, complete, and timely reporting.				
Journal Entries	Complete	An accounting schedule is communicated to those who have to prepare, review and approve journal entries. Review accounting instructions and guidance for completeness, accuracy and compliance with GAAP.				

(Continued)

Process / Account	Control Objective or Risk	Control Activity or Test	Sample Size and Results of Testing	Control in Place (Y/N) if No Type of Exposure	Process Owner	Remediation Actions	Next Follow up / Due Date
Journal Entries	Accurate	All journal entries are balanced with debits equaling credits. Only valid and authorized account codes are eligible and accessible for use. Select a test sample of journal entries and review to ensure appropriate level of supporting documentation, review and approval was performed.					
Journal Entries	Accurate	Journal entries are accurate, initiated, authorized, recorded and processed appropriately in the general ledger.					
Journal Entries	Accurate	Accruals are adequate, accurate, have adequate support and approvals, and are recorded in the appropriate accounting period. Select a sample and review calculations and accounting treatment.					
Journal Entries	Authorize	Only authorized employees have access to prepare, review, approve and/or post journal entries. A list of approved employees is maintained by financial reporting.					
Journal Entries	Reconciliation	Accounts are reconciled or analyzed in detail to ensure account balances are correct and recorded in the proper period.					
Journal Entries	Information Technology	If journal entries are prepared using Information Technology applications, there are controls to ensure that only complete, accurate and timely journal entries are processed for a given period. Select a sample and conduct a walkthrough of transaction through the technology process.					
Journal Entries	Information Technology	Ensure that only accurate account codes are used for journal entries. Review and analyze the company's chart of accounts and general ledger.					

Category	Type	Description						
Journal Entries	Information Technology	Data entry loads or journal entries are accurate, initiated, authorized, recorded and processed appropriately in the general ledger.						
Payroll	Compliance with laws and regulations	Review process to ensure appropriate accounting treatment and reporting of those payroll checks required to be segregated for escheat treatment.						
Payroll	Compliance with laws and regulations	Review accounting treatment and escheat reporting.						
Payroll	Compliance with laws and regulations	Review processing procedures where local jurisdictional laws and regulations are different than company standard practice.						
Payroll	Compliance with laws and regulations	Review and reconcile tax and jurisdictional reporting with actual payroll amounts. Ensure the appropriate recording and payment of non-standard requirements.						
Payroll	Complete, Accurate and Timely	Payroll processed or paid is accurate and complete. Payroll calculated based on approved rates and formulas input to the payroll system, including additional pay and deductions. Review and analyze period over period control totals, variances to planned spending. Select samples and follow the process from time recording, to calculation to payroll disbursement.						
Payroll	Complete, Accurate and Timely	Review and analyze the timing of funds transfer between Company bank accounts to cover payroll.						
Payroll	Complete, Accurate and Timely	Review employee dispute logs to ensure timely, accurate resolution and root cause analysis and continuous improvement to the payroll process.						
Payroll	Authorize	Review and analyze payroll policy, procedures and instructions for processing payments.						

(Continued)

Process / Account	Control Objective or Risk	Control Activity or Test	Sample Size and Results of Testing	Control in Place (Y/N) if No Type of Exposure	Process Owner	Remediation Actions	Next Follow up / Due Date
Payroll	Authorize	Manual checks are authorized and approved by two authorized signatories as named within the Treasury guidelines. Observe and review the manual check process. Select a sample of checks and validate the calculation, management review and authorized signatories.					
Payroll	Authorize	Review all journal entry methodology including expense, liabilities and cash produced for payroll processing. Select sample journal entries for review of supporting documentation and processing of the transactions.					
Payroll	Reconciliation	Bank reconciliation of the payroll processing account is performed after each payroll check run. Select bank reconciliation and review for accuracy, management review and authorization and appropriate journal entry treatment.					
Payroll	Reconciliation	Review the processing and reconciliation trail by following totals and selected sampling through the cycle which calculates disburses payroll to recording of journal entries to reconciliation of bank statements.					
Payroll	Safeguard Assets	Check paper stock and signature plates are retained in a locked safe with limited access by authorized personnel. Perform a physical inspection of these assets.					
Payroll	Segregation of Duties	Segregation of Duties tests are performed by observing roles and responsibilities, reviewing documented flowcharts and/or procedures. Segregation of Duties exists between employees who have access to:					

Payroll	Segregation of Duties	access to systems and those who process the data				
Payroll	Segregation of Duties	employee master data, identifying eligible employees and approved pay rates				
Payroll	Segregation of Duties	authorize and input data				
Payroll	Segregation of Duties	approve and oversee change data or system maintenance and those who input or process the data				
Payroll	Segregation of Duties	review and reconcile reports				
Payroll	Information Technology Controls	Review access controls and the list of authorized employees between the Company's payroll system and Human Resource employee records.				
Payroll	Information Technology Controls	IT processing and calculation controls are built into the payroll calculation which identifies amounts in excess of approved thresholds.				
Payroll	Information Technology Controls	Review and analyze IT control logs. Review and analyze selected system control reports and follow the process to resolve issues on exception reports.				
Payroll	Information Technology Controls	If any part of the process is outsourced, review the SAS 70 report provided to the company to ensure that the outsource provider has adequate internal controls in place. Select samples to ensure consistent processing of information.				
Procurement	Compliance with contract terms and conditions	Review and ensure all vendors have valid procurement contracts and where there are non-standard terms and conditions, those contracts have additional finance and legal approval.				

(Continued)

Process / Account	Control Objective or Risk	Control Activity or Test	Sample Size and Results of Testing	Control in Place (Y/N) if No Type of Exposure	Process Owner	Remediation Actions	Next Follow up / Due Date
Procurement	Complete	Walk through and observe the purchase requisition to purchase order process. Select a sample of approved POs and review for accuracy, completeness and timeliness of processing.					
Procurement	Complete	Walk through and observe the goods receipting process and closing of open POs by requesting departments. Select a sample and review for accuracy, completeness and timeliness of processing.					
Procurement	Accurate	Review procurement activity reports and performance measures to ensure accurate, complete, timely reporting. Review remediation actions and plans.					
Procurement	Accurate	Review the chart of accounts and the application of the account assignment on approved POs.					
Procurement	Accurate	Review exception reports from A/P signaling quantity, quality differences between the PO and the invoice. Select a sample and review for resolution, remediation and action plans.					
Procurement	Authorized	Select a sample of POs and review for completeness, accuracy and authorization. Review that POs are placed with qualified and approved vendors.					
Procurement	Authorized	Select a sample of changes to POs and validate accuracy and pre-authorization.					
Procurement	Authorized	Review exception reports and remediation plans for POs are placed after the goods and/or services have been received.					

Procurement	Authorized	Observe and walk through the vendor qualification process. Review and analyze vendor performance reports, vendor site visit reports and remediation action plans.						
Procurement	Authorized	Review exception reports and remediation plans for POs placed with unqualified vendors or for unauthorized products or services.						
Procurement	Segregation of Duties	Segregation of Duties tests are performed by observing roles and responsibilities, reviewing documented flowcharts and/or procedures. Segregation of Duties exists between employees who have access to:						
Procurement	Segregation of Duties	Vendor master data and maintenance (owned by Procurement department) and employees who have access to process vendor invoices (Accounts Payable department)						
Procurement	Segregation of Duties	Request goods and/or services via Purchase Orders (PO) (owned by Procurement Department) and employees who place the order with the vendor						
Procurement	Segregation of Duties	PO approval (performed by business area requesting the goods and/or services) and employees who have access to process vendor invoices						
Procurement	Segregation of Duties	The procurement professionals who negotiate the contract terms and conditions with the vendor are separate from the employee who requests the goods and/or services.						
Procurement	Segregation of Duties	Process vendor invoices and employees who have access to Goods Receipt on a PO (performed by the receiving department or business area requesting the goods and/or services).						

(Continued)

Process / Account	Control Objective or Risk	Control Activity or Test	Sample Size and Results of Testing	Control in Place (Y/N) if No Type of Exposure	Process Owner	Remediation Actions	Next Follow up / Due Date
Procurement	Information Technology controls	In accordance with Company policy and procedure and at least quarterly, the file share owner's) perform a documented review of the procurement system and file share access to ensure access is restricted to authorized personnel.					
Procurement	Information Technology controls	Additional procurement system controls are designed which:					
Procurement	Information Technology controls	Do not allow for changes to the purchase order during the goods receipt process; e.g., changes to products or services orders, quantities and/or amounts as previously approved.					
Procurement	Information Technology controls	Tracks the remaining balance of blanket purchase orders with recurring payments and closes the PO when the balance becomes zero.					
Revenue	Compliance with Contract Terms	All customers have a valid and approved contract. Customers requesting non-standard contract terms and conditions require additional financial and legal approval. Review exception report for customers without valid contracts and remediate for resolution.					
Revenue	Compliance with Contract Terms	Review Customer dissatisfaction and escalation reports to identify the types of issues customers are having with the Company's products and/or services. Analyze how the Company investigates the root cause of these issues, improves the process and resolves the issue with the customer.					

Revenue	Complete	All sales orders are input to the sales database and once accepted by the Company, the sales order is released to distribution for fulfillment. Review exception reports and follow up with remediation plans. Select and sample to test sales orders for complete, accurate and timely processing.
Revenue	Complete	Zero dollar sales orders are reviewed for accuracy of revenue and inventory accounting treatment. Review the zero dollar sales report and validate the reasons provided for zero dollar fulfillment. Select a sample and test accuracy of reason classification.
Revenue	Complete	Completed sales orders are reconciled to the original contract with differences explained, authorized and documented. Contract and supporting documentation including approvals are retained and maintained with the customer file according to sales order. Review peer-to-peer or self-assessment checklists. Select a sample and verify reconciliation reports and remediation plans.
Revenue	Timeliness	Instructions as to revenue cutoff periods are communicated prior to each month-end closing. Review communications and schedules.
Revenue	Accurate	Review and analyze the company's policy and procedure for revenue recognition. Select a sample of revenue recognition checklists to ensure that the revenue recognition criteria have been met. For a selected sample of transactions, review and follow cradle-to-grave supporting documentation including customer contract, sales orders, shipping and fulfillment orders and customer correspondence.

(Continued)

Process / Account	Control Objective or Risk	Control Activity or Test	Sample Size and Results of Testing	Control in Place (Y/N) if No Type of Exposure	Process Owner	Remediation Actions	Next Follow up / Due Date
Revenue	Accurate	Review and analyze estimate and reserve accounts for compliance with company policies and procedures, accuracy of calculation and timeliness of processing. Recalculate estimate and reserve amounts for accuracy and consistency.					
Revenue	Authorize	Select a sample of sales orders and review for completeness, accuracy and authorization prior to processing.					
Revenue	Authorize	The revenue segmentation reporting by product and geography is reviewed for compliance with consistent application of company methodology. The VP Finance or corporate controller reviews, signs, and dates the detailed schedules and financial disclosures.					
Revenue	Reconciliation	Account analysis and reconciliation is performed between the:					
Revenue	Reconciliation	Sales order database and revenue booked and recognized					
Revenue	Reconciliation	Accounts receivable and recognized revenue					
Revenue	Reconciliation	Sales and use tax and revenue					
Revenue	Reconciliation	Intercompany revenue and Intercompany receivables					
Revenue	Reconciliation	Revenue and royalty payable					
Revenue	Reconciliation	Sales orders, revenue and incentive compensation					
Revenue	Segregation of Duties	Segregation of duties tests are performed by observing roles and responsibilities, reviewing documented flowcharts and/or procedures. Segregation of duties exists between employees who have access to:					

Revenue	Segregation of Duties	Prepare and enter sales orders and those who fulfill the sales order and those who record the related accounting transactions.				
Revenue	Segregation of Duties	Invoice the customer and those who collect and process customer payment.				
Revenue	Segregation of Duties	Record the accounting transactions and those who reconcile the accounts				
Retail Sales Orders	Compliance with Contract Terms	Retail partner list is complete and accurate and represents authorized retail partners who have valid master sales agreements with the company. All business partners have a valid and approved contract. Business partners requesting nonstandard contract terms and conditions require additional financial and legal approval.				
Retail Sales Orders	Complete	Business partner product and pricing lists are complete and accurate and represents products the company is authorized to sell to retail partners. Review the product and pricing list for authorization, communication, and to ensure that these products and prices are included within business partner orders.				
Retail Sales Orders	Complete	The sales order manager reviews and approves sales orders prior to forwarding the sales order to distribution for fulfillment. Review the completed sales order checklists to ensure that the company may fulfill requested product quantities at quoted prices and validate calculation extensions. Select a sample and test supporting documentation.				

(Continued)

255

Process / Account	Control Objective or Risk	Control Activity or Test	Sample Size and Results of Testing	Control in Place (Y/N) if No Type of Exposure	Process Owner	Remediation Actions	Next Follow up / Due Date
Retail Sales Orders	Accurate	All shipments are recorded accurately, in a timely manner and in the appropriate period. Review shipping reports and select a sample to review supporting documentation.					
Retail Sales Orders	Accurate	Walk and observe the process from when the company receives and processes the sales order to fulfilling and shipping the order to recording journal entries. Document control issues and findings.					
Retail Sales Orders	Authorize	Business partners are qualified, preapproved, and undergo credit authorization.					
Retail Sales Orders	Authorize	In accordance with company policy and procedures, as these require additional review and approval; sales order reports are generated to identify those sales orders less than or greater than general sales order volumes and amounts. Review and analyze these reports for additional management review, approval, and supporting documentation.					
Retail Sales Orders	Reconciliation	Reconciliations are prepared, reviewed, and approved between sales orders received and orders fulfilled; unreconciled items are aged for resolution. Select reconciliation, review source data, recalculate and validate approvals.					
Retail Sales Orders	Reconciliation	Reconcile fulfilled sales orders and business partner account receivable data flow. Select a sample; review calculations, approvals, and supporting documentation.					

Retail Sales Orders	Segregation of Duties	Segregation-of-duties tests are performed by observing roles and responsibilities, reviewing documented flowcharts and/or procedures. Segregation of duties exists between employees who have access to:		
Retail Sales Orders	Segregation of Duties	Evaluating and approving business partners and those processing sales orders, shipping product or Accounts Receivable processing.		
Retail Sales Orders	IT Controls	The system automatically monitors customer credit limits and designates a customer as "hold over credit limit" if the customer purchase order exceeds the approved credit limit in the system.		
Retail Sales Orders	IT Controls	Only valid and accurate purchase orders are entered into the system. Orders are reviewed for accuracy and validity prior to entry into the system as evidenced by sign-off of the purchase order.		
Income Tax	Compliance with laws and regulations	Tax schedules are prepared which represent the company's jurisdictional obligations for income tax preparation and filing. The tax department can demonstrate adherence to the schedule. Review and analyze the list of jurisdictional filings.		
Income Tax	Compliance with laws and regulations	Tax research is documented identifying company specific procedures to implement tax requirements into operational and tax processes. Review the list of tax items researched and assessment as to whether the researched item needs to be incorporated into the company's policies and procedures. Senior executives are assured that all available and appropriate tax advantages are included within income tax preparation, tax submissions, and disclosures.		

(Continued)

257

Process / Account	Control Objective or Risk	Control Activity or Test	Sample Size and Results of Testing	Control in Place (Y/N) if No Type of Exposure	Process Owner	Remediation Actions	Next Follow up / Due Date
Income Tax	Complete	There are established lines of communication between the tax function and the functional and geographic business units, providing clear instruction as to required input for income tax preparation. Review policies and procedures for inclusion of tax considerations where and as appropriate.					
Income Tax	Complete	The tax management compares the forecasted pretax income with the tax provision work papers. Review peer-to-peer or self-assessment checklists to determine if the work papers are complete. Verify the use of the income tax checklist and supporting documentation.					
Income Tax	Accurate	The tax provision calculation is properly documented, accurately determined, supported and properly recorded in the general ledger. Review the assumptions and process used to calculate, review and approve tax provisions. Select sample calculations for recalculation.					
Income Tax	Accurate	Sales and use tax liabilities are captured and recorded completely and accurately with payments submitted in a timely manner. Review and analyze sales and use tax work papers and presentation of liabilities.					
Income Tax	Accurate	Business unit and tax management verify the integrity and completeness of gathered data. The tax function performs timely recalculations to assess the accuracy and reasonableness of computations. Internal controls reviews the data input and tax calculations.					

Income Tax	Accurate	To serve as a check and balance and for purposes of accuracy, those who prepare income tax computations/work products and those who review and approve tax submissions and those who approve and/or reconcile journal entries. Walk through and observe the process from receiving data input to preparing journal entries from tax submissions and disbursement of taxes payable.						
Income Tax	Authorize	The tax VP reviews and approves the income tax rate which must be used for budget and forecasting purposes. This rate is reconciled to the actual calculated year-end rate.						
Income Tax	Authorize	The tax VP reviews and approves the income tax journal entries and classification between current and deferred, short-and long-term obligations.						
Income Tax	Authorize	The tax VP reviews and approves the blended statutory state income tax rate.						
Income Tax	Authorize	The CFO quarterly reviews and approves the contingency reserve noting support in accordance with SFAS5 and the related effects on the tax accounts.						
Income Tax	Authorize	Company policies and procedures (e.g., intercompany transactions, cross-border and transfer product pricing) are adequately reviewed and approved for income tax implications.						
Income Tax	Authorize	The income tax provisions, presentations, and disclosure required are reviewed for completeness, accuracy, and compliance laws and regulations. The VP Finance or corporate controller reviews, signs, and dates the detailed schedules and financial disclosures. Review the disclosure and supporting documentation.						

(Continued)

Process / Account	Control Objective or Risk	Control Activity or Test	Sample Size and Results of Testing	Control in Place (Y/N) if No Type of Exposure	Process Owner	Remediation Actions	Next Follow up / Due Date
Income Tax	Reconciliation	Reconciliations are performed between the financial data submitted by the business units and the information submitted to the tax department. Review and analyze selected reconciliation.					
Income Tax	Reconciliation	The Tax VP reviews and approves the roll forward schedule and analysis which includes current taxes payable, deferred taxes and the tax provision. Review and analyze selected reconciliation.					
Income Tax	Reconciliation	The Tax VP reviews the reconciliation of the requested tax entries to the balances reflected on the general ledger to confirm that the information was posted accurately and that the tax accounts are correctly stated. Review and analyze selected reconciliation.					
Income Tax	Reconciliation	The accrual for sales and use tax contingencies is reconciled monthly to supporting schedules or general ledger to ensure the accrual is complete and accurate. Review and analyze selected reconciliation.					

Internal Control – Result of Control Activity Testing

As the Internal Control representative tests each control objective, they should keep track of the tests and results by completing the Result of Control Activity form. This form serves as the cover sheet for evidence collected to support the assertion made about the control objective.

The results of each test, whether positive or negative, must be recorded to demonstrate that the internal control representative exercised an appropriate level of due diligence when reviewing the process. In addition, those items which indicate a deficiency need to be identified and classified for remedial action.

Internal Controls – Result of Control Activity Testing

Company	Location	Financial Period	Prepared by:
		Date	Reviewed by:

Purpose:

Scope or Process description:
Policy and Procedure references

Result of control activities tested

Number and identify each control objective and activity being tested. Follow or create a cross reference to the control objectives and activities as listed on the Test Guide.

Result of the Control Activity should identify the size of the sample, criteria used for sampling and the finding; reference findings as (E) controls were found to be in existence, (CT) controls were found to be executed completely and in a timely fashion, (VA) controls were found to be validate and accurate. Include other assertion levels as appropriate to your test plans.

Assessment refers to your evaluation as to whether the control is working as it should be. Ratings are 1 to 4 defined as 1 for a significant deficiency, 2 as a material weakness, 3 as a reportable condition or 4 as an effective control.

Result of Control Activities Tested

Description of Control Tested	Assertion	Result of Control Activity Tested	Assessment 1, 2, 3, 4
1			
2			
3			

Evaluation: In my opinion, the overall control assessment for the process described above is rated as < insert rating 1, 2, 3, 4 > and describe why you reached this conclusion.

Prepared by: _____   Date: _____

Reviewed and approved by: _____   Date: _____

Once complete, attach the Test Guide as a cover sheet to the supporting evidence and forward to Internal Controls.

Reporting Scorecard			
Company	Location	Financial Period	Prepared by:
		Date	Reviewed by:

Distributed to:

Chief Executive Officer, Chief Financial Officer, Executive Team and Process owners

Purpose: Consolidate the findings from the Result of Control Activity Testing and report on the progress made to remediate open issues.

Goal: Zero material weaknesses and zero significant deficiencies

Testing is current as of <insert date matching to the internal control testing schedule>

Findings:

Process	Total # Controls	Rating 1 SD	Rating 2 MW	Rating 3 RC
Total				

Ratings are 1 to 4 defined as 1 for a significant deficiency (SD), 2 as a material weakness (MW) or 3 as a reportable condition (RC).

Actions:

Process	Process Owner	Remediation Actions	Expected Completion Date	
Internal Control comments or observations				

Acronyms

AP or A/P: accounts payable
AR or A/R: accounts receivable
BOD: board of directors
BS or B/S: balance sheet
CAO: chief accounting officer
CAO: chief administrative officer
CEO: chief executive officer
CFO: chief financial officer
CIP: construction in progress
Company – IDEAL LLC
COO: chief cperating officer
COSO or Framework: Committee of Sponsoring Organizations of the Treadway Commission
CT: complete and timely
DOA: delegation of authority
DPO: days payable outstanding
E: existence
EBS: electronic bank statements
EUC: end-user computing
FASB: Financial Accounting Standards Board
FCPA: U.S. Foreign Corrupt Practices Act
GAAP: generally accepted accounting principles
GL: general ledger
ICOFR: internal controls over financial reporting
IDEAL: Instruction, Design, Evaluation and Assessment for Leadership
IFAC: International Federation of Accountants
IIA: Institute of Internal Auditors
IS: information services
IT: information technology
Legal: legal department
Letter: quarterly subcertification letter or the letter of representation
Matrix: process owner matrix
MBA: master of business administration
MD&A: management discussion and analysis
MW: material weaknesses
PCAOB: Public Company Accounting Oversight Board
PO: purchase order
Program: internal controls program
RASCI: responsible, authority, support, counsel, and inform
RC: reportable condition

SAS: Statement on Auditing Standards
SD: significant deficiencies
SEC: Securities and Exchange Commission
SOX: Sarbanes–Oxley Act of 2002
U.S. GAAP: United States generally accepted accounting principles
VA: validate and accurate
VP: vice president

References

Visit the following sites for additional information on:

Sarbanes-Oxley
www.sec.gov/spotlight/sarbanes-oxley.htm
http://thecaq.aicpa.org /Resources/Sarbanes+Oxley/

Securities and Exchange Commission
http://www.sec.gov/

COSO
http://www.coso.org/

PCAOB
http://www.pcaobus.org/index.aspx

For program support and information, contact
IDÆAL via Policyguru@idealpolicy.com or via http://www.idealpolicy.com

Index